Andrew Dawson is Senior Lecturer in Religious Studies at Lancaster University. He is the author of *New Era-New Religions: Religious Transformation in Contemporary Brazil* (2007) and *The Emergence and Impact of the Base Ecclesial Community and Liberative Theological Discourse in Brazil* (1998).

'*Summoning the Spirits* brings classical theories of spirit possession into lively dialogue with new forms of spirit communication emerging in locales as disparate as Sudan, South India and Silicon Valley. The book's rich diversity of approaches and case materials makes it an indispensable resource for anyone interested in the nearly universal human desire to establish direct contact with unseen powers and forces, however understood.'

Michael F. Brown, Professor of Anthropology, Williams College, Massachusetts, and author of *The Channeling Zone: American Spirituality in an Anxious Age*.

'This welcome multidisciplinary work – richly nuanced and wide-ranging, yet sharply focused – examines spirit possession rituals in relation to interpersonal, institutional, structural and expressive processes, and underscores the potential of possession to adapt to changing circumstances. Each chapter offers ethnographically grounded and theoretically engaged analyses of possession in relation to commoditization, globalization and cultural encounters, placed within contexts of cultural intimacy, symbolism and power. The writers' diverse insights into the roles of tradition and innovation emphasize the ability of possession rituals continually to re-invent themselves in dialogue with personal, political and religious currents.'

Susan J. Rasmussen, Professor of Anthropology, University of Houston, and author of *Spirit Possession and Personhood among the Kel Ewey Tuareg*.

D1607492

Summoning the Spirits

Possession and Invocation in Contemporary Religion

EDITED BY
ANDREW DAWSON

I.B. TAURIS
LONDON · NEW YORK

Published in 2011 by I.B. Tauris & Co Ltd
6 Salem Road, London W2 4BU
175 Fifth Avenue, New York NY 10010
www.ibtauris.com

Distributed in the United States and Canada
Exclusively by Palgrave Macmillan
175 Fifth Avenue, New York NY 10010

Library of Modern Religion: 15

ISBN: 978 1 84885 161 0 (hb)
       978 1 84885 162 7 (pb)

A full CIP record for this book is available from the British Library
A full CIP record is available from the Library of Congress

Library of Congress Catalog Card Number: available

Printed and bound in Great Britain by TJ International Ltd, Padstow, Cornwall

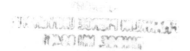

For spirits everywhere,
free or otherwise.

CONTENTS

ACKNOWLEDGEMENTS

As with any book, this one reaches completion thanks to the work and sacrifice of others. My thanks go to the book's contributors. Without their generous cooperation and patience this project would not have been possible. Thanks are also due to Alex Wright and Jayne Ansell of I.B.Tauris and Kim McSweeney of Bookcraft for their timely advice and encouragement. By way of friendship and intellectual challenge, I'm indebted to the members of the Reading Group, not least Arthur Bradley and Mick Dillon. Finally, I thank Debbie for her unstinting support and unrelenting positivity.

INTRODUCTION

Possession and Invocation in Contemporary Context

Andrew Dawson

If the combined outputs of the academic community and popular culture are anything to go by, contemporary interest in spirit possession is on something of a high. With respect to popular culture, heightened interest in printed media and gaming – both computer and board-based – treating spirit possession and its attendant occult motifs is evident in many urban-industrial societies across the world. It is, though, through the visual media of the cinema and, especially, TV that possession-related themes are enjoying real popularity. Like the current batch of vampire-related movies and TV series, televisual and filmic representation of spirit possession represents part of popular culture's ongoing (re-)engagement of supernatural themes and occult motifs.[1] Admittedly, popular cultural production relating to spirit possession is dominated by an English-speaking voice and chiefly refracted through a Christianised worldview. Irrespective of linguistic context or religious heritage, however, the themes dealt with and the manner of their treatment resonate with varied aspects of contemporary experience across the urban-industrialised world.

In academic terms, ongoing interest in spirit possession complements a longstanding track record in which cultures at home and abroad have been subjected to detailed scrutiny, documentation and analysis of a wide variety of ritual activity orchestrated by and orientated to interaction with the supernatural sphere.[2] For some, academic engagement with spirit possession is driven by a desire to demonstrate the overwhelming historical presence which beliefs and practices of spirit possession once enjoyed both within established religion itself and throughout society as a whole (e.g. Goldish,

2003; Klaniczay and Pocs, 2005; Sluhovsky, 2007). Various repertoires of spirit possession have also been studied by way of cataloguing disappearing practices and beliefs which are gradually dying out or rapidly mutating in the face of modernity's encroachment. Both through the detraditionalising proc-esses of urban-industrial creep and the ideological intrusion of proselytising religion – Christianity in the case of South America, central and southern Africa and Australasia and Islam in the case of northern Africa, Indonesia and Malaysia – long-established spirit possession practices have been massively eroded or undergone widespread transformation in relatively short periods of time (e.g. Emoff, 2001; Nicoletti, 2004; Rasmussen, 2006; Wastiau, 2000).

For other academics, the study of spirit possession provides opportunity to explore the 'intriguing' (Behrend and Luig, 1999: xiii), if not paradoxical, increase in spirit possession activity within a purportedly secular modern environment (see also, Crapanzano and Garrison, 1977). As Howard and Mageo remark, 'as any observer of postmodern cosmopolitan society can attest, mystical folk beliefs have not only survived but have flourished along-side high religions and science. Rather than vanish, spirits have been assigned different roles in contemporary society' (1996: 4). At the same time, academic interest in spirit possession undoubtedly reflects broader society's curiosity for things perceived as 'exotic' (Smith, 2006: 33), 'strange' (Lambek, 1981: 4) or plainly 'bizarre' (Keller, 2002: 3). Far more than a mawkish preoccupation with the peculiar, however, academic studies of spirit possession introduce variegated ways of interpreting the world, its contents and what lies beyond. By providing often painstaking description and analysis of ritual repertoires and the socio-cultural contexts in which they occur, academic treatments of spirit possession offer us alternative frames of reference through which our own experiences, be they religious or otherwise, might better be understood.

Summoning the Spirits responds to the ongoing presence of ritualised forms of spirit possession within the contemporary social landscape. This pres-ence, however, is by no means static. It is constantly changing in respect of how spirit possession manifests itself ritually, where and by whom it is prac-tised and what it signifies both to those taking part and in relation to over-arching social structures and dynamics. Given the constancy of change and the variety arising from it, our treatment situates its subject within a broad spectrum of disciplinary, thematic and socio-cultural contexts which might best capture the highly variegated character of spirit possession as it occurs today. Of course, what follows is not exhaustive – far from it. At the very least, though, the overall contents of this book aspire to offer a representative sample of an altogether diverse and fluid phenomenon. To best communicate this diversity and fluidity, *Summoning the Spirits* operates with an inclusive understanding of what constitutes spirit possession in its contemporary forms. Such inclusiveness is necessary to capturing the variegated contemporary terrain through which we travel (see also, Hüwelmeier and Krause, 2010; Johnson and Keller, 2006; Schmidt and Huskinson, 2010).

At the same time, the inclusive understanding employed by any analysis should not be so broad as to be analytically vague and, thereby, hermeneutically useless in respect of the light it sheds – or fails to shed – upon spirit possession. To this end, and by way of orientation for what follows, it is worth pausing to reflect upon both the general terminology used in respect of spirit possession and the manner in which it is framed by the academic approaches brought to bear. Boddy perhaps offers one of the most user-friendly, non-specialist definitions of spirit possession available. Spirit possession, Boddy says,

> commonly refers to the hold over a human being by external forces or entities more powerful than she. These forces may be ancestors or divinities, ghosts of foreign origin, or entities both ontologically and ethnically alien...*Possession*, then, is a broad term referring to an integration of spirit and matter, force or power and corporeal reality, in a cosmos where the boundaries between an individual and her environment are acknowledged to be permeable, flexibly drawn, or at least negotiable... Taking the givenness of spirits as a matter of salience, three parties of variable inclusiveness are implicated in any possession episode: a self, other humans, and external powers. (1994: 407, 422)

Developing Boddy's definition in respect of what follows, spirit possession may be said to comprise four constitutive components: the spirits or supernatural forces which possess; the person or persons possessed; the local context in and by which possession is both enacted and interpreted; and the broader social context within which individuals and local communities exist amidst a range of overarching (e.g. economic, political and socio-cultural) processes and dynamics (see also, Behrend and Luig, 1999: xv). In combination, the construals of spirit and self at play within a given locality constitute an interpretative nexus which sets the conditions of possibility within which spirit possession can be both enacted and understood. At the same time, however, the practice and construal of spirit possession undertaken at the local/communal level occurs against the backdrop of overarching economic-political structures and socio-cultural processes. Mediated by the community and individuals who comprise it, these structures and dynamics impinge upon the practice and interpretation of spirit possession in a variety of ways. Whether through gender dynamics, caste hierarchies, ethnic identities or class relations, for example, overarching social processes influence not only how spirit possession is practised and interpreted, but also by whom and at what cost.

Academic Approaches to Spirit Possession

The manner in which academic studies of spirit possession are framed plays a large part in determining how its constitutive components are understood, both individually and in relation to each other. In respect of the most prevalent academic frames within which spirit possession has been traditionally analysed, in her treatment of spirit possession in Madagascar, Sharp identifies four 'dominant themes' of enquiry: 'the relationship between powerlessness and symbolic expression,' 'psychological or psychiatric angles,' 'a biological model,' and 'social roles and function' (1993: 14–15). Writing about spirit possession in West Africa, Stoller lists 'five dominant forms of explanation to analyze spirit possession.' They are: the 'functionalist,' which focus upon social structures/processes and their consequences; the 'psychoanalytic,' which concentrate on the psychological dynamics of the one possessed; the 'physiological,' which seek biological explanations; the 'symbolic,' which focus upon the cultural context within which spirit possession is interpreted; and the 'theatrical,' which concentrate upon the performative aspects of spirit possession (1995: 17–21). In his study of deity and spirit possession in South Asia, Smith enumerates five 'interpretative frameworks' within which 'possession has usually been examined.' Within these frameworks, spirit possession has traditionally been regarded:

(1) as demonic, opposed to God and good; (2) as a medically defined psychological state; (3) as a psychological condition engineered for the purpose of gaining social or even political control; (4) as an aspect of shamanism; and (5) as an existential reality. (2006: 39)

In view of the existing literature treating spirit possession within contemporary religion, and with the following chapters in mind, I think four broad academic approaches are worthy of note. Awareness of these approaches is important because each one frames spirit possession in a particular way. By configuring spirit possession in a specific fashion, each approach emphasises, play downs or ignores certain of its constitutive aspects and their relationship to – or disconnectedness from – each other. As explored further below, each of these academic approaches to spirit possession can be categorised relative to its emphasis upon either the individual dimensions of spirit possession or the collective contexts within which spirit possession occurs.[3]

Individual Emphases

In respect of those approaches which focus upon the individual, two recognisably distinct sets of emphases can be identified: the psychophysical and the agential. The most traditional – and, these days, contentious – of the psychophysical emphases is the medical one. Within the medical paradigm, spirit possession is analysed relative to its psychiatric, psychological and biological dimensions. Regarding spirit possession as pathological, and thereby as a problem to be 'cured,' medical approaches identify underlying psychophysical conditions (e.g. mental illness, dietary deficiency, emotional repression or epilepsy) as responsible for the varied mental, physical and emotional symptoms which, together or in isolation, come to be regarded – albeit, mistakenly – as a real-life interaction with the spiritual realm (see, Lewis, 2003: 160–84; Peters and Price-Williams, 1983: 5–39).

Another approach to spirit possession which concentrates upon psychophysical aspects of the individual person focuses upon the cognitive or mental dimensions of the human being. Within this type of approach, emphasis is placed upon the cognitive structures and mental processes of the brain (e.g. counter-intuition, inference and attribution systems) which both make possible and interpret a range of experiences which ultimately coalesce to constitute the spirit possession event (see, Cohen, 2007). In addition to exploring why and how the individual experiences spirit possession, psychophysical approaches that draw upon theories of mind, cognitive science and neurophysics also regard transcultural features of spirit possession (i.e. similar characteristics appearing in different socio-cultural contexts) to be ultimately grounded in a universal, 'panhuman cognitive function' (see, Cohen and Barrett, 2008: 246–67).

The second set of approaches belonging to the individual frame of reference concentrate upon the opportunity for subjective-expression, self-assertion and identity-construction which spirit possession affords the individual. Given their shared concentration upon the individual, as with psychophysical approaches, those which treat possession as a site for self-expression focus upon the embodied nature of the processes involved. Unlike psychophysical approaches, however, those wishing to underline the subjective character of spirit possession do so by stressing the centrality of individual agency to what occurs (e.g. Firth, 1967; Kramer, 1993). Appropriating social scientific insights into the individual as both an active maker of meaning and agent in the construction of her own subjectivity, agential interpretations regard spirit possession not as something which happens to the individual but as something which he plays a fundamental role in initiating, directing and concluding (e.g. Taussig, 1987; Wafer, 1991). Here, then, the body is treated as a means by which the individual both expresses and asserts herself through the 'mimetic' (Stoller, 1995) and 'instrumental' (Keller, 2002) possibilities afforded by the spirit possession repertoire.

Collective Emphases

Although focussing upon the role of subjective agency within spirit possession, the aforementioned studies nevertheless freely acknowledge that the constitutive activity of the individual subject can only fully be understood with reference to the broader socio-cultural contexts within which s/he is situated. In so doing, they point us to a second set of approaches which, though mindful of the embodied nature of spirit possession, place their emphasis on the collective context within which spirit possession is played out. As with individual-orientated approaches, two collective-minded emphases are worthy of note: those who concentrate their studies of spirit possession upon its communicative dimensions; and those who situate spirit possession within prevailing social processes of – usually unequal – power-relations.

In respect of the first set of foci, the most influential approaches have been those using textual, idiomatic and dramaturgical models to explicate the communicative dimensions of spirit possession. As Lambek states:

> In order to approach the social basis of possession, it is helpful to view it as a system of communication. By this I mean simply that possession operates to transmit messages (verbal, material, etc.) between senders and receivers along particular channels. (1981: 70)

Within such approaches as Lambek's text-inspired analysis, spirit possession is understood as inextricably woven within a complex web of interpersonal, material and symbolic processes. Indeed, such is the importance of this communal matrix that failure to chart and navigate its complex and often contradictory – polysemic – currents directly undercuts the ritual efficacy of the possession event. As Levy, Mageo and Howard maintain,

> Full possession behavior is highly skillful. It requires mastery of role playing and of subtle kinds of communally significant communication...Possessed individuals operate as competent persons in the moral realm in established webs of communication...The idea of possession as a skillful communicative act implies an audience in a relatively integrated community for its full flourishing. (1996: 18–19)

Reflecting the hermeneutical turn and its semiotic preoccupations which have so influenced communicative approaches, Crapanzano argues that the spirit possession repertoire might best be regarded as a kind of 'idiom' which embodies 'traditional values, interpretational vectors, patterns of association, ontological presuppositions, spatiotemporal orientations, and etymological horizons' (1977: 11).[4] 'Polysemic' in nature, the 'language of spirit possession' must be mastered in both its 'technical' and 'symbolic' dimensions if the one possessed is to achieve anything approaching success (1977: 15). In addition to stressing its idiomatic nature, those underlining spirit possession's communicative character have also emphasised its performative dimensions. As hinted at by the above quotation's use of the terms 'role playing' and 'audience,' communicative approaches often draw direct parallels between spirit possession and theatrical processes and dramatic staging. Typical of the communicative frame's preoccupation with the interpersonal dynamics of hermeneutical exchange, performative approaches to spirit possession appropriate a range of dramaturgical concepts and theories which underscore its theatrical ethos and intent. Just as the actor in a piece of drama, the possessed person assumes a role which plays to its respective audience, is directed by a given script and enacted relative to its props and staging (see, Laderman and Roseman, 1995; Rouget, 1985; Stoller, 1989).

Writing on the Nuer religion of northeast Africa, Evans-Pritchard describes the spirits manifest through possession as 'refractions of social realities' (1956: 106). In the same vein, others regard the spirits as 'metonyms' which – as the term suggests – symbolise unnamed processes and dynamics which both frame and are mediated by respective possession repertoires (e.g. Howard and Mageo, 1996: 4). Such comments, however, do not intend to reduce spirit possession to the status of epiphenomenon whose existence can be explained away through causal reference to prevailing socio-cultural contexts or overarching political-economic structures. Rather, they serve to underline the fact that a rounded appreciation of spirit possession relies upon understanding its beliefs and practices as articulating a varied range of processes and dynamics which impinge upon individual and community alike by way of, for example, caste hierarchies, class conflicts, gender relations, intergenerational frictions, and ethnic-racial prejudices. Although not the first work of its kind, it was I. M. Lewis' *Ecstatic Religion* (first published in 1971) which truly succeeded in establishing the socio-structural gaze as an essential component of any rounded analysis of spirit possession.

Typical of the functionalist paradigm which informs his analysis, Lewis' principal contribution to possession studies was to understand spirit possession relative to the role (or 'social function') it plays in respect of overarching societal processes and structures. Distinguishing between 'central' and 'peripheral' forms of religion, Lewis argues that 'central possession religions' – also termed, à la Durkheim, 'main morality possession religions' – perform an essentially conservative function in that they legitimise and, thereby uphold, prevailing social systems (2003: 29). In contrast to central possession religions, 'peripheral' forms of spirit possession are populated overwhelmingly by powerless and marginalised members of society. Although uncoupled from mainstream morality – and thereby unconcerned with upholding the status quo – peripheral possession practices nevertheless continue to function in a way which conserves rather than undermines prevailing social systems. By providing an outlet for the otherwise irresolvable frustrations, anxieties and grievances of those without recourse to more efficacious means of satisfaction, peripheral possession practices provide an 'institutionalized means' through which potentially destructive socio-cultural pressures can be channelled (Lewis, 1986: 30). Despite their manifest unpredictability and anarchic appearance, peripheral possession practices fulfil a latently conservative social function by offering a ritualised safety valve which ultimately circumvents the need for a thoroughgoing reform of existing structures of inequality and prevailing processes of disempowerment.

Upon situating spirit possession within the unequal power relations of prevailing social systems, Lewis' *Ecstatic Religion* set the scene for much of what was to follow. The vast majority of what followed, though, moved beyond the conservative, functionalist reading of spirit possession offered by Lewis and is, instead, inspired by a variety of post-1960s' emancipatory paradigms such as feminist theory, postcolonial studies and subaltern analyses. While the focus on power used by Lewis continues centre stage, contemporary studies of spirit possession – informed also by the recovery of agency and the hermeneutical turn – are much more inclined to interpret its subject matter through the lens of strategic resistance, self-conscious subversion and constructive appropriation of liberated space (e.g. Braude, 1989; Comaroff, 1985; Ong, 1987; Owen, 1989; Palmié, 2002; Shaw, 2002). The spirit possession repertoire, then, is no longer regarded solely as a systemic preservative, but one that also furnishes opportunity to oppose, circumvent and undermine the powers that be. In addition to rejecting Lewis' understanding of spirit possession as an inherently conservative phenomenon, some scholars have also been at pains to qualify his linkage of many spirit possession practices with peripheral status and powerlessness. Although not denying the relevance of prevailing systems of inequality and exclusion such as caste, patriarchy and ethnic-racial discrimination, these scholars question the often uncritical identification of particular possession practices as straightforward expressions of marginalisation and existential despair. Rather than seeing spirit possession as automatically reflecting or making up for some form of socio-cultural privation, they argue, it might better be regarded as just one among a number of available lifestyles which practitioners have adopted as a means of self-expression or communal celebration (see, Boddy, 1989; Brown, D. D. 1994; Sered, 1994).

Typologies of Spirit Possession

Irrespective of actual conditions on the ground or the particular academic frame through which they are interpreted, spirit possession events the world over appear to have at least one common denominator. This common denominator comprises some kind of alteration, transition or difference occurring in the individual which signals that a step change has taken place and the spirit possession episode begun. As Bourguignon puts it,

> We shall state that a belief in *possession* exists, when the people in question hold that a given person is changed in some way through the presence in or on him of a spirit entity or power, other than his own personality, soul, self, or the like. (1976: 7)

Whether perceived as coming in from outside or making their continuous presence felt in a heightened way, the activity of the spirits is held to involve some form of transformation in and to the one whom they possess. As Crapanzano notes, although common to many forms of spirit possession, this transformation does not necessarily involve the possessed individual entering a trance. He also goes on to acknowledge, however, that 'even in those societies where possession states are near-daily occurrences, possession, whether in ritual or in isolation, always marks an exceptional state that fascinates both participants and observers' (2006: 200–1). Exceptional in character, possession always embodies something of the extra-special, beyond the norm or out of the ordinary.

Although not necessarily connected with spirit possession events, transformations in subjectivity which occur as part of the possession episode often involve some kind or degree of change to individual consciousness. Known by medicalised approaches as 'dissociation' or 'displacement,' but also labelled 'trance' by a number of important studies – not least Bourguignon's (1973 and 1976) – transformations in subjectivity connected with spirit possession are most commonly termed 'altered states of consciousness.' Following Ludwig's understanding of an altered state of consciousness, Crapanzano reproduces a list of its characteristics which includes

> alterations in thinking such as disturbances in concentration, attention, memory, and judgment as well as an impairment in reality testing and a marked tendency toward archaic modes of thought, a disturbed time sense, loss of control, changes in emotional expression (ecstatic

and orgiastic feelings, detachment, etc.), changes in body image, perceptual distortions, changes in meaning or significance such as an increased evaluation of subjective experiences, ideas, and perceptions, a sense of the ineffable, feelings of rejuvenation, and hypersuggestability. (1977: 8)

A fundamental component of a great many spirit possession repertoires, altered states of consciousness and conceptualisations thereof furnish an important theoretical backdrop to the majority of academic treatments of possession, particularly as they relate to the theoretical framing of self – spirit relations.

Self – Spirit Relations

As they are understood relative to a vast range of practical and symbolic co-ordinates, configurations of self – spirit relations at the heart of the possession event are potentially limitless. Among the myriad determinants which frame self – spirit relations, a number of conceptual distinctions are worthy of note. Perhaps the most enduring, yet controversial, of these distinctions is the traditional contrast drawn between *enstatic* and *ecstatic* forms of spirit possession. This contrast was theorised in its most influential form in the mid-twentieth century by Eliade's discussion of possession practices among the arctic Tungus (2004). Here, 'enstatic' forms of possession are held to involve the spirits entering the individual from without, while 'ecstatic' practices involve the individual – or aspects thereof – journeying to meet the spirits in their native, supernatural environment. Although criticised for a variety of reasons, Eliade's work has drawn most fire by virtue of its restrictive association of shamanism with ecstatic forms of spirit possession (see, Lewis, 2003: 43–50). As demonstrated by numerous studies of shamanism in various parts of the world, shamanic possession practices are not restricted to ecstatic conceptualisations but also involve enstatic notions of both a punctual (i.e. short-term) and extensive kind (see, Chilson and Knecht, 2003; Kim, 2003; Langdon and Baer, 1992).

Another enduring, though less contentious, dichotomy employed to conceptualise spirit possession is that of the *involuntary – voluntary* distinction. As implied by the terms themselves, the former mode of spirit possession refers to an event or process which occurs against the will of or without being solicited by the one possessed, whereas the latter kind is initiated and/or controlled by the individual or individuals concerned. Some forms of this dichotomy link 'involuntary' or 'unsolicited' possession with evil/lesser spirits and 'voluntary' or 'solicited' possession with good/higher spirits (e.g. de Heusch, 1981; Staemmler, 2009). Others, though, treat 'involuntary' possession as a kind of 'primary phase' process which affects the unprepared, sometimes in adverse ways, until its dynamics are understood and controlled. At this point, spirit possession becomes a 'voluntary' process effected relative to the will of the possessed individual, at which point it is understood to enter its 'secondary phase' (e.g. Oesterreich, 1930; Lewis, 2003: 83).

Like the involuntary – voluntary distinction, the contrast drawn between what might be termed *unconscious* and *conscious* forms of spirit possession relates to the nature and degree of individual agency at play in the possession event. Within unconscious forms of possession, the mind, self or subjectivity of the one possessed is rendered insensible by the possession event. As a result, the possessed individual is unable to remember anything at all from the onset of the possession episode to its completion. Indeed, among many communities across the world, such is the importance accorded unconsciousness that the insensibility of the possessed individual is regarded as the most important marker of a possession event's authenticity (see, Bastide, 1985; Keller, 2002; Lambek, 1981). In contrast, however, certain communities or particular forms of spirit possession hold the continued awareness of the one possessed to be a vital component of the possession event. While the degree, if not also the manner, of consciousness expected of the individual differs between communities and kinds of spirit possession, the significance attached to sensible agency as a guide to the possession episode remains constant. Although subjective awareness tends to be valorised by typically modern possession repertoires (e.g. spiritist mediumship, new age channelling and neo-pagan invocation), a significant number of traditional paradigms – certain kinds of shamanism predominant among them – do not automatically disparage conscious forms of possession (see, Adler, 2006; Brown, M. 1997; Cavalcanti, 1983; Sullivan, 1988).

The distinction between what are often termed *positive* or *negative* forms of spirit possession is perhaps the most variegated of all the conceptual polarities employed (see, Bourguignon, 1976). Contrasts between positive and negative forms of possession are also drawn using pairings such as 'good' – 'harmful' and 'benign – 'destructive' (e.g. Kapadia, 1996: 423–45; Smith, 2006). The variegation in these particular forms of possession arises from the fact that what might be considered positive or negative about the possession event is determined by a number of different variables, each of which is pluriform in character. For example, spirit possession might be classified as 'positive' or 'negative' relative to its intent, the kind of spirits involved or the type of person being possessed. Among other things, and in explicit contrast to positive/benign forms, possession practices which intend harmful effects have been variously termed 'black magic,' 'witchcraft' and 'low spiritism'

(Evans-Pritchard, 1950; Voeks, 1997). At the same time, of course – as, for example, in the case of a cuckolded partner inducing a third-party spirit attack by way of exacting revenge – what is considered a harmful outcome to some may well be regarded as a positive result by others (see, Brown, D. D. 1994).

In the same vein, the distinction between positive and negative forms of possession drawn by some communities is made relative to the kinds of spirits involved. Here, taxonomies of evolutionary status (e.g. high and low) or categories of being (e.g. good and bad) are usually employed. Within the ethical monotheistic traditions of Christianity, Islam and Judaism, for example, possession by spirits is almost universally regarded as bad because the possessing entities are held to belong to the demonic rather than angelic realm of spiritual beings (see, Goldish, 2003; Sluhovsky, 2007).[5] However, for other religious worldviews (most notably, North American and European spiritist traditions), as disincarnate human beings, spirits are understood not as good or evil but as *more* or *less* evolved (Owen, 1989; Santos, 2004). The majority of indigenous African and South American religions, though, tend to think neither dualistically (as per ethical monotheism) nor monistically (as with spiritist forms) in respect of the spirit-world. In contrast to both of these northern hemispheric paradigms, a good many indigenous religions regard spirits as morally ambivalent agents whose actions, though to an extent biddable, are never wholly predictable. One and the same spirit, then, can be responsible for both good and ill (Crocker, 1985; Wright, 2002: 221–35). As in relation to voluntary – involuntary distinctions, understandings of possession as either positive or negative are also linked to the particular types of person involved. Noted above, the possession of an untrained or unwary individual is often regarded as having negative connotations. While voluntary possession by experienced practitioners resonates more positively, this form of possession can be further divided relative to the different kinds of ritual specialist involved. Within some communities, for example, expert practitioners are distinguished by virtue of their specialisation in bringing about either harm or healing (Dawson, 2005: 114–19).

Neither as established nor as popular as the above explanatory distinctions, a further categorical contrast is nevertheless worthy of note. This contrast relates to the distinction drawn between what might be termed *gnoseological* and *therapeutic* forms of possession. Within the former type, possession is held primarily to comprise the imparting of knowledge or moral instruction not readily available to human beings in their present (e.g. material, immature or sinful) condition. As they are orientated to delivering knowledge or moral instruction, gnoseological forms of possession exhibit typically oracular and discursive characteristics which lend themselves to its communicative aspirations (Brown, M. 1997; McGarry, 2008). Chiefly orientated to bringing about healing – understood broadly to include physical, emotional and material wellbeing – therapeutic forms of possession tend to utilise a more varied range of activity than their gnoseological counterparts (Brown, D. D. 1994; Lewis, 2003). Most commonly with shamanism, these forms of possession often appear within the same ritual repertoire. Some socio-cultural contexts, however, demonstrate noticeable patterns in which certain – usually, better educated – groups exhibit an affinity for gnoseological forms of possession while others favour therapeutic kinds (Camargo, 1961; Cavalcanti, 1983).

Ideal Types of Spirit Possession

In an attempt to capture the multiple configurations through which self – spirit relations are articulated by possession events, academics have formulated or, more commonly, appropriated a number of models. As one would expect given the variation of conditions on the ground, a broad range of alternative models exists (see, Nabokov, 2000). By virtue of their relative popularity, however, three particular forms stand out; they are, 'spirit possession,' 'spirit mediumship' and 'shamanism.' Before looking at a number of examples in which these models are used, two points are worthy of note. First, the types of spirit possession identified are not always mutually exclusive. While different forms of spirit possession may well be practised by distinct communities, other kinds may be enacted not only within the same ritual repertoire but also by the same ritual specialist. As Lewis observes, the various 'mystical encounters' comprising spirit possession 'are *not* characteristic of different cultures, evolutionary stages, modes of production, and so forth, but regularly (although not invariably) coexist in a single cultural setting and period' (1986: 89). Second, each of these models comprises an 'ideal type.' Established by Weber as a key tool of social-scientific analytical description, ideal typing relies both upon the bracketing out or elision of some characteristics and the 'one-sided accentuation' of others (Weber, 1949: 89). By virtue of this bracketing out and accentuation, ideal types never completely match the empirical terrain they seek to map and, as a result of what they seek to achieve, can sometimes appear static. At the same time, because they are context-sensitive ideal types can only ultimately be understood relative to the actual context from which they have been abstracted and upon which they seek to shed interpretative light. Although limited both as empirical descriptors and generalisable models, as we shall see, ideal types are nevertheless extremely useful analytical devices.

The analytical utility and context-relative nature of ideal typologies of spirit possession can be demonstrated through reference to four examples.

The following examples are used because each offers a different configuration and hermeneutical construal of the particular ideal types employed. One of the most referenced ideal typologies of spirit possession is the threefold model offered by Firth (1967). Using all three of the most popular types, Firth distinguishes between 'spirit possession,' 'spirit mediumship' and 'shamanism.' Associated most with non-specialist (i.e. untrained) individuals who are involuntarily inhabited, spirit possession exhibits a lack of control, has no evident ritual function and is generally imbued with negative connotations. As each of the other two types is marked by a greater degree of self-control and clarity of ritual purpose, they are both more predictable in character and regarded in a positive light. Spirit mediumship, however, is chiefly orientated to the conveyance of information and is thereby principally oracular in form. Shamanism, on the other hand, has a much broader social remit and – by virtue of this – a more extensive repertoire of action and greater versatility in handling the spirits under its control (1967: 296).

In his treatment of spirit-orientated activity in Chinese religion, Paper distinguishes between 'shamanism' and what he terms 'mediumism' – i.e. mediumship (1995). Echoing the categorical distinctions employed by Firth, Paper argues that the principal differences between the 'shaman' and the 'medium' are: i) shamanic possession tends to be initiated by the individual concerned, whereas mediumship – 'at least at first' – tends to be of an involuntary nature; ii) the shaman 'remains aware' throughout the possession episode while the medium does not; iii) following on from this, the shaman has more control over the spirits than the medium; and iv) orientated chiefly to communication, the medium's repertoire is more restricted than the shaman's whose principal concerns lie with meeting the general 'needs of the community' (1995: 86–7). Likewise working with a twofold model, Claus contrasts 'spirit mediumship' with 'spirit possession' (1979). Employing many of the distinctions noted above, Claus describes spirit mediumship as a 'legitimate' (i.e. positive) and 'expected' (i.e. voluntary) phenomenon, involving a trained 'specialist' whose 'mastery over the spirit' allows possession to be undertaken with a clear 'purpose' in mind – here, 'soliciting the aid of the supernatural for human problems.' As an 'unexpected, unwarranted intrusion of the supernatural into the lives of humans,' however, spirit possession 'creates a disturbance' which affects the unprepared, holds negative connotations, is experienced involuntarily, and lacks explicit ritual purpose (1979: 29). This time contrasting shamanism with possession, Bourguignon describes 'shamanic trance' as preserving the shaman's subjective differentiation from the spirits, such that the shaman 'sees, hears, feels, perceives, and *interacts*' with the supernatural entities involved. During 'possession trance,' however, the individual enjoys no such subjective differentiation as s/he, in effect, loses all sense of self and '*becomes*' the spirit by whom s/he is possessed (1979: 261).

As every ideal type used to model spirit possession is only understandable as abstracted from a particular socio-cultural context, no single practice or belief can automatically be associated with any given term. Theoretical models such as spirit possession, spirit mediumship and shamanism are ultimately of value, then, only to the extent that they are grounded in a specific socio-cultural context made up of the concrete practices and actual beliefs of individual human beings and the communities of which they are a part. As these models are inherently context-sensitive, and thereby not to be reified, estimations of their utility are best made relative to their analytical efficacy in understanding the concrete phenomena to which they refer. This is a better approach, I think, than holding these models to embody an absolutised definitional standard which claims to capture the essence of what 'possession,' 'mediumship' or 'shamanism' really is.

With this point in view, and mindful of what follows, the diagrammatic schema reproduced below offers an overarching framework against which might be plotted the aforementioned categorical distinctions and the ideal typologies they inform. The diagrammatic schema takes as its principal point of reference the myriad configurations of the self – spirit relationship which contemporary possession repertoires articulate. Allowing for different kinds and degrees of consciousness existing within each of the categories it encompasses, the schema nevertheless comprises a continuum or spectrum of agency which moves from one polar extreme to another. Spirit-dominant forms of possession are situated at one (here, the left-hand) end of the spectrum, while the other end is occupied by typically late-modern (i.e. post-1950s) conceptualisations of possession in which individual agency is in the ascendancy. Between these poles sits a middle sector populated by modes of possession in which spirit and self are more equally active. In addition to moving from the spirit-dominant to the self-possessed, the diagrammatic schema includes three overlapping sections – the *occupational*, the *interfacial* and the *rhetorical* – in which self – spirit interactions are conceptualised in a variety of ways.

Possession Continuum

Within occupational understandings, possession occurs by virtue of a spirit or supernatural force entering or residing in the body of an individual who, because of this spiritual presence, is considered to be possessed. As indicated by the following diagram, the mode of occupation which possession involves can be understood to comprise varying degrees of agency on the part of both

Occupational			Interfacial			Rhetorical
Suppressed	Marginal	Co-operative	Locomotive	Static	Hybrid	Individualised
• Majority of traditional forms • Trance channelling	• Some traditional forms • Trance mediumship	• Enstatic shamanism • Conscious mediumship • Invocation	• Ecstatic shamanism • Astral projection • Neo-shamanism	• Mental mediumship • Telepathic channelling	• Expansion of Conscious	• Psycho-spirituality • Rave-trance

Spirit ← Possession Continuum → Self

the possessing spirit and the possessed host. Although modes of occupational possession in which the agency of the host is understood to be in some way *suppressed* are most common among traditional repertoires, a number of modern forms – e.g. trance channelling – likewise articulate a temporary loss of conscious agency during the possession event. Whether traditional or modern, experiences of suppressed agency are commonly expressed as a blotting out, displacement, loss, overpowering or absence of conscious subjectivity on the part of the possessed person (see, Csordas, 1994; Brown, M. 1997; Keller, 2002; Klimo, 1998; Lambek, 1981; Lum, 2000; Owen, 1989; Stoller, 1989).

Within *marginal* forms of occupational possession – found in some traditional and particular modern repertoires – although the host remains fully aware during the possessing spirit's presence, s/he plays no active part in the possession event. In effect, the possessed individual's agency is marginalised during the possession episode, such that the host is no more than an onlooker or bystander passively observing what the possessing spirit is doing through her body (Brown, D. D. 1994; Santos, 2004). *Co-operative* modes of occupational possession are so-called because the possessed host is understood to work actively with the possessing spirit. Here, possession is a co-agential process in which self and spirit play equal or differential parts in directing each other relative to the particular task at hand.[6] Within traditional possession repertoires, the shaman's relationship with his auxiliary spirits – who reside permanently within the body – is perhaps the most typical form; whereas spiritist notions of conscious mediumship and certain neo-pagan invocatory practices are typically modern versions of co-operative occupational possession (Adler, 2006; Sullivan, 1988; McGarry, 2008).

Unlike their occupational counterparts, interfacial representations of possession understand its processes as unfolding beyond the psychophysical confines of the human body. Although the body retains its significance as both the seat of subjectivity and the ultimate mediator of the materials furnished by possession, it is no longer the principal locus of the possession event. As the interface of self and spirit requires significant degrees of self-management on the part of the individual concerned, subjective agency is valorised as an important part of the possession episode. Within *locomotive* forms of interfacial possession, the human self – or aspects thereof (e.g. soul, astral body or inner self) – undertakes a journey comprising both a dislocation from its physical moorings and a relocation to a dimension, time or place understood as categorically different from the material world of the here and now. Representations of shamanic soul-flight and the ecstatic relations it enables with guardian spirits are typical of traditional locomotive forms of interfacial possession (Chilson and Knecht, 2003; Kim, 2003; Langdon and Baer, 1992). Typically modern versions of locomotive interface between self and spirit are articulated by esoteric notions of astral projection and new age, neo-shamanic practices (Hanegraaff, 1996; Lindquist, 1997; Wallis, 2003).

Static forms of interfacial possession replace the notion of psychical locomotion with an emphasis upon the interface of subject and spirit which does not rely upon the former moving towards the latter. Most popular among established Spiritualist (e.g. mental mediumship) and contemporary new age (e.g. channelling) repertoires, static modes of interfacial possession rely upon the establishment of some form of remote connection through which a spirit or supernatural force is able to communicate with its human interlocutor. The messages transmitted to and ultimately through this psychic connection come usually as concepts or words to be spoken and written, but might also arrive as images or symbols to be drawn (Brown, M. 1997; Klimo, 1998). *Hybrid* representations of interfacial possession employ both locomotive and static tropes. Perhaps the most typical of the hybrid representations of self – spirit interface is the notion of expanded consciousness. On the one hand, the connection established with the spiritual sphere results from the expansion of consciousness towards something held to exist beyond – both outwardly and inwardly conceived – the everyday/ perceived psychophysical boundaries of the self. However, unlike static modes of interface – e.g. mental mediumship or telepathic channelling – expansion of consciousness involves the self – or an aspect thereof – moving toward something which is not ordinarily held to be part of it. On the other hand, the self – spirit connection established by expanded consciousness does not require locomotion on the part of the subject concerned. In contrast to locomotive forms – e.g. ecstatic shamanism or esoteric astral flight – expanded consciousness involves no actual dislocation of the self from one spatio-temporal domain to another. By connoting both locomotion and stasis, then, the model of expanded consciousness furnishes a mixture of both immediate and remote interface between the self and the spiritual sphere (see, Metzner, 2008).

I use the term rhetorical possession to designate a range of contemporary discourse and practice which employs vocabulary and activity directly associated with spirit possession but does so in a way that does not connote belief in or engagement with actual spirits or supernatural forces. The most established forms of rhetorical possession I've come across occur in Brazil among adepts of new age, psycho-therapeutic religiosities who regularly participate in spirit possession rituals as part of their highly eclectic spiritual repertoires (see, Chapter Eight). These non-mainstream spiritualities are principally orientated toward the annihilation of the ego – understood as socially formed and thereby spiritually impure – and the resulting emancipation of the inner, higher or true self which remains untainted by relations with the material world. Although freely participating in spirit possession rituals, many of these adepts prefer to regard the experiences which occur not as arising from contact with independently existing spirits but as psychophysical expressions of inner, but previously suppressed, dimensions of the higher or true self. So, and while not gainsaying the actual existence of spirits or supernatural forces, psycho-therapeutic adepts are likely to interpret their experiences not through traditional hermeneutical models of spirit possession but by employing new age paradigms such as spiritualised readings of Jungian archetypes and depth or transpersonal psychology (see, Dawson, 2007; Labate, 2004).

At the same time – and indicative of wider popular cultural appropriations of non-mainstream supernaturalist narratives – the rhetoric of possession is used by both practitioners of and academic commentators upon contemporary rave culture. Writing about forms of dance which take practitioners 'beyond their normal consciousness into a powerful ecstatic state,' Sylvan reproduces a number of first-hand descriptions which, he says, 'seem to confirm that something akin to possession is happening' (2005: 20, 93). In the same vein, Rietveld's discussion of the 'possession-trance' induced by rave music argues that '[r]oused by sensory over-stimulation, a dancer can be overcome by a state of trance, ranging from emotional/orgasmic ecstasy to, indeed, a type of possession' (2003: 52). Comparing the physical effects of 'electronic dance music culture' (EDMC) described by 'clubbers' with the altered states of consciousness associated with established spirit possession repertoires, Till likewise maintains that 'EDMC shares many similarities with possession trances in traditional cultures' (2009: 178). As with the psycho-therapeutic adepts mentioned immediately above, while employing the rhetoric of spirit possession the overwhelming majority of those involved with contemporary rave culture would not readily associate themselves with an understanding of possession as an encounter with actual spiritual forces whose existence is independent of particular human experience. For both groups, spirit possession is less a means of interfacing with the supernatural realm than a mode of expressing, if not fabricating, a revitalised self.

Content and Structure

The chapters commissioned for this book were chosen from a broad range of proposals and are included because, collectively, they offer a representative sample of contemporary academic reflection upon possession and its cognate beliefs and practices. Together, these chapters articulate disciplinary perspectives, address themes, adopt theoretical frames, and engage geographical contexts typical of the many other approaches, issues, theories, and socio-cultural terrains which likewise relate to spirit possession but for which this book – albeit sadly – has no room. By way of disciplinary sweep, the following chapters draw respectively upon cultural and linguistic anthropology, sociology, performance studies, human geography, and cultural studies. In respect of geographical coverage, what follows treats South, Central and North America (Brazil, Cuba and the USA), Europe (England and Sweden), Africa (Sudan), Asia (India), Australia, and Japan. Due to the socially-engaged focus of this book, I have elected not to include psychophysical approaches such as the medical and cognitive frames mentioned earlier. Other afore-mentioned academic frames (i.e. agential, communicative and societal) are, however, well represented. Likewise present are variegated representations of particular aspects of self – spirit relations and ideal typologies outlined above.

Such is the nature of spirit possession and its academic treatment that – irrespective of disciplinary approach, geographical context, thematic focus or theoretical framing of the chapter in question – a number of issues reappear in various parts of the book. As will be seen, for example, the transgres-sive character of possession and its relativising of existing hierarchies and structures are broached throughout the text. Likewise recurring is the porous or permeable ontology of the self which spirit possession so often presup-poses. In the same vein, possession's communicative dimensions are empha-sised by a number of chapters, as is the fact that its performance takes place in associational contexts comprising conflictual, competing and, at times, contradictory dynamics. Issues pertaining to agency and identity also repeat themselves. In view of this iteration, the overall structure adopted here is partly incidental in that many of the chapters lend themselves to standing alongside or being grouped with a good number of others. Yet, the tripartite structure adopted by this book does have an inherent logic.

Mindful of inevitable overlap and thematic repetition, the book's structural logic nevertheless encourages readers to reflect upon spirit possession as it relates to three complementary dimensions which play out in various contemporary contexts. As the rationale for each section is explicated in its respective introduc-tory overview, detailed commentary can wait. Suffice to say here, though, that the central theme of Part One concerns the manner in which local practices of possession relate to overarching dynamics of socio-cultural transformation. Here, focus rests upon spirit possession as a locally grounded and collectively orientated negotiation of typically modern macro-structural processes. By no means ignoring this approach, Part Two nevertheless focuses upon spirit posses-sion as a means of self-construction. In so doing, this section concentrates upon individual agency and identity formation as they unfold in relation to other selves, both living and 'dead.' Part Three comprises three chapters engaging contemporary milieux which non-specialists might not immediately associate with spirit possession. Here, focus rests upon contemporary expressions of possession as indicative of modernity's progressively radicalised condition.

PART I

POSSESSING THE PRESENT

Local Negotiations of Transnational Processes

Focusing principally, but not solely, upon the communal contexts in which spirit possession occurs, the following chapters collectively lend themselves to an appreciation of a number of complementary dimensions. Fjelstad and Hien's engagement with a Vietnamese-American community in Silicon Valley, California, for example, concentrates upon the encounter between an American woman and would-be medium – called Elise – and the *len dong* religion derived originally from Vietnam. Here, the communicative dimensions of spirit possession come to the fore as Elise is faced with the need to become intimately familiar with both the idiosyncratic markers by which the spirits are identified and the technical mastery of their ritual performance. Tracing the beginning of Elise's mediumistic apprenticeship, Fjelstad and Hien demonstrate how the interplay of transnational dynamics and multi-cultural processes is negotiated by both Elise and established *len dong* practi-tioners. Drawing upon stereotypical representations of the spirits, this local negotiation is further aided by the increasingly hybrid and progressively fluid character of the socio-cultural identities at play in the deeply diverse context of Silicon Valley.

Garbin's treatment of a London-based congregation of the Congolese Kimbanguist church likewise explores spirit possession – 'spiritual manifesta-tions' – as a localised negotiation of otherwise translocal processes. Situated within the 'deterritorialising' processes of international migration, the spir-itual manifestations of deceased Kimbanguist leaders are regarded by Garbin as part of a 'reterritorialising' dynamic in which formerly displaced persons begin to construct a new home-base. At the same time, Garbin's chapter high-lights the transgressive character of possession practices. Here, the spiritual manifestations occurring in the London-based congregation are read by the Kimbanguist leadership as a direct threat to both established authority structures and emergent international arrangements centred in the spiritual homeland of the Congo. The official response and subsequent banning of these spiritual manifestations represents for Garbin the (re)assertion of institutional order and ritual management over an otherwise unpredictable and thereby potentially transgressive phenomenon.

Kenyon's engagement with zar possession practices in Sudan, Africa, focuses upon the newfound prominence of a number of traditionally lowly slave spirits. Exploring the reasons behind this newfound prominence, Kenyon identifies a number of economic-political and socio-cultural developments which frame the everyday experience of those who are possessed by or ritually interact with the slave spirit Dasholay and his siblings. As with many of the other chapters in this book, Kenyon's treatment underlines the prevalence of women in relation to spirit possession practices across the globe. Implicated in both private-domestic and public-economic practices, the women discussed by Kenyon relate to spirit possession as a resource distinct from prevailing power structures and established authorities. More than a simple break with the past, the ritual ascent of once marginal slave spirits signals a localised renegotiation of tradition in the face of widespread and rapid social change.

Examining elements of possession practices enacted by Tamil Hindu diaspora communities in London, David touches upon a number of themes highlighted by preceding chapters. The performance of possession stands to the fore here, as does its transgressive character. Born of the fusion of possessed host and possessing deity, spirit possession is shown to provide a means of experimental expression which first relativises then refashions existing categories of gender, caste and class differentiation. At the same time – and despite the potentially anarchic effects of possession-trance – David underlines the importance of performative control and communal order to the ritual efficacy of spirit possession. David also relates changes in Hindu diaspora possession practices to a range of experiences arising from the Tamil experience of often far-reaching social change. Here, the elevation in status and collective effervescence furnished by spirit possession are understood to resource both individual and communal resilience in the face of the privations, hardships and adaptations associated with forced displacement and international migration.

1

LOCAL SPIRITS/MULTICULTURAL RITUALS

The Dynamics of Place and Identity in Vietnamese-American Spirit Possession Rituals

Karen Fjelstad and Nguyen Thi Hien

Introduction

Two unusual events occurred when members of a Vietnamese spirit possession temple were having New Year ceremonies in Silicon Valley, California. First, people who gathered to usher in the Year of the Pig did not seem at all surprised when Elise, a 47-year-old German-Spanish woman, entered the temple with offerings for a baby spirit. In fact, most members of the temple had already met Elise because she had performed one ritual to honour the spirits (*doi bat nhang*) and another to cleanse the temple with a Tibetan Buddhist ritual she had learned from a gypsy in Spain. Later that same day, the master medium of the temple introduced one of the authors to Billy, another newcomer to the temple. Billy was thrilled because Little Dark Princess (*Co Be Den*), the spirit of an ethnic minority, had incarnated into him while shopping at Office Depot. Apparently, Little Dark Princess started crying when she saw a disabled man walking down the aisles. 'Tears really came from my eyes,' Billy exclaimed proudly. When the temple medium introduced Billy, who is ethnic Chinese from Vietnam, she said, 'he's not Vietnamese either!' These events are unusual because Elise's presence marked the first time, to the best of our knowledge, that a Caucasian American expressed a participatory interest in the *len dong* spirit possession ritual, and it was the first time that an ethnic Chinese at this temple was introduced as 'not Vietnamese.'

This chapter explores the crossing of ethnic borders in a Silicon Valley temple. It considers the complex relationship between ritual practice, place and ethnicity and explains how a traditional ritual that is usually associated with the Viet people is becoming a multicultural practice. Understanding this transition, we argue, entails consideration of the unique environment of Silicon Valley, an area that is characterised by 'deep diversity' (English-Lueck, 2009). Deep diversity occurs where there is so much diversity, and so many alternative ways that people connect to each other, that ethnicity becomes negotiable, people switch their identities and ancestral heritage becomes only one of many sources of identity. As English-Lueck explains,

> As categories multiply and become dense within a particular region, maintaining discrete identities becomes more difficult. Aspects of particular heritage identities are exaggerated, minimised, co-opted, and contested. (2009)

This chapter examines how some spirit mediums have begun to exaggerate certain ancestral identities. Paradoxically, their goal is not to enhance boundaries between ethnic groups but to make those boundaries more permeable.

We also explore how archetypical images of spirits play an important role in ethnic border crossings. Mediums learn about the spirits through visions, which are perceived as gifts from the spirits; listening to songs or stories about them; looking at statues of spirits that are placed on altars; or by interacting with spirits during their incarnations at possession ceremonies. Many characteristics of the spirits reflect standardised, archetypical images of gender, age and ethnicity. This generic nature makes it possible for outsiders to understand and identify with the pantheon. The Mother Goddess religion and the *len dong* ritual thus become 'transposable' – meaning that they have appeal in different cultural settings (see, Csordas, 2009: 7). The spirits are local and very much tied to specific places in Vietnam, but they are able to cross ethnic and national borders because they are generalisable and non-specific.

Data for this chapter were collected in 2003–09 through participant-observation and ethnographic interviews with mediums and disciples in Silicon Valley and northern Vietnam.[1] Although much of the background information was obtained during fieldwork with mediums in a variety of different settings, this research focuses on one temple in particular. The temple was established in Silicon Valley in 2001, but has twice since divided. The master medium is a senior citizen, but the temple is mostly frequented by mediums in their thirties who have spent most of their lives in the USA. They are fluent in English and Vietnamese (although some are better at English), self-identify as Vietnamese-American and are bicultural. They are also mostly well-educated professionals who are comfortable in a variety of cultural and linguistic settings. Although this group is young compared with other Silicon

Valley temples, they describe themselves as spiritually conservative. They like to 'follow the rules' while practising rituals and do not like to 'take shortcuts.' At the same time, they describe themselves as 'more open' and 'different' from other mediums because they are bicultural Vietnamese-American. Although this research focuses on an atypical temple – and the question of whether or not non-Vietnamese peoples can become mediums is currently being negotiated – the move toward multiculturalism is emerging in other *len dong* temples in the USA. This chapter is the first to examine this phenomenon. It will introduce the spirits and their mediums and rituals, explore the association of spirits with specific places and ethnicities and discuss the case of Elise, the first Caucasian woman in Silicon Valley to consider *len dong* mediumship. This study will explore how and why the spirits and mediums cross ethnic borders and the role of imagination and deep diversity in such border crossings.

Spirited Representations of Place and Ethnicity

Practitioners of the *len dong* spirit possession ritual follow the Vietnamese Mother Goddess religion (*Dao Mau*) that worships goddesses of Four Realms of the Universe (*Tu Phu*) – sky, earth, water, and mountains and forests. A goddess and her celestial helpers, many of which are cultural and historical heroes, govern each realm. A number of these spirits incarnate into a medium during a *len dong* ritual that is sponsored by a medium as a means of fulfilling an obligation to the spirit-world. Spirits descend into mediums in established sequences and although there is some variation, mediums are usually possessed by the same spirits. During the highly stylised incarnations the spirits like to dance, read fortunes, listen to songs, and distribute blessed gifts (*loc*). Spirits call mediums into service and although the financial cost of mediumship is often quite burdensome, mediums with a heavy calling (*can nang*) cannot escape their destiny. After initiation, mediums must have at least one (in the USA) or two (in Vietnam) yearly ceremonies (Nguyen, T. 2002).

The *len dong* ritual is associated with the ethnic Viet (Kinh) people. The majority of the practitioners are Viet, the spoken language is Vietnamese and songs praise the spirits in Vietnamese. Traditional Vietnamese clothing is often worn to the ceremonies and Vietnamese foods are consumed. Refugees brought the ritual to the USA during the post-war diasporas of the 1970s and 1980s (Fjelstad, 1995 and 2006: 95–110). Studying the ritual as it is practised in Silicon Valley, Fjelstad writes,

> The first time I attended a possession ceremony I felt as if I was in a
> world unrelated to Silicon Valley, the area where I grew up. I wondered

if people there felt comforted because going to the temple was, in some ways, like going to Vietnam. Everything is decorated in primary colours; the air is thick with incense, fresh flowers, and fish sauce (*nuoc mam*), and several different conversations take place at once, mostly in Vietnamese. (2006: 100)

In the environs of Silicon Valley the *len dong* ritual seemed to be a way of celebrating, as well as maintaining, Vietnamese culture. However, a closer look at the religion and ritual reveals a more complex relationship with ethnicity.

Although many spirit mediums and some scholars (e.g. Ngo, 1996) view the Mother Goddess religion as the most basic religion of Vietnam, it may not be very old and it might have originated in China. Dror notes that 'there is no mention of it in any source earlier than the nineteenth century' (2007: 74). She further asserts that the religion and the ritual probably began in the late-seventeenth or early-eighteenth centuries, and may have been introduced from southern China where there is also the concept of the pantheon of three (or four) domains (2007: 74). Other scholars have suggested that the Vietnamese term for spirit medium (*dong*) may be a derivative of the Chinese word *t'ung* ('a boy of less than fifteen years who has been chosen to become a medium'). This perhaps indicates the Chinese origins of the ritual (Durand, 1959; Nguyen, K. 1983: 23–30).

The len dong ritual is mostly practised by Viet people. Although ethnic minority spirits are incarnated by Viet mediums, it has been rare, although not unknown, for someone from another ethnic group to become a *len dong* spirit medium in Vietnam. One exception is the ethnic Chinese (Hoa) who practised *len dong* prior to the 1979 war with China. Sometimes they performed the ritual in their own temples and other times they performed it in temples of Viet mediums. After the ethnic Chinese were forced out of Vietnam in 1979 it was rare to find Chinese practitioners of *len dong*. In contrast, there are several ethnic Chinese spirit mediums in Silicon Valley. Although some Hoa people have ceremonies in an ethnic Chinese temple in Sacramento – located about one hundred miles from Silicon Valley – many have their ceremonies in Viet temples. They speak the Vietnamese language and are considered as Vietnamese because they came from Vietnam. Because ethnic Chinese are integrated into Silicon Valley communities of spirit mediums, it seemed strange that Billy was described as 'not Vietnamese.' Was it to emphasise the belief that multiculturalism has always been part of the religion and ritual?

Regardless of where the religion and ritual originated, scholars agree that the Mother Goddess religion is syncretistic, easily incorporating local spirits into its pantheon (Nguyen, T. 2002; Ngo, 1996). The pantheon includes goddesses, culture heroes, local divinities, and Buddhist and Taoist figures. The number of spirits is not fixed but depends upon region and individual temple variation. Generally, there are nine hierarchical ranks of spirits including four mother goddesses, one Saint Father with his three royal ladies and a young boy, ten mandarins, twelve ladies, ten princes, twelve princesses, ten or twelve young princes, and two kinds of animal spirit. In addition, the pantheon includes the Taoist Jade Emperor and two Star Spirits, the Buddha, and the bodhisattva *Quan Am*. There is a possible total of seventy or seventy-two spirits, but only thirty-nine of these spirits actually possess mediums. Those spirits that do not possess humans are less well known to mediums. The spirits vary not only by their place in the hierarchy, but also in their origins, which may be either celestial or earthly.

All spirits belong to one of the four realms of the universe and are responsible for activity in those realms. Spirits of water, for example, are associated with oceans, lakes, streams or ponds in any geographical area of the world. Likewise, spirits of forests can be found in any forests of the world. This omnipresence stands in contrast to the fact that many spirits are also identified with specific Vietnamese locales. For example, *Lieu Hanh* (goddess of the sky) is associated with Nam Dinh province where she was incarnated as the daughter of a mandarin in 1557. Approximately half of the spirits have active principal temples, which are located throughout Vietnam (Nguyen, T. 2002). The temples are situated in areas where the spirits once lived or died and temples built on these places are believed to have more efficacy than others (Chauvet, 2007). Master mediums organise pilgrimages to primary temples (Larsson and Endres, 2006: 146–60) and there is an annual cycle of pilgrimages that begins in Hanoi during the lunar New Year (Chauvet, 2007).

Although most spirits of the pantheon are of the Viet majority, several are associated with other ethnic groups, including the Tay, Muong, Dao, Hmong, and ethnic Chinese. Most of the ethnic minority spirits are female, and many are linked to the spiritual Realm of the Mountains and Forests and to the northern and central highlands of Vietnam. This distribution of the spirits is told in the origin story of Vietnam (Ngo, 2006). When the fairy princess *Au Co* married the Dragon King they had one hundred offspring. She took fifty to the mountains and he took fifty down to the sea. According to legend, this is why the ethnic minorities are associated with the highlands of Vietnam and the Viet (or Kinh) majority dominate the coastal and delta areas. Spirits of the mountains and forests have distinctive characteristics. During possession ceremonies they are distinguished by their clothing, style of dance and by the blessed gifts (*loc*) they distribute to the audience. They are known for generosity and abundance – characteristics that also apply to the forests in which they live (Chauvet, 2007). Forest and mountain spirits are also associated with a distinctive style of possession music (*chau van*) that musicians describe as 'lively' and 'colourful.' As Norton remarks,

> The happy, lively and simple character of the Xa melodies fits with the image portrayed by the actions of the mediums when the mountain spirits enter them. When a mountain spirit is incarnated, the medium wears ethnic minority costume, dances energetically and is generally more vivacious than when other spirits are incarnated. Female mountain spirits also distribute natural products to the disciples, such as fruit and betel nut, in contrast to the packaged food and drink distributed by other spirits, thus emphasising the connections between female mountain spirits and nature. The Xa melodies, then, along with the behaviour and dress of the female mountain spirits, promote a feminised pan-ethnic minority stereotype of natural, happy, simple, colourful, and lively ethnic minorities. (2000: 10–11)

Imagination plays a role in how mediums understand place and ethnicity. Mediums gain knowledge about spirit places and identities through songs of the spirits, observing spirit incarnations during *len dong* ceremonies, dreaming, and 'sensing' or visualising what a particular spirit or place is like. Standardised, even stereotypical, ideas sometimes inform these experiences. For many mediums in Silicon Valley, the Realm of the Mountains and Forests is associated with mystery, darkness and hidden forms of knowledge. It is perceived as natural and wild, and is represented on altars by caves that are dark and secretive and possibly full of wild animals, hanging plants, climbing vines, and wild fruits. Ethnic minority spirits who occupy the Realm of Mountains and Forests are often viewed as bearers of 'natural' healing knowledge. Some of the spirits are herbalists, others are fortune-tellers and some are known for having compassion for the ill and infirm. For example, the Ninth Prince (*Ong Chin*) is a collector of herbal medicines. Whenever he is incarnated in possession ceremonies he carries a knife used to collect wild roots in the forest. He 'sells' these plants, represented by potato slices, for one dollar to people at the ceremony. The Little Dark Princess (*Co Be Den*) is an ethnic minority who was disabled as a young girl. Partly because of her disability she became a healer who travelled from village to village to help poor, ill and wounded people. Other forest spirits bestow their mediums with divinatory powers; e.g. the *Chua Boi* spirits who are a group of female forest spirits associated with healing and divination.

The Little Dark Princess who visited Billy at Office Depot.

Ethnic minorities are often portrayed in archetypical ways. The Seventh Prince (*Ong Bay*) is an ethnic Viet spirit who lives near the Chinese border. Because the Chinese influenced him he likes to drink dark tea and smoke cigarettes laced with opium. Often thoroughly intoxicated, he stumbles about the temple in a drug-induced haze. The ethnicities of mountain and forest spirits are often blended, merging several cultures into one, and there is little concern with ethnic authenticity. A single forest spirit might wear clothing from Dao, Tay and Flower Hmong, all at one time, and mediums are usually unable to designate the ethnicity of a particular spirit. Instead, they are all melded together. Although mediums are not concerned with accuracy in the representation of ethnicity, they are very concerned with other forms of authenticity. It is extremely important, for example, that a spirit's personality, temperament, interests, and abilities are correctly represented in possession ceremonies.

Gender distinctions are also represented in archetypical ways, as male and female spirits stress their difference by exaggerating their gender characteristics. Male spirits, for example, have a more serious demeanour than females,

The Ninth Prince (with pipe) differs from ethnic Kinh spirits.

smoke cigarettes and more frequently make demands of their mediums, while female spirits are graceful, feathery and light. As Norton explains, such gender differentiation is expressed in the songs of the spirits.

> Many of the texts for male spirits extol stereotypical masculine char-
> acteristics, such as strength and prowess in the art of war and in some
> cases scholarly and artistic activities, like painting and poetry, which are
> associated with the historically 'male' tradition of civil examinations. In
> marked contrast to the texts for male spirits, those dedicated to female
> spirits often describe stereotypical feminine characteristics, such as
> gracefulness and physical beauty. (2006: 62)

Although *len dong* rituals entail gender traversing – so that female spirits possess males and males incarnate the spirits of females – the gendered behaviour of possessing spirits is consistent with conventional constructions of gender.

The ability to imagine place and ethnicity is important to ritual practice in the USA, especially for mediums who have been unable to travel to Vietnam.

Although the spirits are omnipresent, their US appearance is dependent on a few factors. Spirits must have an altar or a temple where they can be presented with appropriate offerings, and they have to be channelled by a medium. In both cases, specific knowledge of place and ethnicity are important. How, for example, can a medium build an appropriate altar for spirits if she does not know what the particular realm looks like? What kinds of flora and fauna are in the forest realm? What kinds of boats do the spirits row? How can an ethnic minority spirit be represented if a medium does not know how such a person dresses or what the spirit might look like? Although some of this information is gleaned from possession songs, the remainder must be imagined.

Imagining Vietnam is important to many Vietnamese in the USA, and images of Vietnam have long been informed by music videos. Vietnamese communities in California have had access to such videos since the late 1980s and watching them is a popular pastime. Vietnam is often represented in such videos as a rural country full of rice paddy and water buffalo where many of the people are ethnic Viet females wearing traditional dresses (*ao dai*) and conical hats. Ethnic minorities are portrayed as residents of the highlands who wear indigenous clothing, carry tools or baskets with which they collect flowering plants or fruit, while caves, waterfalls, birds, fish, and other wild animals surround them. For Silicon Valley mediums, like other migrant populations (see, Schein, 1998), video has been an important means through which the terrain, peoples and spirits of the homeland are visualised and remembered. But many of these images are archetypical and resonate with non-Vietnamese populations who can also relate to the 'simplicity' and beauty of rural life, 'gentle and nurturing' female spirits, indigenous peoples who are more 'natural' than others, and the secret healing abilities of ethnic minorities residing in remote mountainous areas. Perhaps this helps to explain why Elise felt so comfortable the first time she went to the Silicon Valley temple.

'You Don't Have to Be Vietnamese…'

In February 2006, Elise – a German-Spanish wife and mother who had been raised in Germany and El Salvador before moving to the USA – went to the temple for the first time. Elise had been harassed and bothered by an envious co-worker and was unhappy with the social environment of her accounting job. One day, while discussing these problems with another co-worker who happened to be the sister-in-law of the temple medium, Elise learned that she could go to the temple for divination and spiritual advice. Elise had been born into a spiritually orientated family that practised Catholicism and evangelical Christianity, and because she had always been a sickly child she was familiar with the laying on of hands and other forms of healing and divination. She went to the temple the following week 'just to see what it was like.' When she walked in, she was unprepared for the sense of familiarity that enveloped her.

Looking about the altar, many of spirits seemed recognisable. She said the Young Prince (*Cau Be*) was 'peeking at her from behind some carnations' that had been placed on his altar. Elise explained that she could tell the spirit was coming into her because she had had mediumistic and divinatory abilities since she was seven years old. Indeed, she started having visions and predicting the future while studying at a Catholic school. Elise said,

> The minute I got in there I felt something good. I felt the spirits, especially the little boy, he was very playful and he was getting into my body. I couldn't explain it but I was just laughing and laughing and laughing. I was acting like a kid!

During subsequent visits to the temple Elise was possessed by several other spirits. Since then she has performed a ceremony honouring the spirits (*doi bat nhang*), which is often the first step to mediumship. Although she has not yet fully committed herself, Elise may become one of the first Caucasian American *len dong* spirit mediums in the USA. It is significant that her first connection with *len dong* spirits was through the Young Prince. Often referred to as a baby spirit, the Young Prince is known for being playful, petulant and demanding. The spirit easily crosses other social and cultural borders, such as those between Vietnamese and Vietnamese-American spirit mediums, because he is fun and expressive and most people can identify with the cute baby spirit (Fjelstad, 2010: 52–66).

Elise learned about the spirits by talking to mediums and watching their incarnations at possession ceremonies but much of her knowledge is derived from personal experience. When she meditates she receives messages from several different spirits including the Young Prince, the Ninth Princess and Little Dark Princess. Many of her visions of spirits are remarkably similar to those of spirit mediums, but they are also comparable to Western images of indigenous persons. For example, when asked to describe the Ninth Prince (*Ong Chin*), Elise said that

> he lives in a mountain in a hut. He has herbs tied up and hanging upside down from the roof. There's some dried herbs and animals hanging upside down and he's working on a wooden table and he has a stove or ceramic pot and he's mixing the herbs.

Although Elise has dreams about the Ninth Prince, he does not eagerly accept foreigners. She said that 'he got mad at me for trying to get in his hut. He doesn't like people that he is not too familiar with to enter his place. He wouldn't let me in.'

The Ninth Princess (*Co Chin*) also incarnates into Elise. Known to be compassionate and loving, the spirit embodies all that is stereotypically feminine, even to the point of wearing pink clothing and using pink feathered fans. When describing the Ninth Princess, Elise says,

> This lady is such a loving person. She caresses me all the time. I know that she's close because I can feel it. Whenever I am sad she comes and caresses me. She always wears a dress. When she caresses me her touch is so soft and gentle.

Asked to clarify her attraction to the religion, Elise said that she cannot explain it but that she 'identified with the environment' even though she had never seen it before. When asked if she felt she had lived a previous life in Vietnam she said she had already been 'regressed' by a hypnotist who discovered that she was the incarnation of a great grandmother who had died during the Spanish civil war. Still, she said,

> I do have to admit that I have Oriental feelings. I do like Oriental things a lot and it could be that in a previous life I might have lived in an Oriental city or I might have come from an Oriental. Who knows? I am very attached to Orientals.

This helps to explain, Elise says, why she likes to burn incense in her home, resulting in teasing by her Chinese-Nicaraguan husband.

Although Elise has difficulty explaining why she is able to channel the *len dong* spirits, other members of the temple are more certain. The temple medium believes that Elise has a great gift because she is able to divine, and says that Elise was chosen by the spirits to help the temple where, on weekends, she reads fortunes for people of several ethnicities. Other mediums view Elise's taste for things 'Oriental' as an indicator that she may have lived a previous life in Vietnam. At the very least, her attraction to the religion and ritual suggests that she has the calling to become a medium.

Elise's active interest lends legitimacy to the religion, something that is very important to mediums. The logic is that if the spirits can come into an outsider – someone who knows nothing about the peoples and cultures of Vietnam – the religion must surely be true. As the temple medium explains,

'She is not Vietnamese but god still comes to her, you can't say anything, you *have* to believe.' Elise's participation has even caused other members of the temple to re-evaluate their own commitments to the spirit-world. Thien, a young male medium, said that Elise 'confirmed' the religion for him, making him think more about how he can spiritually better himself. 'There's a definite reason why she came,' he explains, 'it's to validate.' 'She really believes,' he says, 'sometimes she believes more than us.'

Although the temple welcomes Elise and members view her presence as extremely positive, they do not accept all the changes that she introduces. During the New Year, for example, she asked to perform a cleansing ritual to rid the temple of negative energy. While this rite has not traditionally been part of *len dong*, the temple medium said it would be alright because she knew Elise had good 'intent.' Nevertheless, permission (*xin phep*) would need to be asked of the spirits. The New Year ritual involved the use of myrrh, dried flowers and cinnamon that were placed in various locations throughout the temple. It was to be practised every day for three consecutive days but because Elise could only perform the rites for one day, she asked the temple medium to do it for her. The temple medium, however, was 'too tired' to carry out the ritual and asked Elise to do it herself. This tiredness, the temple medium said, was probably spirit induced. By saying this she was indicating that although it was acceptable for Elise to perform an outside ritual, it was not something the temple medium could do. Also, on at least one occasion, Elise interpreted a spirit in a manner that is inconsistent with the mediums' knowledge of spirits. While describing the Ninth Princess (*Co Chin*), Elise said that she wears a long Chinese gown and she explained that the spirit is 'more Chinese than Vietnamese.' Upon hearing this statement the temple medium quickly responded with authority, 'But she is Vietnamese.' After further discussion they realised that the confusion over the spirit's ethnicity had to do with the Mandarin collar of her dress. Elise interpreted the collar to mean that the dress was Chinese when in fact it is traditional Vietnamese dress.

Although Elise has a great deal to learn about the religion and the ritual and she is eager to increase her knowledge, she already has a strong familiarity with many of the spirits. In the view of mediums, this is a gift from the spirits and a sign that Elise is meant to become a spirit medium. At the same time, it can also be noted that Elise's new understanding is enhanced by the archetypical characteristics of the spirits that make crossing ethnic borders that much easier. Elise and the other mediums can each imagine an indigenous healer living a solitary existence in his mountain hut, a lady in pink whose caress is gentle as a summer's breeze or the self absorbed and petulant child.

Elise has been given a bell-stick, a sign of recruitment to mediumship.

Why Multiculturalism?

Elise's presence in the temple helps to validate the ritual for other mediums and adepts and promotes the image of *len dong* as a multicultural ritual. People in Vietnam and the USA have multiple and overlapping reasons for emphasising multiculturalism. Vietnamese scholars have tried to enhance the status and legitimacy of the ritual by describing it as a form of ancestor worship that honours *all* the peoples of Vietnam. The ritual was once classified by the Vietnamese government as a superstitious practice and was banned for several decades. It was legalised in 2006, partly because scholars were able to convince government authorities that the ritual was a form of national theatre celebrating the cultural diversity of Vietnam. Ngo Duc Thinh, one of the scholars most influential in promoting this view writes that,

> in feudal society the Viet majority, who had a higher social and economic level than the ethnic minorities, had an ideology that discriminated against other ethnic groups in all social relations. However...in the religious beliefs of the four palaces we find the spirit of equality; there

is no discrimination against any other nationalities. Because of this, the activities of...*len dong* contribute to cultural exchange and increase understanding between different ethnicities. (1992: 140)

Interpreting *len dong* as multicultural is one way that researchers have attempted to legitimise the ritual (Norton, 2000: 12).

Spirit mediums in Silicon Valley also have a multicultural agenda – the spirits want to attract people of different ethnicities to show the world that the *len dong* ritual is not just for the Vietnamese, but that it is for everyone. 'Why else,' asked one medium, 'does *len dong* exist in America?' She went on to say, 'You don't have to be Vietnamese to worship or channel the spirits, if you have the heart you have it.' This desire to include members of diverse ethnic and cultural groups has led to the exaggeration of certain kinds of identities. The following case involving Billy illustrates this point.

In the introduction to this chapter we mentioned Billy, a thirty-seven year old Chinese-Vietnamese man who is one of the new regulars at the temple. When Billy was first introduced to the authors the temple medium said, 'He isn't Vietnamese either.' Why would she say this about Billy, a man who is ethnic Chinese, grew up in Saigon and has a deep familiarity with Chinese and Vietnamese cultures? Was the temple medium trying to say that Billy and Elise are equivalent to each other because they are not Vietnamese? One reason this comment stood out is that one of the other long-term mediums is ethnic Chinese but she is never described as 'not Vietnamese.' Why did it suddenly become important with Billy? Perhaps it is because by exaggerating the ethnicities of Billy and Elise, mediums are showing that the religion and ritual of *len dong* are not restricted to individuals with Vietnamese heritage – they are available to everyone.

The recent emphasis on multiculturalism is also emerging in Vietnam. In the northern provinces some ethnic minorities are becoming disciples and initiates. They have been exposed to the religion through interactions with the Viet and tend to live in towns or along roads where such contacts are increased. Through these interactions they learn about the ritual by hearing stories from people who are spirit mediums or from those who have had contact with mediums. Although ethnic Chinese were mediums in Vietnam prior to 1979, individuals from the Tay, Muong and Thai ethnic groups have only become practitioners during the past ten years. In addition to the escalating contact between different ethnic groups, this increase is related both to recent changes legalising the ritual and to state recognition of *len dong* as national theatre.

The multicultural agenda also fits with Silicon Valley where 'deep diversity' is a way of life. A concept introduced by philosopher Charles Taylor and later developed by Clifford Geertz, deep diversity posits that,

> The very complexity of diversity in a global city makes it much less predictable and more ambiguous. Alternative forms of identity, not based on heritage, interact with traditional categories of ethnicity as emerging identities compete or are coupled with those ancestrally-based statuses. (English-Lueck, 2009)

Calculating the possible forms of heritage identity in Silicon Valley, English-Lueck found that by 'using a conservative minimum of fifty linguistic/ethnic categories, 1,125 quadrillion interactions were possible.' In such situations, people value mixing ethnic identities and they may even think it to be 'cool' (English-Lueck, 2009). At the same time, people have multiple, overlapping forms of identity. When asked if they were concerned with preserving their culture and Vietnamese traditions embedded in the *len dong* ritual, the mediums said, 'Yes, but we are Vietnamese from America. We're multicultural and we're open to new things. That's what makes us different.' Their religious identity is intertwined with an ethnic Viet identity that is simultaneously multicultural. Such ideas are, however, contested.

Some mediums in Silicon Valley say that *len dong* should be restricted to those people whose ancestors came from Vietnam. One person explained that every culture has its own religion. The spirits are the same, he said, but reveal themselves differently to different peoples. 'If you are American, the spirits are Christian. If you are Vietnamese, they are the Mother Goddess spirits.' 'How' he asks, 'can an American understand Vietnamese spirits? They don't even speak English!' Although this medium excludes Americans from *len dong* mediumship, he includes as Vietnamese someone from any ethnic group who has grown up in Vietnam or speaks the Vietnamese language. To be a medium, in his view, one has to have strong ties to Vietnamese culture. These diverse views can be partly attributed to experiences with multiculturalism. The temple that Billy and Elise attend is atypical in that many of the mediums are young and bicultural. Mostly raised in Silicon Valley, they share values of other Silicon Valley youth. Diversity is more than cool. It is a fact of life that people can traverse heritage identities. Other mediums are not as comfortable with this, perhaps because they are less exposed to ethnic border crossings. Such exchanges are relatively new in Vietnam and some US mediums may have never heard of this phenomenon in the USA or in Vietnam. It is our prediction, however, that the *len dong* ritual will be practised by increasingly diverse groups of people in the near future partly because it supports the cultural and ethnic diversity that arise from increased global flows of people.

The transition to being a multicultural temple will probably be a bit bumpy, especially as alternative visions of the spirits are introduced and new rituals are performed. Deep diversity and the archetypical nature of the spirits, however, will help to make this transition smoother. When Elise first came to the temple it seemed to us that she was stereotyping Asians and indigenous peoples, and we wondered if she was imitating the practices of spirit mediums in ways that were well intentioned but nonetheless disrespectful. At times she failed to acknowledge the deep cultural and historical contexts of the ritual and she introduced changes that were not readily accepted. However, upon further reflection we saw that Elise visualised the spirits in ways that were similar to other mediums, and this was facilitated by the archetypical nature of the spirits. Imagining Vietnam and its spirits is, in fact, a common and accepted form of knowledge which helps to make the religion accessible to all.

Elise was eagerly accepted for multiple reasons, notwithstanding her warm personality. The Vietnamese-American mediums had much to gain from her participation in their rituals. She was able to lend legitimacy to the ritual, validate the 'truth' and universality of the spirits, and support their image of the temple as 'new' and 'different.' Furthermore, by exaggerating Billy's Chinese – but not Vietnamese – heritage, mediums were able to emphasise the multicultural nature of their temple and their religion.

Conclusion

This chapter has illustrated that the *len dong* ritual can have meaning for people in different cultural settings. The ability to cross ethnic and cultural borders is related to two important factors. First, the ritual has internal characteristics that make it readily transposable from one socio-cultural context to another. Second, many mediums are, for a variety of reasons, motivated to practise multicultural rituals. In relation to the first factor, the stereotypical nature of the spirits, the ways that knowledge of the spirits is gained and the mutability of ritual practice contribute to the ability of *len dong* to traverse ethnic borders. Although the spirits are tied to specific cultures and locales in Vietnam, they are represented with conventional (and sometimes exaggerated) models of age, gender and ethnicity. This standardisation makes its possible for members of other cultures to relate to and identify with the spirits. Also, because mediums gain knowledge about the spirits through dreams, embodiment and imagination, the spirits are available to members of any ethnic group open to such experiences. Furthermore, *len dong* spirit mediums are also accepting of ritual change – albeit within certain limits. Members of other ethnic or cultural groups can introduce their own rituals into religious practice as long as they do not threaten the integrity of the ceremonies.

In respect of many spirit mediums and adepts being motivated to hold multicultural rituals, certainly, the view of *len dong* as a national theatre which celebrates cultural diversity has contributed to the legitimisation of the ritual in Vietnam. At the same time, multiculturalism also expresses the values and self-perception of young mediums in Silicon Valley. Having grown up in an environment characterised by deep diversity, these mediums are both familiar with traversing ethnic borders and value multiculturalism as an integral part of their daily lives. In addition, because they regard border crossings as evidence of the 'truth' of their spirits, multiculturalism affirms their religious beliefs. By emphasising or even exaggerating ethnicity they are able to illustrate that their spirits are able to cross borders, their rituals are multicultural and they have relevance to today's world.

2

EMBODIED SPIRIT(S) AND CHARISMATIC POWER AMONG CONGOLESE MIGRANTS IN LONDON

David Garbin

Introduction

This chapter examines the dynamics associated with the contested definitions of embodied charismatic power among Congolese migrants belonging to the Kimbanguist church, one of the largest African Initiated Christian churches. Initially a prophetic movement led by Simon Kimbangu in the then Belgian Congo, Kimbanguism has developed to become, in postcolonial times, a religious institution with numerous parishes in the Congolese diaspora throughout Europe and North America. Located in a London Kimbanguist diasporic sphere, my case study explores the different discourses and meanings associated with the phenomenon of the *molimo* (plural, *milimo*). Often referred to as *manifestations spirituelles* ('spiritual manifestations'), this phenomenon comprises the ritualised embodiment by several female mediums of the spirits (*milimo*) of the Prophet-founder Simon Kimbangu and his sons – known collectively as the *Papas*.

Comprising the two dimensions of healing (*nsadisi*) and divination (*mbikudi*), these *manifestations spirituelles* lasted from the early 1990s to the early 2000s, when the practice was 'officially' banned by the Kimbanguist clergy in the Democratic Republic of the Congo (DRC). Drawing on an ethnography of the Kimbanguist church in the UK and in the DRC and on an oral history of the *manifestations spirituelles* in the London context, I wish to shed light on the tensions over the boundaries of spiritual power and authority among Kimbanguist leaders and worshippers. These tensions had an important impact since they eventually triggered a major conflict leading to the first division of the church in London. Linked to the mobility of spiritual forces across different socio-spatial scales and realms, this conflictual dimension is a key component of my analysis. Of course, spirit possession may be considered an 'integral part of socio-religious representations and practices' and viewed as a 'mode of contact' between God/spirits and humans (Tarabout, 1999: 17). In this chapter, however, I wish to focus on the politics of the spirit(s) and the ways in which the *molimo* phenomenon is bound up with the idioms of order, charisma and public prophetic performance. This is important to consider as practices linked to spirit possession have often been conceptualised cross-culturally as expressions or metaphors of (changing) social realities and as forms of counter-discourse and counter-agency calling into question explicit or implicit hierarchies (Boddy, 1994: 407–34; Osella and Osella, 1999: 183–210). In the case of divination, for example, Winkelman and Peek regard it as

> a field of struggle among multiple interpretations...[that] is potentially a venue of the powerless against the powerful through the constructive and adaptive roles of possession and the associated divinatory revelations. Divination reveals a process of making life subjectively meaningful while providing a social critique and a mechanism for revealing the implicit contradictions in society. (2004: 8)

Considering the realm of possession and divination as a 'field of struggle' between different interpretations and understandings is crucial for our case study. Indeed we shall see how debates around the contested nature of the spirit(s) reflect wider politics of sacred – profane distinctions and spiritual authority. However, I do not want to reduce the analysis to an understanding of individual empowerment through the control, channelling or use of supernatural energies. Rather, I also wish to examine, perhaps more crucially, how this politics of the *molimo/milimo* is entwined with the collective experience of migration, urban modernity and diaspora as a 'horizon of expectation' which provides 'solidarity, purpose, identity, and futurity' (Johnson, P. 2007: 37).

Before examining questions related to the diasporic politics of the *milimo* I wish to discuss a set of issues raised by the production and reproduction of religious belongings in diasporic settings. Following this discussion, I will then provide some background on the emergence of Kimbanguism in the Congo and in the diaspora, before presenting the temporal and spatial backdrop of the spiritual manifestations in London. The initial 'coming into presence' (Lambek, 2010: 17–36) of the *milimo* in London occurred in a particular temporal context. Since the *manifestations spirituelles* took place at the beginning of the diasporic experience when the *bandimi* (worshippers) were (re)organising the church in new settings, the articulation between migration, diaspora and spiritual forces will also be examined as well as the status of migration in the Kimbanguist ethos. To what extent has the migration experience shaped debates about the emergence of the spiritual forces in the new urban landscape of the global city? Finally, in addition to analysing the ways in which the *molimo* phenomenon is bound up with this migration experience, the last section of the chapter focuses on the dynamics linking prophetic territorialisation and embodied power. When unpacking these dynamics it will be necessary to take into account the context of the *Pentecostalisation* of the Congolese religious landscape both in the homeland and in the diaspora and, above all, the contemporary symbolic and territorial (re)centring of a particular Kimbanguist prophetic order.

Diasporic Religion and the Reterritorialisation of the Sacred

In the early 1990s, recreating the *lingomba* ('community of the church') in London represented a reterritorialisation of the sacred which also provided a sense of 'home' for the newly arrived Kimbanguists. Most of these migrants, many initially asylum seekers, had fled the declining Mobutist dictatorship and the economic collapse of the then Zairian state – soon to be followed by the overthrowing of Mobutu by Joseph Kabila's rebel army.[1] These pioneers of the diaspora had made their way to London, following a variety of migratory routes, across Africa (mainly via Nigeria, South Africa and Angola) and/ or Europe (via Belgium, France, Portugal, and Switzerland). The production of a particular religious time-space linked to this 'sacred reterritorialisation' in the British context paved the way for a more explicit search for continuity in terms of organisation, tradition and ritualisation between the diasporic 'periphery' and the spiritual 'centre' in Africa. Indeed, the question of institutionalising this centre – periphery relationship started to emerge since the structure of Kimbanguism has been increasingly defined by the symbolic, theological and sacralised 'centring' of Nkamba, the birth village of the movement's founder Simon Kimbangu. Today, Nkamba is considered the 'Holy City' (*Mbenza Velela*) of the movement. The current spiritual leader of the church – one of the grandchildren of Simon Kimbangu – resides in Nkamba, which is now the major place of pilgrimage for members of what is today a major transnational religious institution with parishes in many African countries – the largest of which are in the DRC, Angola and Congo-Brazzaville – and across the Congolese diaspora in Europe and Northern America.

In their analysis of the Kimbanguist church in the Angolan context, Sarró and Blanes rightly point out that one of the fundamental challenges for

Nkamba temple during a major pilgrimage in 2008.

prophetic movements such as Kimbanguism was the question of surviving the (physical) death of the founding prophet to become established religious institutions (2009: 52–72). While we shall see how conflicts and schismatic dynamics have been shaped over the years by the crucial issue of succession of ecclesiastical and spiritual authority, we may add the effect of 'diasporisation' and uprooting in the contemporary globalised context to this challenge of prophetic inheritance and its eventual routinisation. Thus, in an era of time-space compression, disjuncture, hybridisation, and renegotiation of core – periphery systems, how can the centralised Kimbanguist systems of norms, values and identities be reproduced in new diasporic settings (see, Appadurai, 1996)?

This question appears to be key and not only for the Kimbanguist leaders of the diaspora involved in the power structure of institution and clergy. It is also key for ordinary worshippers (*bandimi*) concerned by the transmission of a Christian Kimbanguist ethos to the emerging 'second generation' in a 'Western' post-migration environment sometimes perceived to be dominated by secular – if not, profane or evil – influences. However, despite the challenge induced by deterritorialisation, it would be wrong to assume that the transnationalisation of Kimbanguism – created by the migration of its members – involved the latter being the receiving end of global forces as the passive subjects of a powerful diasporic dislocation. Indeed, and as a growing body of literature now shows, migrants and minorities are actively involved in the making and remaking of religious geographies, contributing to a contemporary 'globalisation of the sacred' (Vásquez and Marquardt, 2003). These transnational religious fields represent particular landscapes within which the ideas, values, objects, capital, image, and spirits/deities of religious actors circulate (Levitt, 2007; Hüwelmeier and Krause, 2010: 1–16). Intensified by new technologies, these flows constitute pathways which are integral to the relocation and spatial integration of 'migrant faiths' in new national contexts.

As defined by Paul Johnson (2007), the notion of 'diasporic religion' is relevant here for an understanding of another dimension of the individual and collective experience of 'religion in motion' – the realm linking collective memories, sacred or 'sacralised' heritage and (de)territorialised modes of belonging. For Johnson, diasporic religion delineates a space for the renegotiation of 'traditions' and the reworking of sacred references as a symbolic sphere where religious belongings are shaped by the tension between often contested visions of (authentic) 'home' and *mélanges* linked to the migrant 'practice' in a plural urban environment. In this sense, diasporic religion consists both of a 're-rooting' and 're-routing' experience of collective belonging; it involves 'identifications created and maintained through the work of memory, transit, communication, consumption, political contest, and, not least, ritual' (2007: 42). Kimbanguist modes of identification articulate ancestral (Kongo), colonial, post-colonial, Afro-centric, and biblical references, which operate as connected and connecting narratives in the current diasporic context. They produce meaning, filling the voids of the diasporic condition as they construct the migration experience against a wider perspective and a deeper history. Since they are interweaving notions of spatial ancestrality and sacredness with a set of collective memories, these 'diasporic horizons' – these *imaginaires* – also tend to reinforce the centrality of Nkamba. The pivotal symbolic position of the Holy City provides, in turn, the possibility for narrating a 'stable' community in a context of post-migration territorial instability, crystallised, for instance, by often temporary and precarious religious 'emplacement' in the post-industrial spatial interstices of the 'global city' (Garbin, 2010: 145–65; Krause, 2008: 109–30).

This vision of a 'stable' Kimbanguist universe centred on a powerful Nkamba represents a real symbolic resource in a context of crisis, mainly resulting from tensions over the leadership of the church among the descendants of 'Papa' Simon Kimbangu. Over the years, these tensions have dramatically eroded the unity of the church and the Kimbanguist *Kintuadi* – a sense of brotherhood linked to a 'golden age' of solidarity during the colonial repression when Kimbanguists were forced to worship underground. In this context of crisis, there is a clear tendency for the reaffirmation of the particular prophetic territorialisation of Nkamba and the charismatic authority of the spiritual leader (*Chef Spirituel*) who inherited the power to regulate the use of spiritual gifts. In addition to the renegotiation of centripetal diasporic horizons in a post-migration context, this specific Kimbanguist geography of the sacred represents, as we shall see, a crucial backdrop for our understanding of the politics of *molimo*, especially given the progressive diasporisation of Kimbanguism.

Kimbanguism and its 'Diasporisation'

The origin of Kimbanguism as a prophetic and messianic movement has been well documented (Asch, 1983; Balandier, 1955; Banton, 1963: 42–55; MacGaffey, 1983; Martin, 1981; Mokoko Gampiot, 2004). Mokoko Gampiot characterises Kimbanguism as an 'independent African religion born in the Belgian Congo out of the reaction of a Congolese leader against the colonial order' with 'spiritual and historical roots in this Congolese attempt of mystical and political reconstruction of the Kongo Kingdom' (2004: 49). While Balandier (1955) described Central African messianic movements in terms of symbolic resistance and political counter-forces resulting from the 'colonial situation,' Sarró and Blanes (2009: 52–72) rightly note that Kimbanguism managed to adapt to the postcolonial period through its routinisation, while keeping a strongly affirmed prophetic dimension even in its diasporic form (see also, Jules-Rosette, 1997: 153–67; MacGaffey, 1983).

Like most African independent religious movements, Kimbanguism emerged in an area where Christian missions were active. Thus Simon Kimbangu had been educated in the Baptist Missionary Society station in Gombe-Lutete, near Nkamba. He received a call from God (*Nzambi*) in 1918 and in 1921 started a ministry of faith-healing which soon brought thousands of pilgrims to Nkamba from the Lower Congo and what is today known as Congo-Brazzaville and Angola. Perceived as posing a threat to the colonial order, Kimbangu was arrested by the Belgian army and after 30 years of imprisonment died in jail in 1951. Most of his followers had been forcibly displaced across the country, yet ironically, as Tishken notes, 'the state's repressive tactic of forcing Kimbanguists into exile spread the movement throughout the Congo' (2002: 84).

Marie Muilu, the wife of Simon Kimbangu, played an important role in organising the movement from the time of the repression, when Kimbanguists had to go underground, until the official recognition of the Kimbanguist church as the 'Church of Christ on Earth by His Special Envoy Simon Kimbangu' – *Église de Jesus Christ sur Terre par Son Envoyé Spécial Simon Kimbangu* (EJCSK) – in 1959; one year before Congolese independence. From this period onwards and until his death in 1992, the youngest son of Kimbangu – Diangienda Kuntima ('Papa' Diangienda) – occupied the leadership of the church, assisted by his two brothers Kisolokele and Dialungana. Diangienda transformed the once localised messianic movement into one of the largest African Christian churches, gaining the official recognition of the Word Council of Churches and encouraging its expansion outside the Congo, in Africa and then Europe; a process which started with the migration of students to Belgium, France and Switzerland. It was thanks to these students that the CIK (*Cercle International Kimbanguiste*) – an organisation linking Kimbanguists in Europe with the church in Zaire – was created in 1976 (Mokoko Gampiot, 2008: 304–14). Working towards legal recognition of the church in France and Belgium, the organisation obtained the keen support of Diangienda, who travelled with a 250-strong delegation of Kimbanguist pastors, musicians and deacons to visit the newly constituted 'parishes' (Diangienda Kuntima, 1984: 218–25). This first generation of Kimbanguist 'pioneers' was soon joined by a growing number of migrants and asylum seekers, among them individuals who would become pastors and deacons and contribute to the recreation of a Kimbanguist diasporic moral order.

As the bulk of Congolese migration to the UK occurred from the early 1990s, the first British branch of the Kimbanguist church was created – later than most of its French and Belgian counterparts – in 1991. At that time, London was generally considered 'safer' than Brussels or Paris, where Mobutist agents were said to be actively trying to suppress the exiled resistance to the Zairian government (Styan, 2003: 17–37). Kimbanguists in London had started worshipping in home prayer circles before moving to a rented community hall and a Methodist church in 1991, both in east London. Links were established with Kimbanguists in Belgium and France and different sections were progressively set up within the church (e.g. youth, musician and choir groups). Money to develop the church soon began to be collected through regular *nzinsani*, the Kimbanguist rituals of offerings, where worshippers compete in a joyful atmosphere. Part of this *nzinsani* money could also be converted into 'sacred remittances' transferred to Nkamba, a practice still essential today since it is a sacred duty for Kimbanguists to strengthen their holy city, the symbolic and sacred centre of global Kimbanguism (Garbin, 2010: 145–65; Mélice, 2006: 67–76).

This centralised structure of the church revolving around the sacred power of Nkamba was eroded by a conflict directly linked to the inheritance of the leadership among the descendants of 'Papa' Simon Kimbangu. After the death of Diangienda and his brother Kisolokele in 1992, Dialungana, the last remaining of the three sons of Simon Kimbangu, became the head of the church. When Dialungana passed away in 2001, his younger son, Simon Kimbangu Kiangiani, took control of the church. This move was soon contested by the children of Diangienda and Kisolokele. Eventually, this conflict led to a schism which saw the emergence of two different branches: the 'official' church – also termed the '3=1' (in reference to the Kimbanguist 'trinity'[2]) – led by Kiangiani; and a group regarded as 'dissident' by the 'official' branch and – in reference to an ideal unity of the 26 cousins who were grandchildren of Simon Kimbangu – called the '26=1.' In the Congo as well as in Angola, confrontations, often violent, erupted over the definition of embodied spiritual power, but also for the control of the resources of the church between the members of the two branches (Sarró, Blanes and Viegas, 2008: 84–101).

The *Milimo* in Context: from Unity to Division

While the schism triggered by the conflict of leadership also provoked a division of the church in London, it is during the early 1990s that emerged the first real conflict among the Kimbanguists in the UK with the '*molimo* practice.' The first spiritual manifestations occurred when several women interrupted the service and started prophesying in their native language of Lingala. In an unconscious state of ecstatic trance, these women were possessed by the spirits of Papa Simon Kimbangu and Papa Diangienda. Prophesying (*mbikudi*) took the form of revelations about what Kimbanguists often refer to as 'secrets;' i.e. the otherwise hidden past of members of the church or messages about the future. They also had visions and revelations about the situation of the church both in the UK and in the Congo. In addition, they would assume the traditional role of the 'Papas' and thereby be individually consulted for advice or healing through prayers or by using the sacred water of Nkamba.

At first, the *bandimi* (worshippers) welcomed these *manifestations spirituelles* for several reasons. For instance, the apparition of the *milimo* through the body of several women was linked to one of the many prophecies made by Papa Diangienda, leader of the church for more than 30 years. Well known by Kimbanguists and based on the biblical book of Joel (chapter 2, verses

28–9), this prophecy predicted that 'young women would receive the Spirit' (*les jeunes femmes recevront l'Esprit*). Another important element of the initial consensus about the *molimo* phenomenon is linked to the coming of the spirit of Papa Diangienda, who had died in 1992 during hospital treatment in Switzerland. Indeed, the apparition of his spirit in the midst of the London diaspora was interpreted as an accomplishment of his earlier unfulfilled promise of visiting the Kimbanguists in the UK during his stay in Europe. Even Pastor A. – one of the fiercest opponents of the '*molimo* parish' and who played a key part in the division of the church – reflected on the coming of the *molimo* of Papa Diangienda in these terms.

> We thought that Papa Diangienda was coming in spirit, as he said he would be coming here in London. In fact, everything was prepared for Papa Diangienda, the house, the car, but then he died before he could come to London. He died in Switzerland. We were so surprised... So when he appeared as a *molimo* we thought it was *him* coming. We thought he was visiting us, but in spirit – we were really happy.

Another important aspect of the initial context of the apparition of the *molimo* in London is related to the lack of knowledge on how to deal with this phenomenon. Prior to their migration to London, only a few Kimbanguists had the experience of witnessing *molimo* possession first-hand. Among them was Pastor B. who, as an *encadreur* (see below), had been in charge of the supervision of spiritual retreats introduced during the mid-1970s. During these collective retreats, usually held in remote forest areas, worshippers showed intense devotion consisting of fasting, prayers, singing, and public confessions of sins 'fed by the hope for the healing of individual and social ills' (Mélice, 2001: 40). Many Kimbanguists would be touched by the spirit(s) – of Kimbangu or Marie Muilu, for instance – subsequently speaking in tongues, entering into trance or having visions. These three of four day retreats were connecting worshippers to the early age of Kimbanguism – an age of sacrifice and struggle but also of the power of *charismata* – and triggered a revival of faith and spirituality. In this sense, then, the presence of the *milimo* in London was perceived as a clear indication that spiritual energy was operating within the church and that the 'work' (*misala*) of prayers and intense devotion had been rewarded. Consequently, it was seen as a positive sign, providing the possibility for renewed spirituality and the re-moralisation of the community in the new diasporic context.

Sharing the knowledge linked to his experience as a spiritual supervisor (*encadreur*), Pastor B. contributed to the routinisation of *molimo* possession.

The spirits appeared during *beko* (prayer circles) as well as during Sunday services and séances became gradually organised and ritualised over time. Through the female mediums (*mamans basadi*) the *milimo* of Papa Simon Kimbangu and his sons were conveying 'messages' directly to the worshippers or through *encadreurs* who would write them down. Male and female, *encadreurs* were also responsible for making sure that the bodily trance of the medium remained 'controlled' during both the possession and the critical moment of the departure of the spirit from the body of the medium – the liminal stage between the end of the possession and the regaining of a 'normal' state of consciousness. *Encadreurs* would also play the role of 'assistant,' holding the Nkamba water used for healing (*nsadisi*) sessions.[3] Circulating within the Kimbanguist transnational space, Nkamba water and earth are essential sacred elements which reflect the importance of the 'portability' of the Holy City in the everyday diasporic context.

The conflict emerged out of a debate among London Kimbanguists about the veracity of the *milimo*'s prophecies and whether their actual origin was evil or divine. It is also important to note that initially there was no clear 'official' line about the *molimo* phenomenon in the Kimbanguist church. While only a minority of Kimbanguists had, because of their immigrant status, the possibility of travelling outside the UK, the London parish managed to organise a small delegation to accompany one *maman basadi* to Nkamba in order to get the opinion of the, then, spiritual leader, Papa Dialungana. Kimbanguists are still divided today about what the opinion of the spiritual leader actually was, with many arguing that he asked Kimbanguists to 'keep praying' to get an answer about the origin of the spirits. However a group blamed the *milimo* for 'producing disorder' and 'spreading lies' when condemning the supposedly immoral behaviour of members of the church who were accused by the spirits of, for example, theft, adultery and, in some cases, consulting witches and *féticheurs*. On the other hand, another group saw in the *milimo*'s revelations a divine intervention from the 'Papas' to restore discipline and moral order within the community of the church. The conflict eventually became violent and led to the first division of the Kimbanguist church in the UK. The group opposed to the *milimo* left the church, which, at that time, was situated in the Docklands area of east London. In 1995, this group created their own parish in Ilford (also in east London) in a rented Baptist church and managed to get the support of several 'elders' (members of the clergy in the Congo) who started openly to criticise *molimo* practices.

Opposition grew throughout the 1990s in a context of the increasing 'centring' of the power of the *Chef Spirituel* in Nkamba (Eade and Garbin, 2007: 413–24). In 2002, an official document (*Les Résolutions*) was released from the Holy City which sought to regulate the institutional structures of the church. The document confirmed Simon Kimbangu Kiangiani as the new and only spiritual leader, causing the schism with the other grandchildren of Simon Kimbangu – who saw in the decision a way for the 'elders' to marginalise members of *la descendance*. The document also comprised an article which, for the first time, officially banned *molimo* possession in places of worship. This decision reflected the extent to which – given a clear process of renewal of both bureaucratic and charismatic power associated with the notion of the ancestral prophetic centre of Nkamba – individual embodied charisma had become more and more problematic. Since the *molimo* embodiment entails prophetic performances linked to the gift of *charismata* such as healing and prophesying, its appearance in the public space of the church could well represent a symbolic challenge to the ongoing concentration of spiritual power around the leader of the church headquartered in Nkamba.

The publication of *Les Résolutions* had an important impact in London. The Docklands *milimo* gradually stopped appearing in public during services, prayer meetings and retreats. When they did appear, the pastors or *encadreurs* would stop the possession by touching the body of the medium. As Pastor A. told me: 'because the body that touches another possessed body is a body which is not inhabited by the *molimo*, if this foreign body touches the possessed person, automatically the spirit should go.' For Kimbanguists who opposed the *milimo*, the new spiritual leader had managed to put an end to the use of 'destructive' forces, sources of division and conflict within the church. Among followers of the *milimo*, some viewed the diminution of their appearance as a confirmation that the *milimo* were indeed 'real' and of divine nature since they had obeyed a sacred and divine order. Others accepted the decision but deplored the loss of a source of spiritual guidance linked to the presence of the 'Papas' in their midst.

Molimo and the Migration Experience

Since the *manifestations spirituelles* occurred at the beginning of the diasporic experience, it is important to explore the role played by this specific context and the status of migration both in the Kimbanguist symbolic and sacred sphere and in relation to the coming of the spirits in the 'global city' of London. In a wider perspective, the territorialisation (or reterritorialisation) of African churches in Europe is mainly the result of the migration process and the progressive constitution of new African diasporas. Exploring African Christianities in diaspora, many scholars have discussed the ways in which migrant congregations offer possibilities for negotiating the ambiguities and socio-cultural intricacies of the migration experience (Harris, 2006; Maskens, 2008: 49–69; Nieswand, 2005: 243–65; Ter Haar, 1998). Churches in the diaspora are important social spaces as they often involve community (re)arrangements which combine kinship and/or ethnic affiliations with the maintenance or creation of transnational social linkages with the homeland, other diasporic hubs or a sacred centre such as Nkamba. At the same time, the predicaments and opportunities of migration may be addressed through religious discourses – not least Pentecostal ones – which articulate modernity, social mobility, individual success, access to commodities, and prosperity. The localised creation of sacred landscapes in diaspora may also be accompanied by an emphasis on a globalised Christian universalism (Glick Schiller, Caglar and Guldbrandsen 2006: 612–33) or a radical reassertion of links with the time-space of the domestic sphere of the 'homeland.'

Migration also has a specific status for Kimbanguist migrants and the Kimbanguist belief system. Like the New York Black Caribbs/Garifuna studied by Paul Johnson (2007), the Kimbanguists have at their disposal a multiplicity of 'diasporic horizons,' which are both revolving around the tropes of collective migration and exile – e.g. the transatlantic slave trade and forced displacement and deportation during Belgian rule – and framed by a cyclical conception of time through which Kimbanguists are considered the new Jewish nation and Nkamba the 'New Jerusalem.' These powerful symbolic worlds draw the boundary of a 'community of suffering' which is 'updated' in the current context of migration and uprooting (see, Werbner, 2002). In this sense, both notions of 'old' and 'new' African diasporas are entangled and set against the powerful biblical dimension of exile (see, Koser, 2003). In addition, migration represents a way to convey the 'universal hope' of Kimbanguism embedded in its prophetic message. Kimbanguists often evoke Papa Diangienda who was known to encourage Kimbanguists to travel abroad and become *ambassadeurs du Kimbanguisme* by spreading the name of Kimbangu and, perhaps more importantly, by behaving in an exemplary way amidst the new tempting environment.

The coming of *milimo* was also closely associated with this migration experience. As spirit possession operates as a 'meta-narration' of experienced social and cultural transformations, the *molimo* phenomenon may be seen as a way of coming to terms with socio-cultural changes linked to migration. Initially, for many London Kimbanguists it appears that the *milimo*'s messages were indeed providing a way to negotiate the consequences of migration, the sense of loss and the 'cultural shock' which, according to Pastor G., contributed directly to a 'lack of respect' for the Kimbanguist doctrine and the church hierarchy.

There was not enough respect for the Kimbanguist doctrine. There were tensions between people, problems. So in some ways the *milimo* came to help us...The church was a way for some people to show that they had money, because there was easy money [*argent facile*] at that time! *Chekoula* [cheque fraud] and *booku* [benefit fraud]...So these young people were accumulating money, there was no respect...So the *milimo* came in this context, it was to help us, within the church...The spirit of Papa Simon Kimbangu came, to put some order in the church.

According to this particular interpretation of the *manifestations spiritu-elles*, the *milimo* were divine 'agents' of social control with the mission of reviving the faith and the obedience to a strict and 'authentic' Kimbanguist code of conduct (*Mibeko*). In this sense, the *milimo* were helping the moral transition, the reterritorialisation of a Kimbanguist ethos and order in the dangerous and tempting context of migration. The spirits of the 'Papas' were enabling a sense of ancestral 'home' in the diaspora as well as providing hope for the future and divine protection in times of uncertainty resulting from the 'in-betweeness' of the condition of migrants in Britain. Indeed, while retaining a Kimbanguist moral order in the 'risky' environment of Britain was seen as an essential part of the work of the *milimo*, difficulties linked to the incorporation in the new society were also addressed. During the early 1990s, one of the main concerns for Congolese Kimbanguists was linked to their immigration status, not least their asylum claims. The *milimo* were thus consulted by the worshippers asking for spiritual help to regularise their status in the UK.

Pastor G: Thanks to the *milimo*, we were successful with the papers... For example, you have been rejected and you need to leave the country, when you see her [the medium], you pray and she would tell you what to do and to pray, to adopt a good Christian behaviour. Her prayers will help you to get the papers. Nobody in our parish was deported [*expulsé*] because of absence of legal documents, nobody.

Pastor A: What people would ask was to get papers...We were all waiting for the decision of the Home Office. They wanted spiritual help...they were going to see the spirits of the *Papas* to see if they could get the papers...People would come with the letters of the Home Office and she [the medium] would touch the letter and pray...But instead of calling Papa *Mfumu a Mbanza* [Papa Dialungana, spiritual leader at that time] they were asking the *milimo* 'help me with the papers.'

The critique of Pastor A. about the role of the *milimo* – described here as *replacing* the power of the spiritual leader for worshippers seeking help with their immigration status in Britain – reflected the opinion of most of those who joined the Ilford parish after the division of the church. For them, the *milimo* represented uncontrolled forces challenging the (centralised) Kimbanguist body/space matrix of charismatic power (Garbin, 2010: 145–65). As we shall see, the relationship between this dimension of embodied charismatic power and the realms of order and disorder was integral to the politics of spirit possession among diasporic Kimbanguists, especially in the context of growing Pentecostalisation.

Order/Disorder, Boundaries of Embodied Charisma and the Pentecostal 'Other'

Those who strongly opposed the Docklands parish in which the female mediums were communicating messages from the 'Papas' were keen to draw clear-cut boundaries between *molimo* possession involving public perform-ances of healing and divination and other more individualised types of spir-itual gifts practised in the private sphere. While visions and dreams allow Kimbanguists to connect spiritually with Nkamba and with the 'Papas,' one of the charismatic gifts *par excellence* among Kimbanguists is the gift of receiving songs – the sacred hymns – which in addition to the Bible and prophecies of the Papas (mainly Kimbangu and Diangienda) represent the

Kimbanguist choir of the Ilford parish in London singing sacred hymns.

other essential source of Kimbanguist theology (Mokoko Gampiot, 2004: 99). Those who are blessed with this gift – perhaps the most important Kimbanguist oral tradition for expressing the divine – are said to be 'inspired' (*inspiré*). There are no particular ways of identifying 'inspired' Kimbanguists. Those who have the gift tend not to make public testimonies nor do they publicly prophesy during collective séances even if the hymns they receive contain biblical or prophetic messages (see, Molyneux, 1990: 153–87; Mokoko Gampiot, 2004).

This was a clear point of contention for Kimbanguists who saw in the *milimo* a way for the female mediums to publicly claim charismatic authority among the community of worshippers. In their eyes, the *milimo* were not only replacing the power of Nkamba but they were also uncontrolled forces generating disorder and confusion in the sacred time-space of the church service. They would also emphasise that the coming into presence of the *milimo* was unannounced, disrupting the service or the preaching.

Interestingly, a parallel was established with the Pentecostal churches (*églises de réveil*) which constitute the powerful 'other' of the Congolese religious landscape for the Kimbanguists. These *églises de réveil* have had a dramatic impact in the Congo since the early 1990s, especially in Kinshasa where the public and everyday popular spheres have become gradually 'charismatised' (Devisch, 1994: 555–86 and 2000: 119–43; De Boeck, 2005: 11–32; Pype, 2006: 296–318). While the members of the Docklands parish argued that the possessed *mamans basadi* were closely controlled by *encadreurs*, as the trance of the female mediums sometimes involved collapsing on the floor, for those opposing *milimo* possession it was uncomfortably similar to Pentecostal practices of intense bodily devotion. In their eyes, *molimo* trance was out of step with the traditional Kimbanguist 'management of the body' which is characterised by restraint – including the prohibition of dancing – especially during public worship. This particular set of *techniques du corps* (Mauss, 1934: 271–93) represents a crucial boundary between, on the one hand, the idioms of control, (centralised) order, discipline, and 'moderation' in the use and display of charismatic power and, on the other hand, the 'disorder', (individual) lack of control and 'excess' attributed to the theology, organisation and practices of Pentecostal churches.

Perhaps another reason why a parallel was drawn with the *églises de réveil* was the fact that in the early 1990s a Kimbanguist parish in Selembao (a neighbourhood of Kinshasa) also experienced these *manifestations spirituelles* mostly among young women. In the particular context of the Pentecostal boom across the urban landscape of the Congolese capital, the Selembao parish became known for its intense spiritual activity – attracting many non-Kimbanguists eager to consult the *milimo* for healing, prophecy or to get help with visa applications to Europe. Through visits and phone calls, some links were indeed established between the Docklands parish and Selembao, with prophetic revelations from each group occasionally coinciding. Because of the existence of such transnational – or, better, translocal – linkages, those opposing the *molimo* accused members of the Docklands parish of having established their 'holy centre' at Selembao instead of Nkamba. What is interesting here is that certain discourses were constructing an *imaginaire* of two transnationally connected urban hubs, each of which had its own inherent dangers – London, a global city of powerful spirits, and Selembao, an area where *féticheurs* and 'false prophets' of Pentecostalism were said to be active (Garbin, 2010: 145–65).

The potential influence of the *églises de réveil* appeared problematic insofar as in the eyes of most Kimbanguists the claim for spiritual power among Pentecostal pastors and prophets seems solely legitimised by an individual

Spiritual leader dispensing Holy Water to pilgrims in Nkamba.

divine revelation. In this sense, then, the *manifestations spirituelles* – involving depersonalisation of charisma from established hierarchies and its reperson-alisation within the female mediums – were clearly embedded in contested notions of spiritual authority. As mentioned above, the official 2002 ban of *molimo* practice in Kimbanguism is best understood against a specific theo-logical and prophetic order. In the context of the conflict over the leadership of the church between the members of *la descendance*, this order has been reinforced by both bureaucratic dynamics shaped by the Kimbanguist clergy (*Bambuta*) and a particular system of belief bound up with the prophetic embodiment of charismatic power. One of the most crucial beliefs is that the current spiritual leader incarnates the Holy Spirit (*Molimo Mosanto*) and is thereby endowed with the legitimate use of charismatic gifts. Albeit to a lesser extent, even though the leader's siblings also tend to have a sacred character, this endowment comprises precious symbolic capital of religious authority. It is in this context that the individualised embodiment of the *milimo* in the Docklands parish can thus be seen as posing a challenge to the existing terri-torial order. It does so because it involves a type of prophetic performance which symbolically contests existing monopolistic arrangements in respect of both the use and regulation of *charismata* and the status of the prophetic space of Nkamba as the 'authentic,' ancestral source of healing and miracle.

Conclusion

The case study of *molimo* embodiment presented in this chapter reflects the essential ambiguity of the sacred as a 'numinous experience' (Otto, R. 1923) which, in the case of Kimbanguism, is shaped by both Spirit-centred tendencies and a notion of ancestrality linked to traditional Kongo beliefs. Furthermore, this case study raises crucial issues about the relation-ship between the body and the sacred. It appears that the religious body is emplaced in different spheres (public and private), *imaginaires* and symbolic geographies (sacred and profane). At the same time, the body also actively emplaces, since it grounds and locates the spiritual experience by linking the realms of territoriality and sacred identity (see, Knott, 2005). In a plural religious context where Pentecostal Christianities play a crucial, if not quasi-hegemonic, role – in both the religious landscape and the cultural field – the religious body also becomes a marker, a boundary between different ways of performing the sacred. Another dimension of this chapter treats the set of power dynamics associated with the idea of order/disorder and charisma. Insofar as the Kimbanguist church regulates spiritual power and charisma – especially within the place of worship which constitutes not only a religious space but also a space for the enactment of ethnic and diasporic belongings

– the *molimo* phenomenon was directly embedded in the politics of public – private distinctions.

A question remains, though, concerning the extent to which the diasporic condition has shaped the interpretation of the *molimo* as a challenge to a centralised prophetic order. The issue of prophetic legitimacy is of course not new and in the case of Kimbanguism it has been prominent since the start of the ministry of Simon Kimbangu (Mokoko Gampiot, 2004). In his seminal study of prophetic movements in the Lower Congo – from their emergence to the early 1980s – MacGaffey (1983) reports instances of individualised prophetic dispositions linked to 'popular Kimbanguism.' He notes how, in the Kimbanguist church, 'major revelations and ecstatic experiences can constitute a threat to the ecclesiastical order, and must be contained' (1983: 70). The emergence of the *milimo* in the Docklands parish, then, cannot solely be attributed to the diasporic condition. At the same time, of course, the process and project of migration has undoubtedly influenced the tensions and debates about the role of the Spirit(s) within the new urban landscape of the diaspora. Here, the *molimo* phenomenon connects the themes of migration and the portability of religion in an era of global flows with the realm of the embodiment of the sacred in a modern context populated by 'occult economies' (Comaroff and Comaroff, 1999: 279–303). From this particular angle, then, we can see how the circulation of spirits and spiritual energy occurs not only across boundaries between the ethereal and physical worlds but also, and increasingly so, across the boundaries of physical spaces within wider migration or diasporic spheres (Hüwelmeier and Krause, 2010; Johnson, P. 2007; Lambek 2010: 17–36; Saraiva, 2008: 253–69). The presence of the *milimo* expressed a quest for continuity which linked past, present and future while connecting wider spaces of flows and filling moral voids. However, with the growing need for a routinised charismatic order across the Kimbanguist diasporic sphere, the maintenance of centre – periphery relations through bureaucratic conformity now represents a more significant element by which this sense of continuity is defined.

3

SPIRITS AND SLAVES IN CENTRAL SUDAN

Susan M. Kenyon

A Visit with Dasholay[1]

This evening I visited Umiya [zar leader] Sittona. Walking into her compound just after sunset, I found she was already possessed by the *burei zar* spirit Dasholay. At first I couldn't see anything except the glow of cigarettes inside the *rakuba* [lean-to], from where women's voices greeted me. Then Sittona's daughter, Sowsan, appeared to welcome me and led me over to the *rakuba* where Dasholay had come to two women. Sitting on the ground, facing each other, they were dressed in long black robes and head-scarves, smoking cigarettes. Dasholay-in-Sittona greeted me heartily, shaking hands in manly fashion and repeating *Khwaisa*? ['Are you well, is it good?'] as he gripped my hand aloft in apparent delight. Dasholay had also come to my old friend Maha, who was somewhat less effusive. I had clearly interrupted the spirits' conversation with their human guests, who included Hannan (whose baby had died a few days ago), Asia, Zachara, and a couple of others I didn't recognise.

'You're busy,' I protested, 'I'll come another time.'

'No, we're just chatting,' the Dasholays chorused, looking at me expectantly. I told them I'd come to show Sittona film of the zar thanksgiving ceremony held last month in Rajab at her house. Dasholay-in-Sittona promptly announced that he wanted to see it, and clearly so did the women. For the next half hour, they passed around the camera, watching, in the small camera window, video footage of the visit of the great Pashawat [Egyptian/Ottoman] spirits and shouting in delight as they recognised both spirit and human guests. Sowsan and her children wanted to see it too, and then in came Sittona's husband with some of the men who had been sitting outside in the road and they wanted to see it as well. They didn't look at much but instructed me to make a copy of it for Sittona.

When the film show was over I realised that Dasholay had left Maha, who was recovering from a fit of sneezing. She had taken off the black robe and was packing it up, ready to leave, and asked when I could visit her at home. Then she must have recalled our earlier conversation, when I'd worried about not hearing from my family. 'Why don't you ask Dasholay to check on your kids, to make sure they're okay?' she asked. This seemed like a great idea. I'd tried calling Alistair in England yesterday, and spoke briefly to one of his room-mates, but he didn't call back; I haven't heard from Chris in Indiana at all, and been unable to check my email since I came from Khartoum over six weeks ago. So I gave Dasholay 5,000 SDP [US$2], which is a lot [people usually give 500 SDP for this type of request], told him I was worried about my sons, Alistair and Chris, and asked him to see if they were well. Asia brought fresh incense, Dasholay breathed it in deeply and thoughtfully and, after a pause of a few minutes, turned to me, beaming. Shaking my hand heartily, he announced for all to hear, '*Be khair*, they are fine!' We shook hands aloft again, then pressed our hands to our hearts, repeating '*Be khair!*' I suppose it was what I expected, though I'd hoped for a little personal touch too, perhaps some small details about what they've been doing. Yet overall, I admit feeling reassured; and my companions thanked Dasholay profusely for his help, obviously impressed by his facility in grappling with problems of such international scope. (Field-note extract, 23 October 2001)

Background to Zar

The type of spirit possession commonly known as zar (also, *zaar* or *sar*) is found throughout northern Africa, much of the Middle East and in many diasporic communities of Europe, Asia and North America. It is particularly widespread in northern Sudan, related to beliefs and rituals found elsewhere in Africa. The term zar refers not only to a particular kind of spirit but also to the elaborate rituals associated with it and to types of illness or disorder caused by the possessing spirit, which may be appeased (if its demands are met) but cannot be exorcised. More formally, zar is known as the 'Red Wind,' *al-rih al-ahmar*,[2] and the spirits as *dastur*, 'hinge' or 'constitution,' suggesting the articulation of differences, including worldviews. It has been widely described (Lewis, al-Safi and Hurreiz, 1991), particularly for Sudan (Boddy,

1989; Constantinides, 1972; Makris, 2000) where today two related forms – *zar burei* and *zar tombura* – are found.[3] In contemporary Sudan, beliefs in zar are broadly shared among men and women, rich and poor and young and old, but its ritual is controlled largely by middle-aged women. Defying persecution, ridicule, education and modernity, Islamism and other forms of religious conservatism, zar continues to be widely practised and to attract new adepts as well as new spirits and rituals.

This chapter looks at some of these innovations, drawing on extended ethnographic field research in Sudan, mainly in the Blue Nile market town of Sennar where zar has been closely linked with the history of the modern town (Kenyon, 1991: 100–17 and 2009: 33–77). Sennar was founded by the Anglo-Egyptian colonial ('Condominium') government in the early-twentieth century as a settlement for ex-slave soldiers and their families, a few kilometres south of the old Funj capital of the same name. They brought zar with them from Upper Egypt and today's zar practice is directly descended from their ritual. As Constantinides (1972) also observed, the possessing spirits in Sudanese zar represent variously powerful figures present in nineteenth-century Egypt, grouped into seven categories or nations: *al-Darawish,* Sufi holymen; haughty *Pashawat,* Egyptian/Ottoman clerks and medical practitioners; aloof *Khawajat,* European administrators and missionaries; *al-Habbashi,* Abyssinians, ranging from well-dressed sultans to common servants; wild *Arab* tribesmen, brandishing short sharp knives; *al-Sudani,* coarse Black warriors, wielding ancient spears and shields; and the female slaves, *al-Sittat,* mysterious grandmothers, coquettish concubines and glamorous girls. Some spirits are identifiable (such as the Darawish spirit *Abd' al-Qadr al-Jilani*), others are family groups (the Habbashi *Awlad Mama,* children of Mama), but most are nameless individuals who possess traits specific to their group which both identify them and recall memories of their collective past. They most emphatically are not spirits of contemporary groups or individuals. The Sudani, for example, represent not contemporary Sudanese citizens but those people referred to in colonial records as 'detribalised;' i.e. slaves taken by force to the markets of Egypt. Although these spirits are today joined by spirits of later African immigrants and refugees, the appearance of most spirits in formal rituals recalls a place and past all but forgotten; a veritable 'palimpsest' of meanings, as new events are written onto a script itself already superimposed on earlier rituals (Boddy, 1989; Shaw, 2002). In Sennar, however, the core script remains linked to a past period about which people do not otherwise talk. A template, this script continues to address current needs even as the memories it evokes remain oblique, shifting and unsettling.

It was the woman remembered as Grandmother Zainab, a former slave of the Ababda people in Upper Egypt, who came south in the early-twentieth century with ex-army colonists and brought zar to Sennar, directly (in the words of her descendants) from the 'palaces of Instanbul.' Much of today's zar ritual and belief can be traced to Grandmother Zainab's early experiences in Ottoman Egypt. In the intervening years, the town of Sennar has prospered and expanded well beyond its founding families, mainly through colonial attempts to introduce intensive agriculture into the region by constructing a dam across the Blue Nile at this point. Subsequently, migrants from throughout Sudan and beyond have been attracted to the area by economic, health and educational opportunities. For many newcomers, particularly women, the houses of zar have offered colourful drama as well as social support and therapeutic assistance. Despite changes in the background of its participants, formal rituals of Sennar zar continue to bear the imprint of the original settlers' experience. Indeed, many of the spirits who possess people today directly recall nineteenth-century subaltern army life, with all its diversity, tension and unpredictability.

Recent Changes in Zar

In recent years, there has been a significant change in zar. This change comprises the emergence of lowly slave/servant spirits – specifically the siblings named 'Bashir,' 'Luliya' and 'Dasholay' – from the older panoply of zar spirits. Although these spirits are not regarded as new, their newfound prominence and present role signifies a departure from earlier practices.[4] Unlike the past, these slave spirits help people today by directly relaying messages between the 'Big' (i.e. important or old) spirits and their human guests. This development appears to have occurred within the last 30 years. It began when one of the zar leaders had a dream in which the spirit Bashir instructed her to prepare coffee for him so that he could 'come down' to cure/examine (khashf) women suffering from zar disorders.[5] The same spirit then started possessing several other local women on a regular basis, drinking coffee with their invited guests and (for a small sum) offering advice on physical and personal problems. Subsequently, Bashir's spirit sister or twin, the prostitute/bride spirit Luliya, also began to possess a few women outside formal healing ceremonies, offering spiritual help with reproductive matters. By the early-twenty-first century, Bashir and Luliya have been joined in this type of 'work' by their older half-brother spirit, Dasholay – or Azrag as he is more casually known.[6] In the past, women were possessed by Dasholay on important ceremonial occasions, but only within the last decade has he come regularly to examine clients. All three siblings can be coarse and capricious as well as highly sociable, but the informal rituals associated with them have become very popular, largely superseding the more formal, elaborate healing ceremonies.[7] As a result, everyday possession activities are now dominated by the visits of the three slave spirits.

This chapter explores the implication of these changes, in terms of what they reveal about developments in Sudan, about zar itself and about spirit possession in general. Economic, social and religious upheavals have transformed the country and go part of the way to explain what is happening in zar. The spirits and beliefs of zar itself have also adapted to the changing cultural expectations of more literate and affluent adepts, who are far removed from the ex-slave communities in which zar flourished in the early-twentieth century. Yet, this makes the contemporary predominance of servant/slave spirits even more intriguing. Accounts of possession beliefs and practices in other parts of the world, however, suggest that these spiritual developments are not isolated and that insight into the changes affecting zar in Sennar can be found in the ways that global transformations are negotiated at a local level.

Zar in the Contemporary Sudanese Town of Sennar

Sennar is a dusty market centre in Central Sudan, situated on the west banks of the Blue Nile. Today it gives every appearance of an unimposing 'traditional' African town, with unpaved roads and colourful outdoor markets. At the same time, it is an essentially cosmopolitan place, where satellite television makes world news instantly available and positions Sudan firmly in a global culture. Ubiquitous cell-phones link citizens to relatives working in places like Saudi Arabia, Malaysia and North America; rickshaws imported from India jostle with Toyota trucks and Land-Rovers along the highway; macaroni competes with more traditional beans and lentils; and forms of dress reflect fashions found throughout the Muslim world. On the northern outskirts of town, elegant new villas are being constructed – visible reminders of sons working overseas, sending remittances home which are then invested in real estate. This area contrasts sharply with squatter settlements of simple grass huts continuing to expand on the town's southern borders which are testimony to new waves of migrants from the west or south seeking refuge and opportunity. In towns like Sennar, men (and sometimes women) can find work, state education is available for their children and a variety of healing options, including a town hospital, meets their health needs. And for the devout, there are increasing numbers of mosques which offer opportunities for Quranic learning, prayer and the embrace of the wider Islamic community, *al-Jama'a*. There are also four churches catering to the recent influx of

Christian refugees from the south. I did not meet any of these refugees at the houses of zar. Indeed, all of the zar adepts I know are Muslim.

The Politics of Change

In the nearly half century I have known it, Sennar has changed dramatically. The town has almost trebled in size and the lives of its residents – many of them poor rural migrants – have prospered beyond their wildest dreams. Their children are being educated in the expectation that they will become tomorrow's professional class; and they are acquiring some of the consumer wealth that is increasingly regarded as indispensable in today's world. Many of these advantages have been bought by relatives working overseas, in other parts of the Muslim world, in Europe or America. Through these links even those left at home become familiar with the differences, and also the opportunities, in other ways of life, as expectations rise and social statuses fluctuate rapidly. For many women, this comes as no surprise. They and their mothers have been on intimate terms with foreigners for generations, living with them more closely than their expatriate children now experience. The spirit-world of zar – in many ways a parallel world to that of human life (Boddy, 1989) – has long offered adepts some understanding of strangers and the impact they have on local lives.

The nation state of Sudan has also experienced dramatic change. After several years of political insecurity, a successful military coup in 1989 instituted an Islamist government, the National Islamic Front (NIF) – known since 1998 as the National Congress. By the early 1990s, political and economic links with the West were severed, and the country aligned closely with the larger Muslim world. Subsequent crises, notably inflation and commodity shortages, increasing cost of living and unemployment, escalating labour migration, and politico-religious repression have variously impacted upon women's lives. Expanding educational facilities have made higher education more readily available, but expectations have been raised as employment opportunities shrink. Affording even basic staples has become increasingly difficult at a time when male support is often absent. Marriage has been delayed indefinitely because of the lack of suitable partners, and polygyny become more common. Meanwhile, profits from Sudan's new-found oil wealth – located on the boundaries between northern and southern Sudan – have failed to benefit the population at large. Channelled through the north, it exacerbated long-standing differences between the so-called 'Arab' Muslim north and non-Muslim, African south. Civil war returned with increasing intensity and though peace terms were finally agreed in 2005, the situation remains unstable. Furthermore, renewed conflict erupted to the west, in

Darfur. Throughout the country these events are monitored closely on television and radio, and, with young men conscripted into the government armed forces, few families have not experienced loss firsthand.

There was also dramatic global turmoil in the weeks preceding my visit to Dasholay in October 2001. On 11 September 2001, my host family and I watched on their small black and white television screen the shocking images of planes crashing into key US landmarks. Despite al-Jazira's and – courtesy of a neighbour's satellite dish – CNN's exhaustive coverage, the extent of the destruction remained unclear, but our disbelief and anger were widely shared. Over the next few days, people I barely knew stopped in the streets to offer the *fatiha* (Islamic condolences) and express the sincere hope that my children had been spared. Only when the US-led coalition invaded Afghanistan in early October – also covered extensively in the media – did sympathy dissipate. People wondered aloud if Sudan, an equally poor country, was to be attacked next, and shuddered at the incomprehensible but familiar aggression of the West.

The Politics of Possession

Sennar's houses of zar have likewise not been spared upheaval. In the early 1990s, the NIF attempted to reform popular Islam, including suppressing zar activities. Ritual events were forcibly interrupted and women known to be active in zar were whipped and imprisoned. Both zar leaders in Sennar were arrested but – despite the indignities their followers later recalled – government repression only reinforced the authority of the zar. Since the sudden death of Umiya Rabha in 1998, there has been a virtual explosion of activity as four new leaders have been inaugurated in *burei zar* alone. Yet, they also signal a departure from earlier generations of leaders who up until this time have all been descendants of the ex-slave colony. Though the four trained with Grandmother Zainab's successors and practise the form of zar she brought to the town, they belong to so-called 'Arab' tribes of northern Sudan and are from a different social background than former leaders descended from the ex-slave colony. Both the senior leaders in *burei zar* today, for example, have had long careers in zar but not only are they northern Sudanese, they also have independent jobs associated with clinical medicine. Umiya Kandiya, a Mahas woman, was girded as zar leader in 1999, inheriting Bashir as her main servant spirit. She holds coffee parties for him at least twice a week, despite a busy life as a practising midwife, teacher at the local midwifery college and single parent of two adopted daughters. When I have met her at the college, she has a crisp but sympathetic professional manner that endears her to pregnant patients but contrasts with her volatile personality in zar.

Susceptible to possession by spirits from *tombura zar* as well as *burei zar*, Kandiya often struggles with their conflicting demands. This concerns other women in zar, who feel her control of the spirits is sometimes wanting.

Umiya Sittona was only girded in 2000, but is widely regarded as the senior leader because she inherited her knowledge and paraphernalia directly from Grandmother Zainab – the main 'house-post' of Sennar zar. Born in 1940 to a Danagla family, Sittona became ill when still a child and was taken to all sorts of doctors and healers, including Zainab. Sittona only recovered, however, when treated by Zainab's son, Shaikh Muhammad, a powerful leader in the now obsolete form of zar known as *nugara*. According to local exegesis, *nugara zar* came from the heart of Africa, representing very old beliefs and practices. This helps explain why Dasholay is such a powerful spirit for Sittona: he is traced directly back to Muhammad and his mother Zainab. Although for much of her zar career Sittona worked closely with Muhammad's daughter, Rabha, the fact that she was first treated by the former soldier and colonist links her directly to Dasholay.

Charismatic and caring, Umiya Sittona is highly respected in her neighbourhood – a commanding presence despite the fact that in her day job at the hospital she is a mere 'cleaner' (*al-farasha*). Sittona suffers from a range of health problems: a goitre for which she had surgery in 2000, diabetes which is controlled by diet and some undetermined eye disorder (she frequently wears dark glasses). She may be ritually possessed by the whole panoply of spirits (*al-Jama'a*) – including Bashir and Luliya – and is much admired for the control she exerts over them. Sittona's main spirit, however, is Dasholay. Only he comes for the express purpose of examining patients – every Tuesday (and sometimes Sunday), when she prepares bitter (sugarless) coffee for him and his human guests.

The Black Spirit Dasholay: Spirit for a New Century?

Who, though, is Dasholay and why has he become so important? As a Black spirit, Dasholay is often referred to as Azrag, a term with servile overtones used for those 'blue-black' peoples to the south of Sennar. Dasholay, however, is definitely not regarded as belonging to the category of 'black spirit,' as are *Jinn* and Wind (*rih*) – each of whom is associated with evil. In local terms, Dasholay is a 'Black Red Wind,' essentially benevolent and supportive. Indeed, his names carry both affection and respect.

Other aspects of his identity are also important. Dasholay is one of four siblings, of whom Josay rarely appears. Bashir's appearance is often concurrent with or sequential to that of Dasholay, while the fourth sibling, Luliya, comes separately. Primarily associated with the Habbashi group, they are described as 'little' spirits, *khadam*, slaves or servants, since Habbashi spirits, like spirits in Ethiopian zar, include different classes – ranging from the powerful *Wazir Mama* to the lowly siblings under discussion (Leiris, 1934: 96–103, 125–36 and 1938: 108–25; Leslau, 1949: 204–12). When Dasholay 'comes down,' he may possess several women at the same time and I variously found him/ them to be 'very expansive,' 'boisterous and teasing,' 'intense,' and 'forceful.' Dasholay commands respect. Even as he jokes with his guests, they greet him formally – kissing the head of the woman he's possessing as they ask for advice. Both Bashir and Dasholay are served expensive refreshments such as cigarettes, coffee and (when available) local liquor (*araqi*). Today, most animal sacrifices in zar are offered in their name, and they then share meat from the head of the sacrificed animal with each other and with human guests who request it. In the formal ceremony of *Rajabiya*, they are both very visible, opening and closing each day's events and appearing in the interstices between visits from the Big spirits. The appearance of Dasholay and Bashir

The Black Spirit Dasholay.

provides light relief as well as a reasonably cheap opportunity to talk with the spirits. They are greeted enthusiastically by human guests who belt out familiar refrains to the song (*khiate*) summoning them.

Dasholay is always described as the 'biggest/oldest' sibling. He is the senior of the slave spirits, and as such he is more powerful than his siblings. However, he is also a very old spirit, as suggested by the fact that some of the songs for him are in an unknown language. Although most spirits communicate directly only with the Umiya they possess (see, Lambek, 1981), Dasholay, like Bashir, chats openly with people who come to meet him. While his words are based on Sudanese colloquial Arabic – with certain consonants substituted (see, Leslau, 1949: 204–12) – Dasholay's language is best described as *rutana,* one of the archaic tongues associated with peoples to the south. The language of Bashir, said to be Ethiopian, employs similar conventions and while it sounds different from that of Dasholay, the spirits can communicate with each other. After some initial uncertainty, they are also understood by their human guests.

During a healing ceremony in 1984, Dasholay suddenly possessed Umiya Rabha and instructed her to begin making 'coffee' for him. The following refrain, in Sudanese Arabic, greeted him and is probably more recent than the rest of the otherwise unintelligible *rutana* song. 'Dasholay, we are getting back to Dasholay. You are the owner of the cross, you are my supporter. I love you, and I will be back for you.' The reference to the 'owner of the cross' firmly identifies Dasholay as a Christian spirit. At the same time, while the white cross on Dasholay's black robe makes clear that Dasholay (like Bashir) may not be Muslim it also indicates that he is definitely not a follower of Satan. In addition, the verse reminds us that Dasholay had earlier been an important presence.

Dasholay is also a Sudanese spirit. Although he has the same unnamed Ethiopian (Habbashi) mother as his siblings in zar (where maternal links are important)), he has a different father – a Black Sudanese named Buruna (Buruni). Because of the importance of patrilineal descent in the larger society, Dasholay is thus linked to the *Sudani* spirits. Though I have never encountered a spirit named Buruna, the historical referents of the name are striking. 'Burun' was how Arabic-speakers referred to those people whom they enslaved from the Upper Blue Nile (Funj) region. A borderland between the present Sudanese and Ethiopian nation states, this has been a particularly violent and insecure region since the late-nineteenth century, when people like the Uduk were major targets of slave raids. It was also a major conflict arena in the more recent and long-running civil war (James, 1979 and 2007). While Dasholay – or Sholay – was not a name she knew, Wendy James has remarked that 'Da' is a familiar prefix for place names and clan names among the Gumuz, who live upstream from Sennar, mainly on the Ethiopian side of the border (personal communication, 2008 and 2009). Dasholay could, then, have been an actual person. The only records left, however, are the embodied experiences of zar which are notoriously thin on specifics. Few other individual spirits, though, have such a well-defined or intimate profile. Dasholay's blackness, emphasised by his nickname Azrag, is reinforced by both his dress and the sacrifice offered to him: a black male sheep or goat, the blood of which is 'drunk' by needy clients who daub it on their faces or hands. In this way the power of a Black African spirit, a slave, is literally absorbed into their bodies – an act repeated when they later share its meat.

Dasholay's Clients

Typical of those I met at zar events in general, the women who consult Dasholay have confidence that he can deal with the more challenging issues they face today. During my fieldwork in 2001, I met Asia and her sickly baby regularly at the house of zar and often saw her talking with the spirits. She told me that her daughter had been born prematurely in Sennar hospital and was not expected to survive. Two months later, she was small but still alive. Asia worried about her constantly because she could not afford the ongoing hospital care or nutritional supplements doctors told her were vital. She did not have enough breast-milk for the infant and tried to supplement feedings with bottled formula, instructions for which she could not read. The baby thus remained frail, but she was Asia's only child and Asia herself was no longer young, having married late in life. Her friend Hannan had also given birth prematurely around the same time and both women were shaken when that infant died suddenly. Asia turned regularly to Dasholay as someone who not only shared her concerns but had access to alternative therapies to safe-guard her child.

Tall, handsome Maha was another woman I often met at the houses of zar, particularly at Sittona's where she sometimes assisted with the ritual. On one occasion we listened wide-eyed as, highly agitated, Maha detailed her latest problems. Her daughter had been arrested and was in prison, accused of stealing large sums of money from the local government offices where she worked. Maha wanted advice from Dasholay about how to help her, indeed about what she should do. She feared she might lose their home (bought partly by proceeds from her daughter's job) and needed help in understanding how to navigate the legal impasse in which she now found herself. Dasholay's advice, urging restraint and patience, seemed to have the desired effect.

Rather different were the concerns of my old friend Zachara who, despite her newfound Islamic piety, had an ongoing conversation with Dasholay. Of major concern was her son-in-law, not heard from for many years. With their three children, Zachara's daughter had moved back in with her parents, found herself a job and waited sadly for news.

> Drawing on the cigarette she had offered him, Dasholay asked Zachara if there was any news of her daughter's husband.
> 'No,' said Zachara, 'no news for eight years, not since he left her to go back to Libya after the birth of their son. Not a word: no money, no letter, nothing ever since.'
> 'Can he be dead?' I wondered.
> 'No,' said Dasholay firmly, 'there would be news if he is dead. No, he simply has no money, he is lazy, he is ashamed, he is not getting in touch.' (Field-note extract, 23 October 2001)

After this exchange, Zachara admitted that she had visited another woman with strong powers in zar, whose spirit had told her that the husband would come soon. Dasholay disagreed vehemently with what the other spirit said and held out no hope they would hear from the reprobate.

Each of these cases, including my own, involves generational issues, as mothers grapple with the changing, sometimes dangerous world into which their children have been propelled. These women have few precedents for dealing with the challenges daughters particularly face: neonatal advances, expanding opportunities for employment, shifting understandings of legality, absentee husbands, and the encroachment of outside, often foreign, authorities on matters of family life. There is, however, one place to take such issues. The zar have long been a source of sound therapy and advice, even though many of the old spirits are now felt to be out of touch, too old-fashioned to understand new problems. Responding only when the drums are beaten in increasingly costly and infrequent ceremonies, the old spirits are too difficult to contact on a regular basis. Dasholay/Azrag and Bashir command respect for the accessibility of their advice and the forthright way in which they address contemporary problems. While their message is not always as encouraging as in my own case – when Dasholay was shown to be absolutely correct – they seem to understand the difficulties ordinary people face. As spirits of slaves, Dasholay and Bashir are regarded as the ultimate 'fixers,' ready to serve others as they negotiate otherwise inaccessible avenues of power and the complexities of modern life, both home and abroad.

Memory and Ritual in Central Sudan

Slavery Remembered

Several overlapping threads throw some light on the recent prominence of slave spirits. The slave trade, for example, pervades the history and ritual of zar in significant ways. Less well-known than the Atlantic trade, the African slave trade along the Nile was older, possibly dating back to Pharaonic times, and Sennar has long been an important crossroads. The powerful Funj Empire – which dominated much of what is now Sudan until 1821 – depended both on trade in human beings and on its slave army (Spaulding, 1982: 1–20 and 1985; Johnson, D. 1988: 142–86 and 1989: 72–88). After the Ottoman invasion of 1821, slave trading in Sudan increased rapidly and – despite the Ottoman ban on trading in 1854 – slavery persisted in Sudan well into the twentieth century. Although women were disproportionately caught up by the slave trade, other than as commodities their involvement has been ignored in the historical record. We know that there was a ready market for women; for example, concubines from the Ethiopian borderlands commanded the highest prices. The lives of concubines, however, were more privileged than other female slaves who could be prostituted by their owners (Spaulding and Beswick, 1995: 512–34).

Little is known otherwise about the daily lives of slaves from the region. Though slave trading, slave labour and slave suffering all facilitated the enormous economic global transformations of recent centuries, the voice of the slave has rarely been heard. As Lambek (1996: 235–54) and Palmié (2002) point out, while spirit possession is the traditional medium or idiom of the slave experience it is not something which modern experience has been trained to take seriously. Hard to decipher, the rituals of zar nevertheless open a window of 'dramatised history' (Constantinides, 1972) into nineteenth-century subaltern life. Furthermore, as a 'malleable' form of social memory, not least of a past which remains 'imperfect,' zar remains open to reinterpretation as its possession practices continue to weave the historical experience into more recent episodes of Sudanese life (Sharp, 1995: 75–88). As Lambek explains,

> [Spirits] are thus 'living history' in a strong sense; they bring forward and force people to acknowledge the commitments of and to the past. The past is never completely over; it continues to shape the present, even as it is distinct from it, and at the same time it is available to be addressed by the present. Conversely, remembering entails engagement with the past. (1996: 243)

In even simple zar rituals like Dasholay's coffee party, we are reminded that the past continues to affect the way that people deal with the present. Because its ritual suggests a level of meaning understood only in reference to outsiders who exerted control over local lives, zar recalls not simply a local past, but one further removed from present time and space. Through the medium of spirit possession, these outsiders are, among others, embodied by zar in the local bodies of its practitioners. Refracted through the often disconcerting gaze of zar, possessed women become these possessing others and thereby learn something of the difference and power found both in other cultures as well as their shared past.

The perspective of zar offers insight into the frailties of the powerful as well as the strengths of the subaltern. For example, certain Pashawat (Ottoman) spirits exude authority, even arrogance, but can be diverted by a pretty girl; some Arab warrior spirits value valour above discretion, choosing suicide over defeat; and black female spirits wear symbols of servility (ankle bracelets) as they strut proudly around the *maidan* (place of zar). These contradictions offer subaltern groups opportunities for dealing with those who have power over their bodies – something particularly understood by the spirits of slaves, whose unelaborated experiences have prepared them for the difficulties confronting townspeople today. Having suffered a certain fate themselves, slaves can, as spirits, give advice on how to deal with similar issues among the living (Bourguignon, 1995: 71).

Drawing on pivotal experiences of the distant and recent past, zar offers adepts a lens through which to view the transformations that continue to affect the modern-day world. At the same time, it offers a potential means of dealing with these transformations. The rituals in which zar spirits visit by possessing their hosts reflect a world full of tension, strangeness and unexpected turns. The embodied discourse of zar evokes encounters with strangers experienced through disorder, in times of dislocation and dispossession, when familiar resources have failed or collapsed. This is also how a woman talks of her initial experience/ encounter with zar spirits – she becomes ill or upset, but with a disorder that cannot respond to any known curing system. Zar offers a solution, by enabling the patient to bring the disorder back to the Other. By allowing the spirits to take over her body and sometimes be active through her, she is able to appropriate the otherness which first led to her disorder. In so doing, some kind of compromise is usually reached as mutually agreeable terms are negotiated. Consequently, the relationship between possessor and possessed – always, at least superficially, polite – comes to resemble that of guest and host. As in other possession practices, resolution is reached through a bargaining process, a contract with the possessing spirits, whose demands the Umiya interprets and helps implement.

A similar process in Ewe vodu is described vividly by Rosenthal (1998). Here, the spirits of former slaves possess the descendants of former slave owners, remembering an ongoing 'sacred debt' and set of mutual obligations that continue to shape present relationships. Through the shared knowledge inherited from Grandmother Zainab, memories of slavery also persist in Sennar zar. Today, when 'daughters of Arabs' (i.e. descendants of the former slavers) such as Kandiya and Sittona dominate the houses of zar, the increasing importance of slave spirits suggests, as with Ewe vodu, that some old debt is being remembered.

Negotiating Change

The recent prominence within zar of descendants of the Arab peoples of the north perhaps partly answers why slave spirits are choosing to surface now, in the early-twenty-first century. Other factors relating to the prominence of spirits such as Dasholay and Bashir may, however, also be significant. This is a time when the army has apparently consolidated political power in Sudan, and when there are constant threats of violent upheaval from within as well as without. It is also a time when young men are encouraged to work overseas, not always successfully; when local and national institutions are powerless in the face of new imperial threats; when Islamist leaders are redefining, sometimes apparently arbitrarily, social and religious correctness; and when families are broken up and new social orders are emerging as a result of financial remittances from overseas labour or perceived Islamist loyalties. As rough slave spirits with links to army ranks, the likes of Dasholay and Bashir are well-placed to consider individual disorders such as those mentioned above; not least since some of these disorders are, in part, the outcome of the present military-government's policies.

The death of Umiya Rabha (granddaughter of Grandmother Zainab) in 1998 and the demise of the old slave colonies – whose descendants controlled zar ritual for the last century – are also significant factors. As descendants of slaves, Rabha and others shared the knowledge brought from ancestral homes such as Egypt and the southern stretches of the Blue Nile. Interwoven with the broader accommodations made under slavery, this ancestral knowledge informed the social and ritual life of colonies like Sennar (Kenyon, 2009: 33–77). So, even as these early colonies are gentrified through their absorption into spreading urban neighbourhoods, new zar leaders continue to appropriate this knowledge and thereby reinforce their authority through the direct links enabled by the spirits of slaves responsible for their founding.

Current zar leaders like Sittona and Kandiya offer links to other contemporary sources of power, notably clinical medicine. Sittona may be a mere cleaner but she spends much of her day in the hospital, and – while Dasholay is insistent that his clients follow only his advice – she talks knowledgeably about alternative therapies. At the same time, the services offered by Dasholay-in-Sittona are more accessible, financially and socially, than a visit to the hospital or to the Big spirits of formal zar ritual where women may experience condescension and confusion. Furthermore, spirits like Dasholay relate easily to the women who consult them. Daughters of Arabs they may be, but many adepts today are nevertheless feeling economic, political and religious pressures which they need to discuss with somebody not invested in the hegemonic authority of the hospital, mosque or council offices.

In retrospect, my visit to Dasholay in 2001 highlighted some of the attributes that have made him such an effective spiritual support in the early-twenty-first century. In view of ongoing change, people are reminded how the global economy – somewhat different from but no less exploitative than the nineteenth century – is shaping local concerns in ways over which they feel they have little control. One expedient that proved effective in the past – even for slaves like Dasholay and his siblings, who appeared to have lost everything – continues to address the concerns of ordinary people today. As spirits in zar, Dasholay and Bashir speak for times which otherwise seem forgotten and, as spirits of slaves, they have the authority to address issues outside both present and local domains. In Sennar today it is not a collective subconscious guilt that drives women to sacrifice to the spirits of slaves, but rather a shared recognition that such individuals remain part of the larger global community in which they struggle to find their way. While there is no single, simple explanation for why slave spirits like Dasholay and Bashir should now gain prominence in zar, various overlapping threads make their present role appear timely, opportune and ultimately reasonable.

4

GENDERED DYNAMICS OF THE DIVINE

Trance and Possession Practices in Diaspora Hindu Sites in East London

Ann R. David

Introduction

This chapter examines detailed evidence from current and previous fieldwork in East Ham, east London, at sites of religious Hindu practice which offer significant data relating to religious possession.[1] The selected examples of benign possession are viewed as an integral and significant part of religious practice in contemporary forms of British Hinduism – forms that evidence a new growth in religious ritual and more prominent outward display at Hindu religious festivals in the UK. As well as the understanding of gendered issues in contemporary religious contexts, my particular interest is in the embodied and performative aspects of possession as practised in the trance dancing seen at annual festivals such as *Tai Pusam* – a Tamil Hindu festival dedicated to Murugan, Lord Siva's son in the Tamil month of January/February (called *Tai*) – and during summer chariot processions. The chapter examines in detail trance and possession amongst Tamil Saivite devotees at annual Hindu festivals, as well as oracular possession by a guru in a neo-Hindu site of religious expression frequented by female Tamil worshippers. I begin by briefly setting out the historical and cultural context of Hindu possession, and then discuss the part played by the notion of selfhood and individuality in such events.

Examples informing this chapter are taken from current fieldwork in East Ham, east London, from two different sites. The first is a small, newly estab-lished Hindu 'temple' called the Melmaruvathur Weekly Worshipping Centre which is an off-shoot of a well-established Hindu temple in southern India that offers, I would suggest, a form of neo-Hinduism. At this London religious site, Sri Lankan women offer their devotions to images of a male guru – living at the 'mother' temple in India – who regularly becomes possessed by the feminine power of the divine, called *Sakthi*.[2] The women participate fully in all the religious ritual at this setting. Since in orthodox Saivite temples only male priests can play the role of intermediary between deities and worshippers, this small but local site of practice challenges religious norms and offers the women a space where they embody and perform the divine, giving them access to a religious agency that is commonly prohibited in Brahminical Hindu worship. Through their movements, gestures and specific ritual actions, these new forms of feminine worship indicate an emerging divergent process of gendering the divine in current Hindu practice. This example of new gendered/re-gendered dynamics in Hindu expression is situated in a theoretical discussion of the significant and strategic conceptualisation of possession practices.

The chapter then moves on to examine more spontaneous forms of trance and possession at orthodox British Hindu temples amongst diaspora devotees attending annual festivals where possession is a potent signifier of Tamil devotion. These shows of devotion (*bhakti*) by worshippers are becoming more common and are increasingly on public display in the UK and elsewhere in the Tamil diaspora. Here, embodiment by a spirit or by a form of a deity constitutes a specific performance where the body of the individual literally becomes the body of the possessor. Possession is heavily reliant on present experience yet is mediated by a historical and cultural mythology, providing a form where personal and collective are yoked together, as the individual internalises the form of the deity. Public witnessing is of great significance to the event, allowing a corroboration of the extent of the possession. The chapter explores the extent to which possession is culturally and religiously defined and what place such individual transcendent experience has in the contemporary expression of British Hinduism. It interrogates migrant religious experience, seeking to discover what factors are at play in these newly emergent expressions as well as investigating notions of gendered ritual worship.

It is important to acknowledge at the outset of the discussion that possession in both historical and current Hindu practice does not comprise one single, simple category, but rather is a phenomenon which manifests through a complexity of embodied states, emotions, linguistic expressions, geographical locations, and cultural and religious performance. It holds multiple levels of meanings, encompassing the norms and values of religious and spiritual experience within Hinduism that range from Sanskritic Brahminical ritual to local, rural cultural practices. It is a topic that – as Frederick Smith reminds us in his extensive work on the subject – contains many-fold indigenous terms for the category of possession (2006). This kind of detailed analysis of terminology indicates that we need to understand and to view such embodied experiences as far as is possible from within the cultural and religious system of which they are part, laying down our Western notions that perhaps see such possessed states as unusual, threatening or even fascinating. In Hindu ritual, possession beliefs and the enactment of them form part of the 'normal range of human experience' and are a widespread activity affecting young and old, women and men, and those of low-caste, as well as middle and high-caste status (Erndl, 2007: 150). Possession is a temporary state of being that is fully supported by socio-cultural and religious norms, and which draws on an understanding of human life and the cosmos that is inextricably linked, indicating a symbiotic relationship with both natural and supernatural forces. Possession can be malevolent and potentially dangerous yet can also bring auspiciousness, happiness and positivity. As an action, it is transgressive as it allows for behaviour that is for the most part spontaneous, out of control and liminal, yet it is often sanctioned in religious practice and in social situations as a sign of grace. Its presence can indicate a level of purity that is highly valued by Hindu devotees.

Historical and Cultural Contexts of Hindu Possession

The history of possession practices in classical Tamil literature situates the phenomenon firmly within the *bhakti* (devotional) tradition. *Bhakti* expresses a devotional fervour towards the deity to the extent that the devotee may experience union with that deity or being 'possessed' by him/her. Extensive references in South Indian Tamil devotional poetry as well as late-first-millennium Sanskrit literature reveal the significant place of possession as part of such intensely-focused love of the deity by an individual devotee. The famous third-century classical Tamil text *Cilappatikaram* refers to celebratory ritual dances and possession dance, and Sanskritic texts as far back as the *Rig Veda* (1000 BCE) catalogue many instances of possession, thereby locating it in Sanskritic texts and culture. This is an important analysis for our discussion here, as what is being suggested is that the usual binary categorisation of elite Brahminical Sanskritised (male-dominated) culture and the local, vernacular folk practices highlighted in today's ethnographies on possession and in current thinking is in fact an imaginary one (see, Smith, 2006: 147). In relation to this chapter – which examines possession in orthodox Tamil Brahmin religious practice in east London as well as in emergent forms of Tamil neo-Hinduism that draw on vernacular expressions – this is a significant point.

By citing evidence that dissolves the traditional prejudices that possession is mainly for those of lower caste or from village backgrounds, we can view the ever-increasing instances of possession in contemporary British Hindu ritual in a different light. Rather than evidence of low-caste practice as it is often viewed, my ethnographic fieldwork reveals Tamil devotees of varied castes and classes participating in bodily mortification practices such as body-piercing and fire-walking during which some will go into trance or possession states (see, David, 2008: 217–31). As these practices become more emergent in British Hindu religious life and visible to a greater public gaze, there are increasing numbers of Hindu devotees participating in these age-old, yet newly defined, forms of religious possession and related rituals.

Concepts of Selfhood in Hindu Possession

The phenomenon of religious possession calls into question the place of the individual in the cosmos. As Erndl states, 'in Hinduism, there is no clear dividing line between divine and human; gods can become humans and humans can become gods' (1993: 113). Many commentators writing on Hindu ritual draw attention to the fluidity between divine beings and human beings and note how the performance of possession collapses any notion of boundaries of form (e.g. Erndl, 2007: 149–58; Fuller, 1992). We are dealing here with a worldview that sees the embodied human self as a permeable, even porous entity, available for the gods and spirits to enter on demand or spontaneously. This is quite a different notion to Western approaches that value, as Geertz puts it, the 'conception of the person as a bounded, unique, more or less integrated motivational and cognitive universe, a dynamic centre of awareness, emotion, judgment and action' (1993: 59). An ability to enter a state of possession is indicative of socio-cultural beliefs that identify powerful forces and influences outside the individual; in contrast to a Euro-American culture that identifies them within.

Further conceptual examples in Hindu practice which support the idea of the fluidity between the human and divine world are the notions of assimilation and reciprocity. Assimilation is found in exchanges of blessed food (*prasad*), when the devotee partakes of nourishment that the deity has 'eaten' and blessed, thereby imbibing and assimilating the deity's essence, purity and strength. One woman spoke to me of receiving *prasad* through the gift of a saree that had been 'worn' by one of the goddesses in the temple and that she herself would then wear. All such food and objects are considered 'imbued with his or her [the deity's] more purified and more powerful "substances"' (Nabokov, 2000: 9). *Prasad* is the material symbol of the deity's power and purity that has undergone a transmuting process during which the food, drink or clothing that has been symbolically eaten or worn by the god is imbued with divine grace and power (Fuller, 1992). The devotee then absorbs or ingests such divine qualities through the taking (or wearing) of *prasad*. It is a process of temporary divinisation of the human devotee, an impermanent moment of possession.

Additionally, the reciprocal gaze through the unblinking eyes of the deity to the devotee – a two-way exchange and a central part of Hindu ritual called *darshan* – is a receiving of power, of divine grace, with transformative poten-tiality (David, 2009a: 217–31). The deity gazes on the human devotee as the worshipper gazes on him/her. It is a reciprocal relationship, allowing transfer-ence of power, goodness, grace, and purity from the deity to the human, and is, in a sense, like the partaking of *prasad,* a form of temporary possession. It is as much about being seen as the act of seeing, and remains the most impor-tant part of Hindu devotion, whether in public or in private. As Eck notes, such 'visual apprehension of the image is charged with religious meaning' (1998: 3). Such seeing and being seen is a kind of touching – a contact between deity and onlooker – and a kind of knowing or understanding. Thus the concept of exchange between gods and humans, as argued previously, is at the heart of Hindu ritual worship. Smith has noted that the 'concept of divinization of the body is a theme that runs through Indian religion from the middle Vedic literature to contemporary possession performance,' under-lining the notion of total interrelatedness of body and cosmos (2006: 155). In the more spontaneous and easily recognised states of possession described below, the same understanding of the body as sacred space or as becoming divinised pertains. Those possessed are treated at the time *as* the deity and full of divine power, and are not seen just as a human temporarily transformed who still has human failings and who might be ritually impure. For that time, the possession is complete.

States of possession reveal a conceptual understanding of an individual self that can at times embody forms of the supernatural on a temporary basis, and also a belief that the Hindu devotee's body is transformed into sacred terri-tory. Using common ritual purification procedures to invite the deity to enter the body, a sacralisation or divinisation of the human form can take place. One common example of such transformation of the physical and meta-physical body takes place on a daily basis in orthodox Hindu Saivite temples when highly trained Brahmin priests prepare for ritual. Their prescribed ritual actions to purify body, heart and mind, codified by the Sanskritic tradition, appear to, in a manner of speaking, dissolve the human identity and create an invitation to the deity to enter their embodied form. The priests then become fit and purified intermediaries for the all-important relationship between the deities and the devotees visiting the temple. Without this process, ritual worship could not take place, and devotees would have no access to the power of the deity. Here the most valued criterion for possession to take place is one of ritual purity.

Gendered Possession by *Sakthi*

As noted, belief in the power of the deity to take possession of an individual is found in many instances of Hindu religious practice. In one area of East Ham, east London, an unusual Hindu religious scenario exists. The Melmaruvathur Centre is a local offshoot of a well-established South Indian temple, set up eight years ago in a converted house in a residential road near to East Ham High Street. The Centre is a religious 'temple' where Tamil Hindu devotees – predominantly Sri Lankan Tamil women – worship an individual guru as their deity. The man, named Bangaru Adigalar and resident in India, becomes possessed by a female goddess, *Sakthi*, thought to be the feminine power of the divine. When possessed, he talks, walks and acts as a woman and is referred to as 'she.' His is an oracular form of possession – in trance, possessed by the divine goddess he will give guidance to those who come to get his blessing and his words are thought to come directly from the divine. Adigalar sees himself as the humble mouthpiece of the goddess and has a global following of diaspora Tamils who have established similar worshipping centres all over the world. At present, there are over 4,000 Worshipping Centres in India, North America, Malaysia, Singapore, Australia, Dubai, Europe, and the UK. The following description is given by an in-house publication from the USA.

> Arulvaakku (Arul + Vaakku means Divine + Utterances) or Oracles are the sayings of His Holiness Adigalaar in a transcendental state in which, AdhiParaSakthi Spirit enters his body. He becomes She, since She is in Him. In that state, S(H)e delivers Oracles to individual devotees, in which S(H)e cures incurable diseases, solves unsolvable problems, makes the dumb speak, deaf hear, and blind see, gives spiritual guidance and provides solace. (*The Spiritual Beacon*, 2001: 2)

The dominant discourse described here and expressed by many devotees I have interviewed at the London centre is that of the miracles effected by Adigalar's power, particularly through his oracular possession. Since the 1970s, Adigalar has been receiving the goddess – called here by a qualifying epithet that refers to the most 'supreme' form of *Sakthi* (*Adhiparasakthi*, meaning 'first' and 'highest') – and although his state of possession is considered spontaneous, the formal times of his oracular trance have now been

Bangaru Adigalar.

restricted to Fridays, Sundays and Tuesdays at the mother temple in India. This is mainly due to the need to regulate the many thousands of devotees who now come to worship at the Indian temple, but also indicates the rather flexible and pragmatic arrangements in relation to specific embodied possession. Over the years, worshippers have come to see Adigalar as not only being possessed by the goddess *Sakthi*, but now worship him *as* the goddess herself. He is seen as totally identified with her. When going into trance, Adigalar begins by circling the complex of the temple. He then showers and changes into a red dhoti and goes around a second circuit. This is followed by various prayers and the performance of *arti* – the waving of a lighted flame, often camphor, in front of the deity and then to the devotees which symbolises the transference of power and purity between deity and the individual. Further circumambulations of the shrine take place accompanied by full body prostrations. Arriving at the main shrine of the temple, he talks to the goddess and then gently and quietly becomes possessed by her – a process described elsewhere as the 'holy spirit of Adhiparasakthi descending on him' (*The Spiritual Beacon*, 2001: 2).

Through his/her oracular pronouncements, Adigalar has evolved new and detailed forms of rituals and ways of conducting worship (*puja*). This neo-Hindu approach allows worshippers of all castes, of all ages and both genders to engage fully in religious ritual, overruling traditional Brahminical taboos that control women and lower-caste devotees in ritual practice. As the goddess *Sakthi,* Adigalar has vowed to empower Hindu women through religious ritual. At the London site, *puja* is led by a young married Tamil Sri Lankan woman and the majority of the followers are Tamil women. All participate in the ritual worship. On each of my many visits, it is insisted that I too contribute at specific times during the *puja.* As a non-Hindu, not only is this taboo in orthodox practice, but here at the Melmaruvathur Centre it is considered a privileged and auspicious position, and much sought-after by the devotees present. In fact, great pride is taken to note that Melmaruvathur Centres all over the world welcome those of different faiths and ethnicity, although in practice, it is clear that the majority of followers are Tamil Hindus. Ritual worship has been carefully evolved in this neo-Hindu expression so that tradition and modernity are woven into a symbiotic relationship, thereby attracting not only thousands of worshippers from all walks of life in India, but appealing directly to the Tamil global diaspora. It is attractive because of both its open acceptance of devotees of all castes and the guru's stance on women. It places no requirement on followers other than that of devotion.

Gendered Devotions

Unusually, the ritual worship at this centre is carried out by women, without the mediation of any male priests, and women of all ages are allowed into the inner sanctuary, regardless of age or issues of impurity related to menstruation. One of the group's atypical features is that women are trained to carry out public *puja* and fire sacrifices, called *yajnas* or *hommams.* Men are involved too, but the public *puja* is dominated by women. Although the global dissemination of Adigalar's practices follows the mother temple, the diaspora context in London is particular in that it is the first of the centres to be established in the UK and it is situated in a local area where more orthodox Saivite ritual worship is established. Thus, this new worshipping centre offers Tamil diaspora women a significant alternative religious base. Bangaru Adigalar as *Sakthi* has declared a mission to elevate women's status in society and to empower them, not just by seeing them as equal to men, but by giving them preference and priority in their spiritual activities as well as their secular and social roles. This is important, because despite the changing social, political and financial status of many of India's middle and upper-class women, women generally still remain second-class citizens. Discussing the rituals at the Indian temple, Chandrasekharan notes that,

> the Sakthi Path visualizes, and has accorded, a very unique role and status for women – even a preferential place to them – to conduct rituals and participate in all spiritual activities without any restriction whatsoever, as the upliftment of women socially and spiritually is the surest way of transforming and transfiguring humanity. (2004: 190)

In the context of the strict hierarchical systems which have, historically, dominated Indian society, this re-codified system of religious practice appears to reveal new negotiations in both social and religious domains. Narayanan speaks of the temple being 'overtly "feminist" in that it insists on equality between men and women' (2000: 770). There are no barriers of caste, gender or age, so widows, menstruating women and low-caste devotees may all take part, and are not prohibited from the ritual, as in many other Hindu temples. The concept of feminism and the differences in conception of the term in the West and in India is rather too large a subject to discuss in detail here, but it is important to acknowledge how differently Indian feminism has developed, and that it has not necessarily been concerned with Western notions of sexual freedom or opposition to the patriarchal family (see, Hiltebeitel and Erndl, 2000; Robinson, 1999).

Speaking with the women and men of the London temple, the sense of freedom and empowerment in their involvement in ritual practices is a domi- nating theme.[3] This contradicts traditional and current practice in main- stream Hindu temples in India and in the diaspora, where in Brahminical dharmic ritual, male priests direct and control the worship, acting as purified vehicles for the intimate relationship with the deity and offering the only access to divine power for the women. The sacred space of the temple is a highly gendered one, despite the fact that many of the deities worshipped have a female form. As Morin and Guelke acknowledge,

> Religious space often requires a spatial separation of men and women that comes with the associated power differentials. A worship service, for example, may be highly spatialized, as men typically officiate and have control and access to exclusive sites of power (and 'the sacred') within a religious building. (2007: xix)

As *bhakti* devotion allows for different kinds of relationships with God, we can find other examples of the reversal of gender roles, such as male devotees

Tamil devotees performing *puja* at the Melmaruvathur Temple, London.

of Krishna worshipping as females (Young, 1987: 59–103) and Tamil men encompassing 'femaleness' while possessed (Kapadia, 2000: 183). This is apparent in the East Ham centre where the male guru is worshipped as a goddess. Certain folk or rural practices of Hinduism also permit women a greater freedom and authority, where they can function as religious specialists (Sugirtharajah, 1994: 59–83).

Women's place in religious practice in Hindu traditions is a complex subject and clearly cannot be viewed through a lens of Western feminist standpoints that search for women's equality and rights – both 'unfamiliar concepts in a religion that has supported a hierarchical social system based on birth and occupation' (Young, 1999: 3). Despite areas within Hindu religious practice where women have been subjugated – such as in strict Brahminical spaces where men control the worship – Hindu women, as in many other cultures, have also been empowered by religious practice over the centuries. As Narayanan points out,

The Brahminical Hindu tradition has been marked by the curtailing of freedom to women in the spaces connected with dharmic roles. And yet, it may be argued by some that women in Hindu traditions – either because of or in spite of gender, caste, and class restrictions – have continuously found opportunities to create new spaces for artistic expression and paths to salvation. (2007: 180)

I argue here that there are manifold layers of significance in the Tamil women worshipping their guru – a man who becomes possessed by the most powerful feminine energy and force of the divine – as a woman. His evolved neo-Hindu practices offer the women devotees a link with a global religious community and appear to bring confidence and a sense of effectiveness in their complex migratory lives. Always a distinctive feature of Hindu tradition, worship of the goddess is now empowering the women through a new trajectory of ritual worship.

Possession Practices of Hindu Devotees

At the orthodox Saivite London Shri Murugan Temple – newly built according to traditional Hindu architectural principles and the first of its kind in London – over a thousand devotees will gather at their annual *Tai Pusam* celebrations. Each year of visiting I have observed increasing numbers of Tamil devotees attending along with a growing number of those going into states of possession or trance during their religious devotions.[4] The possession states witnessed at the East Ham temple are certainly spontaneous, yet at the same time follow a culturally codified pattern, and are controlled to some degree by fellow devotees who support, both physically and emotionally, those in possession. As people move around in trance, family members or supporters chant the name of the deity to them and protect them from hurting themselves or from falling down. In interviews, people speak also of the control of possession by the priest – if he sees a person in too frenzied a state or perhaps too vulnerable, he will press ash on their forehead with some vigour as they approach the shrine and bring them out of such devotional intensity.[5] Spontaneity is part of the event, as it is unknown who of the many devotees will become possessed, although most will be in a condition of devotional fervour and will have prepared for the day by fasting, bathing and by using further purification disciplines such as abstinence from certain foods, a period of celibacy, meditation, and prayer.

The unpredictable nature of possession – in that it can happen during *puja* (worship) or while singing *bhajans* (devotional songs) or in receiving *darshan* from the deity – allows it to be accepted and honoured in Hindu society, demonstrating that it is possible for a devotee, albeit briefly, to become united with and entered by his favoured deity. This is the sought-after intimacy between worshipper and deity which is the common goal of Hindu worship. One woman told me later that the deity Murugan (son of Siva) was the one carrying her heavy pot (containing mashed fruit) that she had on her head, and that she felt no weight. Another devotee – a young married man in his thirties and a devout devotee of the deity Murugan – each year at this festival undertakes body piercing and carries the *Kavadi* in procession in and around the temple.[6] He regularly goes into a possessed state and dances wildly whilst carrying the heavy burden of the *Kavadi*. When devotees enter possession trance during some of the religious festivals such as *Tai Pusam,* they are seen as embodying the divine by other participating devotees, who will try to touch their feet or actively seek out their gaze as they would do with one of the deities.

As the aforementioned young male became possessed and started to dance, devotees watched, chanting the deity's name and encouraging him in his trance, then proffered their children to him for a blessing. Chris Fuller explains that 'a man or woman, or even a child, who becomes possessed by

A Hindu devotee wearing *Kavadi*.

a deity is, while in this state, regarded as a bodily manifestation of the deity within' (1992: 31). The devotees becoming possessed at the East Ham temple are from all castes, signifying a change in diaspora practices compared to those in Sri Lanka, Mauritius and Malaysia, for example, where possession has been the prerogative of the lower castes and is looked down upon by higher caste Tamils. In a state of possession, then, all boundaries of caste, location, family, age, and occupation recede, bringing a freedom from the heavily bound social and religious status traditionally valued by Tamil Hindus.

Witnessing the preparation for the festival in the temple, one sees devotees already in a heightened state of emotional and religious devotion as they prepare their offerings – the *Kavadi*, the milk pots, their trays containing cut coconuts, fruits, and incense – which the priest then blesses. All the time, there is chanting of devotional songs accompanied by the beating of drums and tambourines and the atmosphere is filled with expectation, with powerful hypnotic sounds and by the pungent smells of incense and cut fruit. A ritual specialist, brought in for the occasion, moves round the room, undertaking the ritual body piercing for those who wish. As he attends to each devotee who is to have a piercing, the sound of chanting and the beats increase to a louder pitch and the priest, who watches attentively, holds the burning camphor close. Friends and supporters surround the person who is usually already in a quiet trance-like state, and then using pressure on certain points, and plenty of sacred ash, the specialist inserts the objects of piercing. In this case, he puts a small silver needle vertically into one young woman's forehead, just placing it through the very top layers of the skin.

The next devotee, a middle-aged woman, has chosen to have a silver *vel* – considered to be Murugan's lance, having a spade-shaped blade at the end to represent the *Sakthi* power of the divine – through her tongue, and is held by her husband as the procedure takes place. Each woman neither winces nor shows distress during the piercing, and there is no sign of blood. Each remains quiet, eyes slightly glazed, and then one woman begins to rock from side to side, in trance. The man continues now with more spectacular piercings of male devotees who are having *vels* through their tongues and cheeks, as well as small needles through their upper arms. Another man has hooks inserted all over his bare chest and back, from which are hanging limes. The accompanying singing and drumming now increases, with chanting of *Vel, vel, vetri vel!* ('victorious *vel*') loudly and more energetically as each person receives their piercings and this refrain accompanies the devotees as they process three times around the temple. Lack of pain or any show of blood is thought to be proof of the purity of the state of the devotee and of the presence of the divine Murugan entering his or her body to possess it. Ward reminds us that there is scientific evidence that 'repetitive auditory patterns' such as drumming and sounds of chanting, clapping and singing are all factors that lead towards producing a trance state (1984: 310). Added to this are the intense use of incense and the burning of camphor – which has narcotic effects – at such times in Hindu ritual, again something proven to have a powerful effect on brain function (see, Ward, 1984: 307–34). Another factor influencing any performance of trance or possession is the devotee's own expectations of such a highly charged event.

The highly elaborate wooden *Kavadi*, carried by many of the male devotees, are decorated with peacock feathers to symbolise the peacock that transports the deity of Murugan, spoken of as his vehicle. The carrying of such *Kavadi* symbolises the devotee's body as a vehicle for the god Murugan; that is, the human body of the devotee is made available to the deity to 'ride' or to possess. One documentary film of the famous *Tai Pusam* celebrations in Kuala Lumpur, Malaysia, records devotees stating that 'Murugan dances on our body,' as if the deity is riding on and in their bodies (Simons, 1973). The sense of being mounted by the deity is also contained in the Tamil word *avecam,* commonly used for possession. Another Tamil term would be 'god-dancing' or 'dancing the god' (*teyyāttam*) which would be appropriate for the descriptions of these devotees performing a trance/possession dance. At the London Shri Murugan Temple, one or two of the male devotees dance ecstatically whilst possessed, all the while carrying the heavy *Kavadi* on their shoulders. One young man even ties bells on his ankles to enhance the sound of his movements in the trance dance. I would argue that such benign trance/possession dancing of Tamil devotees at the *Tai Pusam* festival is a potent signifier of Tamil devotion, a performance of faith in the deity Murugan, expressed in the movements and gestures of their dance. In this instance it reveals more about the nature of religious *bhakti* within Tamil Hinduism as a belief that the powers of the deity Murugan become embodied in the purified body of the devotee during the dance and, more importantly, the devotee's possession. As discussed earlier, it confirms the porosity or fluidity of the embodied individual and transcends the usual notions of boundaries between humanity and the supernatural world. This is perhaps even more important for those who have fled their homes in Sri Lanka, and for whom transcending boundaries of place and space in their diasporic situation are pressing factors.

Diasporic Issues
Factors of life of the Sri Lankan Tamil diaspora play strongly on the changing manifestations of cultural, social and religious practices as seen in the above examples. Many of my informants in East Ham are refugees from the civil

war; others are 'twice-migrants,' having journeyed from Sri Lanka to countries in Europe (e.g. Switzerland, France and Germany) before migrating to the UK. Many have struggled to obtain qualifications, jobs and settled homes. In terms of oracular possession, Patricia Lawrence's ethnographic study of Tamils in Sri Lanka notes that the civil war has brought increased involvement in such ritual, as well as in goddess worship and possession during fire-walking events (2003: 100–23). Bodily mortification practices are also on the increase. These facts of increased ritual involvement and more bodily displays are confirmed too in my ethnographic work in London. Lawrence explains how such events – particularly that of oracular possession – are used as 'therapeutic' tools, enabling devotees to absorb and come to terms with their painful memories and their suffering through collective healing and re-empowering rituals (2003: 114–15).

Certainly, the stories from devotees at both the orthodox Saivite East Ham temple and the new Melmaruvathur Centre reveal the need for 'divine' help with their social problems, such as sickness of family members, the difficulties in gaining employment, inability in becoming pregnant, and so on. The discourse at the predominately Sri Lankan London Melmaruvathur Centre described above seeks to reconcile tradition and modernity, home and diaspora, past and present, and offers new understandings for the contemporary, and often displaced, diasporic devotee. Mottos (in Tamil and English) displayed on the walls of this neo-Hindu temple describing one family, one humanity and one Mother are frequently cited in my interviews with devotees, as are the appearance of miraculous resolutions to their problems. It is a reformulated, re-imagined Hindu doctrine which carefully presents a world that is free from caste, gender restrictions, colour, and creed, thereby appealing to those of lower status (who attend the temple) and those who find traditional Saivite worship restrictive. Dominant themes are of miracles that involve the resolution of health crises, pregnancies in the case of women unable to conceive and job offers where none had been available (see, David, 2009b: 337–55). Underlining the contemporary application of divine power, miracles now include the successful receiving of immigrant visas.

These examples remain essential areas of importance to Hindu life and survival and, nowadays, for those seeking asylum and are proof of the power of the deity intervening in their lives. Furthermore, such divine power offers an apparent route to social freedom for devotees who have very little and find themselves often on the lowest rungs of society's ladder, as well as assisting in healing the traumas of loss of family and home, of displacement and resettlement. As in Lawrence's study (2003: 100–23), here in the UK there is evidence of an increase in ritual practices such as body piercing and fire-walking amongst the Tamil Hindus, not only from Sri Lanka but from Malaysia, Mauritius, Singapore, and South Africa (David, 2009b: 337–55). Perhaps these proud narrations of miraculous powers are for the Sri Lankan refugees a way of reaffirming faith, of providing evidence of divine protection and of hope for the future. Is this a time when such supernatural factors are most needed in the lives of a community who has lived through violent conflict and territorial displacement?

This chapter has looked at contemporary forms of Hindu possession in relatively newly established Tamil religious communities in east London. Both sites explored are home to diasporic groups, with many followers still holding refugee or asylum status, although others are longer-settled migrants. Possession experiences found amongst such Tamil Hindu followers in the UK are, for these communities, living evidence of the power and presence of their deities in contemporary London, and of the auspiciousness and purity of their temples and their religious events. This soothes and eases the passage of those fleeing the difficulties of Sri Lanka and for those whose journeys of migration have been long and troubled. Tamil migrants from Malaysia, Mauritius, South Africa, and southern India join with those from Sri Lanka at festival times, bringing and establishing an eclectic mix of village religious traditions as well as Brahminised Sanskrit practices in these London temples and religious centres. It is evident that increasingly displayed proof of the power of fervent devotion through trance and possession is a central aspect to assist settling socially, culturally and religiously, offering a sacred space where all can be accepted and can unite. Embodying the gods through culturally and religiously defined trance and possession is a powerful way for Tamil Hindus to mark their place in UK life and to re-imagine their solidarity with a global community of Tamil religious worshippers.

In the same way, Sri Lankan Tamil women who unite in their devotions offered to Bangaru Adigalar – as the form of the feminine power of the divine – are establishing their own place and space in a diasporic milieu where they can find a level of religious independence and empowerment. According to informants, the miraculous possession oracles of their guru have brought perceived resolutions to their problems, offspring to childless marriages and allowed for successful job-seeking which have transformed their lives. These stories of possession miracles are framed by certain social and cultural expectations of a 'good' Hindu life. The chapter offers initial findings from such a Hindu female-managed and negotiated space that takes its authority from a godly female power manifest through a human male form. Worship of the goddess, always a distinctive feature of Hindu tradition, is now empowering the women through a new trajectory of ritual worship.

Part II

TAKING POSSESSION OF THE SPIRIT

Relational Selves and Supernatural Others

It is now something of a truism to say that individual identity is forged and subjective agency practised in relation to others – be it in association with or distinction from these others. Within worldviews infused by the presence of the supernatural, the others in relation to whom identity and agency unfold are as likely to be spiritual entities as they are flesh and blood human beings. As the ritualised orchestration of humankind's interaction with its supernatural others, the spirit possession paradigm furnishes a particular kind of resourcing through which identity construction and self-expression are supported. Paying particular attention to the themes of identity and agency, the following three chapters engage a number of assumptions which both underlie and inform the spirits' capacity to sustain individuals in their respective personal projects.

Set in Cuba, Santo's chapter engages the mediumistic practices of Spiritism as directly contributing to the 'production of particular kinds of persons.' By first identifying and then working with the spirits with whom s/he is most closely associated, Santo regards the medium as both producing these spirits through her person while, at the same time, producing his person through the spirits. Such is the case, because Spiritist practices – like other possession repertoires populating Cuba's religious landscape – work with a particular 'ontology of the self.' Here, personhood is constituted through relations of mutuality as much with the spirits of the dead as with the living. Santo identifies the central component underlying this exchange as a conceptualisation of the self as porous to the spirit-world. While furnishing the self with a range of supernatural resourcing upon which to draw, this permeability also entails a degree of subjective vulnerability which must be minimised by learning to know and work with the spirits.

The porosity of the self and the world we inhabit to supernatural influence is explored by Goslinga in relation to assisted conception narratives in south India. Here, Goslinga focuses upon a single story which – narrated by the mother – tells of the god Pandi and his role in the conception of a daughter, Rajathiammal. Woven throughout the story, Goslinga argues, is a richly textured alternative to prevailing 'Euro-American conceits' and their attendant bio-medical presumptions in respect of persons, the body and our material environment. Throughout the narrative, Rajathiammal's mother records various interventions by Pandi in which the god both reasserts and overturns existing arrangements – be they physical, religious, economic or moral. Ultimately, the narrative recounted by Goslinga represents an extended claim to belonging and the myriad obligations implicated by it. At the same time, the narration of Pandi's actions also asserts the complementary role of maternal agency in respect of much that occurred.

Coleman's chapter on a Pentecostal organisation in Sweden reflects a growing appreciation of the ritual and discursive similarities between particular forms of charismatic Christianity and other religious repertoires traditionally associated with possession. Likewise noting the 'permeability of the self' to supernatural 'in-filling,' Coleman employs a 'transactional model of charismatic personhood' in which identity is constructed in relation to a community of fellow believers – each of whom is, likewise, intent on forging his/her own sense of self. Here, the concept of 'meta-possession' is offered to explicate the 'complex invocation of agency' which narrates spiritual inspiration and its concomitant expansion of subjectivity and its reach. Coleman's use of the notion of 'ventriloquism' – being talked through by another – points further in the direction of the Pentecostal discourse at play serving to reinforce the self and its claims upon the world around it. As with other possession repertoires, the supernatural agency which speaks through the human host both underwrites claims to speak authentically 'in the spirit' and absolves the host of responsibility for what is said through him/her. Together, the authenticity of what is said and the absolution for its impact affords the subject a degree of agency above and beyond that of the ordinary, uninspired individual.

PROCESS, PERSONHOOD AND POSSESSION IN CUBAN SPIRITISM

Diana Espirito Santo

This chapter deals with the production of particular kinds of persons in the spirit mediumship practices known in Cuba as *espiritismo cruzado* – meaning crossed or syncretistic Spiritism.[1] These practices furnish the practitioner of the dominant Afro-Cuban religions with a logic for the 'self' and its differentiation. I will argue that it is not enough to ask what Morten Klass suggests is that most uncomfortable of questions – namely, 'What is really happening when someone claims to be, or is said to be, undergoing "possession" by a "god," a "spirit," an "ancestor," or some other variety of invisible or noncorporeal entity?' (2003: 1). Rather, we must first ascertain what kind of ontological premises underpin a notion of the person who is 'possessed,' so that we do not end up by naturalising religious experience according to theoretical pregivens. In the first section of this chapter I explore the importance of ideas of porosity and relationality in the definition of the 'self' among followers of Afro-Cuban religion in general. In the second section, I focus mainly upon Cuban Spiritism to highlight the role that spirit mediums play in the creation of particular religious and personal paths, and thus, persons. In the third, I point to the dynamic character of such self-understandings. In the end, these questions lead us to consider not just the implications of the interconnectivity of mutually constituted – and constituting – cosmologies in Cuba and perhaps elsewhere with respect to the development of selves, but also the relationship obtaining between persons and entities beyond single or event-like moments of possession.

Existence and Relationality in Afro-Cuban Religion

In Havana, adepts and experts of Afro-Cuban religion are avid observers of the interconnectedness of the world of the living and the spirits of the dead and other deities. Religious biographical narratives are testament not just to the myriad signs, proofs and interventions the latter proportion the former, but also to the necessary co-existence of realms of visible and invisible causality, material and immaterial agencies and human and non-human selves where even objects are actors in this stage. José, an elderly and experienced spirit medium and long-time initiate of popular *Santería* and *Palo Monte* practices, tells me the following.

> I have a little anecdote I will share with you. I was in the military once, and they were going to cut one of my legs off because I had a wound in the sole of my foot that was turning gangrenous. I was in the hospital and the doctors gathered to perform the surgery. One of the doctors they called was a close friend of mine, and when he found out it was me they were to perform the amputation on, he came to me and told me I should ask for permission and leave. 'Don't let them cut off your leg, shoot yourself my friend, I prefer you dead than crippled,' he said sadly, and I left. When I got home, I was advised by a cousin to go to the house of a well-known *brujero* [word denoting religious expert that deals in witchcraft, but in this case, a practitioner of Santería], he told me that people arrived there in crutches and left walking, and my father said 'let's go! If there's a chance, we'll take him!' So they took me. When I arrived the man placed a mat on the floor and laid out his cowry shells [divination method in Santería]. He told me to take my shoes off, and then began his ceremony. He tells me – listen to this, these are words I will never forget, forty-three years ago – 'Santa Bárbara says that if you are initiated in the next forty-five days she will save your life and your leg. She says you came here looking for the last solution because you want to kill yourself.' I told him that this was correct, that I would rather die than be lame. But the initiations were close to 4,000 pesos! I told him the *santo* [also known as *oricha*] would have to wait until I had the money. Then the old man threw his oracle once more and he said 'if you say yes now, the *santo* will give you the money you need.' I had 86 pesos in my pocket but I made the promise then. Lying on my bed, for 39 consecutive days, I was visited by people who owed me money and who paid me more than they owed, and I managed to do business with others. In the end, the only thing I had to sell was the gun with which I was going to kill myself, to complete the cash I needed. I sold it to a

cousin of mine, who in turn sold it to a sailor, who, the following day, with the bullet that had been destined for me, shot a woman, his lover. I kept my leg.

The gun, according to José, was fated to kill, but it was not to be him. Santa Bárbara – associated through historical processes in Santería with the virile and fearless male African Yoruba god *Changó* – had kept her word just as he had his. José's story, like those of so many others, indicates that in Havana an individual's path – as also his determination to discern, consolidate or even subvert it for his own good – is influenced by the whim and grace of agencies that parallel but also transcend his.

Whether seen or not, understood in the present or retrospectively, religious practitioners and adepts are finely tuned both to the multiplicity of forms that such agencies can take and to how implicated they are with them – especially once they begin to develop in the Afro-Cuban religious field. Causality here is simply not linear: persons, spirits and deities are chained in processes of mutual constitution that must be respected at all costs and whose effects can be felt in the unfolding of life. That these processes often imply working a delicate balance between understandings of destiny on the one hand and individual choice on the other is evident by José's own warnings: 'I cannot respect mediums who abandon their spirits after they have developed them. There are terrible consequences.' He gave me the example of a spirit medium friend of his who had recently 'seen the Lord.' By this he meant that she had joined a Protestant church and thereby abandoned her long-term faith in spirits. 'She is now a miserable human being,' he said, 'all the talents and jobs she had are gone. She is left with nothing.' From his perspective, his friend had clearly chosen (mistakenly) to forsake a cosmos in which not just her *belief* but also her *existence* had been implicated. At stake, both in José's and his friend's stories, was the consolidation of life itself: in the first case, an embrace of it via an explicit trust in the relations that were defined as constitutive of his person and its physical continuity – in this case with *Changó*/ Santa Bárbara – and in the second, a rejection of a pre-established way of life in which such relations had already been irrevocably and spiritually forged with corresponding results.

Afro-Cuban religious practices both reveal and generate relatedness at all levels: between persons and their guardian deities/spirits, between objects and spiritual powers and between persons and social others. All of this defies conventional understandings of time and space and, more importantly, of the person as a contained, discrete and pre-defined entity. Rather, among a generally fluid Afro-Cuban religious sphere, there is an accepted notion of the person as born from a relational logic underlying all persons, things and spiritual entities; a relational logic that is inherent to their 'making' and not simply a backdrop to their existence. This implies a constant potential for transgressive categories, and mostly, for a transgressive notion of existence. The examples are plentiful.

Also known as *Regla de Ocha*, the religious practices of Santería – associated in Cuba with West African, particularly Yoruba, influences – offers one such example (see, Bolivar, 1990; Brown, D. H. 2003; Lachatañaré, 2001). With Santería, the deities to whom one is initiated – known by the Yoruban term *orichas* or as *santos*, after the Catholic saints with whom they came to be associated – bring *aché*; an energy, life force or even a grace or potency that may be received and given, accumulated or dispersed. In Santería, such life forces can permeate and even become persons and things. This is evidenced by the fact that the *santos* are not just kept in material vessels, but their very essence – their *aché* – takes material form as a stone (*otá*) which is placed inside the vessel. Thus, the existence of thing and deity are here one and the same. Holbraad's analysis of the oracular branch of *Regla de Ocha*, the prestigious Ifá, points in the same direction. In Holbraad's understanding, *Orula* – the divination deity *par excellence* – is understood as motion; here, the markings on the diviner's board through which he is manifest. For Holbraad, the powder on which such markings are effected is also *power* or *aché* (2007: 189–225). But, if we see in these examples an understanding of spiritual existence as enabled by and weaved through materiality and motility (and not just represented by it) we also see the existence of the person herself as subject to the same sorts of oscillations and crystallisations of spiritual existence. In Santería, the neophytes are *born* through initiation as the *oricha* is placed on their 'heads,' signalling henceforth an altogether new existence for both deity and person. In Cuba, the *oricha* is as multiple as the person herself – every *santo* is unique, not simply by way of its often numerous avatars (*caminos*) but in the particularity of each *camino*'s manifestation; such that making one is tantamount to making the other. The flipside of this birth of persons is death; a state of existence clearly imbued with its own advantages and perspectives. In the cult of Ifá, for instance, the diviners (*babalawos*) are – by virtue of the omniscience gained through their initiation to the deity *Orula* – considered paradoxically to be already 'dead.' This is the case because their vision depends on a capacity to transcend mortal knowledge which is available only to those in the 'beyond.' In Santería, too, some initiations require that the neophyte symbolically 'die' and subsequently be buried. Life here begins with death.

A comparable kind of play on the tenuous line between categories of life and death, material and immaterial and transcendent and immanent, is that of practitioners of the *Reglas de Congo* or *Reglas de Palo* (see, Bolivar and Diaz de Villegas, 1998; Cabrera, 1998; Figarola, 2006).[2] As Figarola notes, for *paleros* – followers of Palo Monte – the category of *los muertos* (the dead) already implies a 'life' of sorts (2006: 230). By ritually pacting with particular spirits of deceased persons, the *palero* endows the dead with renewed life on an earthly plane through material incentives such as blood. In exchange, the dead act as messengers and executers of both healing and destructive forms of witchcraft. The well-known 'exchanges of life' rituals (*cambios de vida*), for example, are designed to save an individual by substituting the life of one entity for another – normally an animal for a person, although occasionally, and more ominously, one person for another. These rituals are a further reminder that the boundaries separating inner and outer forms of personhood are often frail. Indeed, *paleros* are expert manipulators of living and dead forms of agency because they recognise that a person, as much as a spirit, is not a bounded creature but one that can leave 'traces' of their exist-ence in the world – as well as absorbing the traces of others – making him or her vulnerable and porous. A name, for instance, just like a hair, nail or piece of clothing, leaves a fingerprint (*huella*) through which witchcraft becomes possible. The ritual recipes (*amarres*) intended to emotionally and sexually 'tie' a person to the one who desires him or her, for example, work on these same 'sympathetic' principles. Although a fundamental spiritual currency in its own right, a person's material continuity 'outside' of him or herself can both protect but also leave him exposed with potentially precarious results. In Palo Monte, the fact that a person's 'self' and its substances may simply *spill out* or distribute itself, if you will, means that it is all the more vital to fortify the protective potential of this self. In other words, this potential must be 'made.'

What follows suggests that the practice of Cuban Spiritism[3] (*espiritismo cruzado*) – which, along with Santería and Palo Monte, is one of the most widely diffused religious practices – presents religious folk in Havana with a mechanism for such 'makings' through which the 'self' is both produced and distinguished from its 'non-self.' To develop in Spiritism is to create bounda-ries, albeit shifting ones, which both extend and render the person autono-mous. In the previous paragraphs I drew on Yoruba influences (which are pervasive in the collective Cuban imaginary) and Palo Monte practices (where life and death are often interchangeable) to outline the importance to Afro-Cuban religiosity of a relational understanding of the self as a connected and porous being. In the following sections I examine more precisely how, in this environment, developing a sense of a self and its boundaries becomes all the more important. It is in this context that Spiritism furnishes the Afro-Cuban complex with the necessary conceptual and ritual technology to develop the self and its boundaries. Spiritism does this by working with arguably the most transgressive category of all – that of the self's protective spirit guides and ancestors whose characteristics overlap in deeply sensorial, psychological and social ways with those whom they protect. Having lived lives and died deaths, these spirits are bearers of unique cultural, religious and ethnic biographies and histories. These spirit identities are at once continuous with and an expansion of the persons they watch over, but whose particulars must nevertheless be actively developed in the process of learning mediumship.

What I also argue is that this process of development is a continuous and double-ended affair, where neither spirits nor persons cease to be 'produced' through their interaction. In Cuba it is not just the case that death is often a source of life or a new potentiality for life (Bloch and Parry, 1982: 8). It is more that death is itself present in the living; it is essential for existence through the voices it carries forth. Just as Kopytoff has convincingly expressed the difficulty of analytically separating the dead from elder living members of a lineage among the Suku of south-western Congo (1971: 129–42), in Cuba, Spiritism – having historically replaced the role of African ancestor cults – likewise enables a vision of cyclicality and continuity that both challenges straightforward divisions of living and deceased and adds to it a concern with this process as 'evolving.' I will also show that the ontological premises of Spiritism's notion of personhood are indispensable to understanding how notions of individual destiny and potentiality can be reconciled with the importance of free will and subversion so prevalent in the Afro-Cuban moral landscape. Situated within an often threatening material and spiritual environment, this reconciliation implies a development of the potential for creativity and control both over oneself and in relation to others.

The Role of the Dead

Although little has been written to examine its significance, in today's Cuba the idea that the *santo* is a different kind of *muerto* is still common. The anthropologist David H. Brown has postulated what he says are often conflicting, but co-existent, understandings of Afro-Cuban religion which he identifies as the 'Ocha-centric' – referring to those who see Santería as its central authority – and the 'Ifá-centric' – referring to those who regard Ifá's ritual divination experts (the *babalawos*) as central (2003: 294). I would further complicate this picture by adding a 'Spiritist-centric' axis. *Iku lobi ocha*, it is routinely said: the dead give birth to/precede the *santo*; the *santos* were once the dead themselves. Cabrera's carefully crafted portrayals of Afro-Cuban religious adepts in her seminal *El Monte* (originally published in 1954), leave no doubt that a deep ritual and cosmological interdependence between Spiritists and other religious practitioners is at stake, historically and contemporaneously, precisely because of the centrality of the dead. The realm of the dead, says Palmié, had hitherto been regarded as a 'wilderness, a kind of primeval reserve into which people venture to domesticate or colonize its denizens' (2002: 195). Providing a means by which to access and appease their needs, Spiritism reintegrated a pragmatic concern with deceased relatives and religious ancestors. It is telling that the most popular forms of Spiritism today (with which I concern myself here) are alluded to as *cruzado* – meaning crossed or syncretistic – confirming the continued relevance of Cabrera's observations. Flexible, and yet ritually separate, if Santería, as Palmié argues, 'lays out the coordinates of a "value space"' (2002: 195) – a moral topography where the *oricha* is defined as the most divine of entities and the Palo dead as its darker counterpart – then Spiritism articulates not just the *language* with which this is achieved (namely, through its classification of spirits) but also a conceptual repertoire through which the person can understand his or her spiritual constitution and gain control over its production.

Historical accounts point to the importation of Spiritist texts from France from the mid-nineteenth century onwards. This was the Spiritism of Allan Kardec (also known as Kardecism), whose main works – *The Spirits' Book* (1857) and *The Mediums' Book* (1861) – had begun to transform European middle-class homes into arenas of amateur spirit séances. This new configuration alluded to laws of communication and influence between spirit and material worlds, processes of reincarnation and progress and an ascending ladder of evolution that could be climbed through the trials and tribulations of successive lives and deaths. Ideas of interconnected social and scientific evolution were seen as potentially all encompassing; modernity was on the loose and science embodied the promise of ultimate measurement, explanation and redemption through progress. According to Peter Washington – and with Christianity no longer fitting the role – all of these trends sought a key that would unlock the occult mysteries of the universe (1995). This approach was to sit comfortably in the New World. On the one hand, as Brandon notes, in a country 'where a Spanish-born upper-class dominated the Catholic Church, middle-class Cubans were the first to become involved' with Spiritism (1997: 86); even if this involvement was eventually to give way to *cruzado* forms of spirit mediumship. On the other hand, as Román shows, we should be cautious about making too fine a distinction between 'pure' and 'syncretic' Spiritist practices in Cuba, even at their inception (2007: 34). This is because Spiritists of all stripes 'invaded the terrain of medical science and astronomy, corroded the natural-supernatural divide, multiplied the spheres of life, disaggregated the soul into multiple components, and denied scientific "materialism"' (2007: 34). The idea of a 'spirit guide' in particular would take on paramount importance as the ontological reorganisation of the Afro-Cuban religious 'self' transgressed its original signification.

Contemporary Spiritism is heterogeneous and fluid. While in Havana a handful of groups define themselves as *cientificos* – following a doctrinal form of Spiritism more closely related to Kardec's initial scientific impetus – for most Cubans an *espiritista* is a medium *par excellence*. Consequently, it is connectivity to the world of the dead, and precision in the acquisition and translation of the knowledge it brings forth, which today defines Spiritism. Mediums can be men or women of any racial identity or background. Good mediums can become famous and their name circulated by word-of-mouth among the city's religious circles and networks. Overwhelmingly, Spiritists are sought-after to impart the dead's advice on matters ranging from health and professional prospects, to love, marriage and family disputes. They elucidate paths of action by clarifying the state of an individual's relationships, perceive and pass on knowledge regarding the existence of jealous neighbours or competitive co-workers, determine whether the individual is being followed by unwanted spirits, and associate him or her with this or that *oricha*. In so doing, the medium creates a portrait which the client develops through subsequent consultations or takes away to build upon through work with other *espiritistas*.

Mediums may also undo witchcraft by performing cleansings with plants and tobacco, prescribing particular baths or remedies to lighten a person's 'energies' or by staging rituals of 'breakage' (*rompimientos*) to cut negative influences which are particularly entrenched. But it is precisely by enabling the client to identify the spirits in his or her *cordón espiritual* (spiritual cordon) that these ends can be achieved, for they are constitutive components of his or her physical and emotional wellbeing. Indeed, a great portion of a medium's efforts go toward both detailing these entities and advising on what they wish those they protect to offer them in order more effectively to facilitate their favours. Often involving the performance of some form of ritual obligation, in cases where the spirit guides identified belong to a different religious lineage such advice might even recommend initiation into another form of mediumistic practice (e.g. Santería or Palo Monte).

What is crucial to note here is that many religious adepts are encouraged to 'develop' their spirits, whether they actively become mediums or not. These protective beings form the basis of all other modes of protection. To recognise them, socially and materially, is to sediment one's own existence. For this reason, as I was told on several occasions, sceptics and disbelievers are the easiest targets for witchcraft and other 'evil works' (obras para el mal). Because they have not 'attended to' their own spirits in ways that properly acknowledge and materialise their presence, sceptics and disbelievers are more vulnerable to domination and coercion by the spirits of others. While espiritistas create the potential for spirit activity through an identification of their characteristics and needs, those who ignore them do not only deny the existence of spirits, they also undermine their own. As one informant put it,

> On many occasions those spirits can simply leave the person's side… because that person has never given them any attention, the spirit may not recognise them at all. For good reason there are ceremonies in Palo and in the santo, as well as in Ifá, so that the entity recognises you.

While this statement – much like José's above – is something of a warning, it alerts us to the fundamental role espiritistas assume in creating the means by which an individual gains ontological 'status' in the Afro-Cuban religious world. While spirit mediums may also 'be' other things, ritually they embody both the clearest example of how the spirits are implicated in the development of 'persons,' and how this, in turn, helps shape the dynamic of Afro-Cuban religiosity in general. As a Santería adept once told me, 'all santeros and paleros are espiritistas, but not all espiritistas are other "things."' As a mechanism by which 'selves' are identified, Spiritism acts also as a motor for their production. Called 'spiritual investigations' (investigaciónes espirituales) by espiritistas, for example, rituals of spirit identification and communication are widely regarded as a necessary preliminary to any other Afro-Cuban rite being effected. Indeed, most santeros and paleros will keep coming back to Spiritist mediums to 'check' on their muertos' statuses and concerns.

Process, Partnership and Personhood

Spiritists often talk of having a facultad (talent) or don (gift or grace), in reference to their abilities to 'see,' 'hear,' 'feel' or 'incorporate;' while others speak of having their Spiritist virtue 'marked' in their paths or destinies. Mediumship, however, is itself not seen simply as an ability, innate or otherwise. It is instead regarded as a set of special relations that cannot be located exclusively inside the person/body of the medium herself. In an essential sense, mediumship is thought to be more about having a capacity to productively engage in these relations than about any pre-given sensitivity. Whether manifest from childhood or discovered and generated in adulthood in a particular social and religious environment, not everyone possesses the gift of mediumship. Those who do must embark on a long-term project of development that is equivalent to their *own* development as persons. Mediumship is, in this light, a type of partnership between a living person and a series of spirits whose effectiveness depends on the strength of the connections between them at any given time. In this partnership, the medium is above all a conveyer of information which clarifies, predicts and prescribes. The medium, then, is not simply a voice: her 'person' – by which I mean both physical body and sense of self – is a fundamental tool and meeting-ground for the unique abilities of each of the spirits belonging to her spiritual cordon. In so being, the medium must not just get to know and master these spirits, but must also *produce* them *through her person.*

The idea that a mutual responsibility is at the heart of this relationship is pervasive: spirits evolve through their mediums just as mediums evolve through their spirits. This double-sided process is not simply an abstraction but is understood as having an undeniably physical, sometimes even *visceral,* dimension. For instance, as a young man, Héctor – a medium in his late thirties – describes how he often felt sharp and inexplicable pains in his heart. Having consulted the doctor and found no reasonable cause, Héctor examined his family history and identified the ominous presence of his deceased grandfather in his midst. Héctor depicts his grandfather as a rough and impulsive Spanish *isleño* (from the Canary Islands), who had run into trouble and fled to Havana at the beginning of the century. Héctor explains that his grandfather's avenger had eventually caught up with him and shot him several times through the heart. By feeling the sharp pains in his heart, Héctor was literally embodying his grandfather's past wounds. A solution to this problem could only be achieved by addressing both ends of the equation. First, the grandfather's ghost had to be ritually recognised and thereby worked towards an acknowledgement of himself as now an integral *part* of his grandson. (Indeed, and as some family spirits are wont to do, the grandfather's spirit ended up as part of Héctor's *cordón espiritual.*) Second, Héctor had to relieve the spirit's pain through whatever actions were available to him. As a result, Héctor quit smoking. Héctor is not alone, as many religious persons in Havana claim to suffer from the excessive proximity of dead kin. Because of this, *espiritistas* are routinely hired to provide relief by either dispatching spirits from the realm of the living or by clarifying their pleas and thereby helping the living respond to their needs.

If Héctor's story deals more directly with the agency of ancestors, it nevertheless introduces the critical idea that whatever forms of mutuality exist between persons and spirits – not least those between a person and his spiritual cordon – these relations have a direct impact upon the living. When talking of the spirits belonging to their spiritual cordon, adepts of Spiritism describe them as being of more or less 'light' and of this or that ethnic and religious background, profession and personality. The most commonly cited spirits are those whose lives speak directly to a Cuban past. Consequently, frequent mention is made of the spirits of African slaves, creoles, indigenous folk, Spaniards and other colonialists, independence martyrs, Catholic clergy, Cuban writers and intellectuals, and those of immigrant worker communities such as the Chinese, Palestinian and Haitian groups. Every *cordón* is thought to be composed of identifiable beings whose experiences and abilities (as well as failings) are unique and to a large extent *transferred* as 'perspectives' and knowledge to those whom they protect. I have also heard of persons having spirits of bureaucrats, casino owners and, most commonly, gypsies, Arabs and Indians. Garoutte and Wambaugh argue that, 'seen from a historic perspective, these entities constitute a rather curious, generic inventory of peoples brought to the island to work' and represent 'a thoroughly Cuban transformation of the spirit guides recognized by Kardec' (2007: 160). However stereotypical they may seem to the outsider, these spirits are more than ideological or historical reminiscences. Rather, their agency is embedded and manifest in the present tense. This 'transferability' of agency is made possible by Spiritism's representation of the 'self' as able to 'connect' itself to the dead through that which both incarnate and disincarnate beings have in common – the spirit. As the principles governing physical demise and spiritual reincarnation regard person and spirit as different manifestations of the same thing, developing within Spiritism requires embracing the dynamic nature of this spirit cosmos and its corollary, the self that emerges from and in conjunction with it.

The notion of 'process' (*proceso*) at work here is connected to a notion of 'evolution' which is at play across the Afro-Cuban religious landscape. All Afro-Cuban religious 'work' is thought to promote a material or spiritual *evolución*. As different scholars have noted, religion 'resolves' (see, Argyriadis, 2005: 29–52; Hagedorn, 2001). But Spiritist cosmology furnishes the religious practitioner with something other than a linear or cumulative view of development. Instead, Spiritism weaves an understanding of 'process' with a concept of the person as *ipso facto* extended through her spirits. That is, the person is defined relationally to entities that transcend his or her own space-time limitations and who are themselves subject to their own 'processes' at both earthly levels and beyond. As Csordas has argued relative to the Protestant charismatics he has followed, it makes sense to ask what the role of the body is in producing this particular 'self;' that is, how does it become 'objectified' (1994: 9)? In agreement with Csordas, I would say that for most *espiritistas* their selves are neither immutable substances nor single entities, but capacities to 'engage or become oriented in the world' (1994: 5). These capacities are revealed retrospectively, for example, in claims that criminals 'have' aggressive spirits, artists creative ones and doctors the spirits of healers or other medical specialists. These capacities might also unfold through life events, as, for example, in causal understandings of particular blockages in love being the result of an 'unattended' enamoured spirit. In all, self-knowledge in respect of one's spiritual capacities is a prime contributor to the way in which such *religiosos* both understand themselves, their characters and their bodies and act upon these understandings. Sara, a young medium I interviewed, for instance, insisted to me that her timidity was a result of the presence of a traumatised *Indio* (indigenous Cuban) spirit whose tongue had been cut off by its master. By overcoming this 'fault' in herself, Sara sees herself as contributing to the 'evolution' of her *Indio*, whose trauma acts as an impediment to its task of looking after and guiding her.

In mediums, the dynamic aspect of their relationships to their spiritual cordon is evident from the fact that the means of establishing and maintaining these relations may change over time. While some mediums are inclined to work with cards if their dominant spirit is that of a gypsy, for example, the mode of divination changes relative to both the spiritual development of the medium and the kind of entity manifesting itself at the time. The ultimate objective of development is that of producing a self-awareness which includes these entities, not simply as concepts, but as *orientational* or behavioural guides This is exemplified by the fact that many would describe a truly developed mediumship as one in which the medium's own 'intuition' acts as the pivotal engine for the generation and retrieval of spiritual information. Consequently, and irrespective of how 'present' a spirit appears, it takes centre or backstage according to the medium's will. When truly developed, the medium has succeeded in producing the smoothest possible overlap or entanglement between her senses and cognition and those of her spirits. As the site of this multiple relationship, the role of the body becomes integral. We could say, then, that the medium's 'self' has become integrated in such a way as to make relations with her spirits an implicit rather than explicit reality.

While the spiritual cordon can be thought of as a kind of 'blueprint' established before birth, as I have suggested, its *existence* as such is not to be taken for granted. In the domain of Spiritism, development (*desarrollo*) requires not just acknowledging the spiritual cordon but also *activating* it. As suggested above, this activation is at once productive of the 'self' and its boundaries.

Both as a means of exchange and as a way of personalising the entities in question, *matter* is held to be central to this 'activation.' Material objects and consumables are not only important go-betweens for the transference of affection and knowledge between spirit and human realms, but essential in themselves in the tangible recreation, if not *enactment,* of existences that come into being only through their engagement in practice. The intertwining of Spiritist and Afro-Cuban religious cosmologies once again becomes evident here. Practitioners of Santería (*santeros*), for example, honour their spirits with specific foods such as rooster and goat meat; while followers of Palo Monte (*paleros*) more routinely use the blood of animal sacrifices. For *espiritistas* also, the dead must always 'eat' first.

Although food is perhaps the most basic of 'activation' procedures – both indicative and *creative* of the spirits' existence among the living – the most important forms of materialisation are those designed to *represent* the spirits. Most significantly, *espiritistas* will dress and care for dolls and icons of all shapes and forms which represent their particular spirit guides. Gifts of flowers, tobacco, rum, and jewellery or attributes such as bows, arrows and miniature weapons are means not just of paying tribute but actually *fortifying* the spirits in question. It is no coincidence that *espiritistas* whose spiritual cordons are well represented are thought to be those better equipped to defend themselves in the battles of everyday life.

Materiality, here, is a way of extending the spiritual world into the physical one. It is, so to speak, cosmogonic because this extension is at once creative and reflective of self-awareness, and thus of the *existence* of spirits and mediums alike. It is creative of spirits because representations also serve as a type of ontological 'mirror' through which spirits recognise themselves as agents *in* and *of* the material world. In so doing, the spirits take shape (materialise) within it. In respect of mediums, it is cosmogonic because material representations are exteriorisations of aspects of themselves as multiple and connected beings – externalisations which solidify these aspects during a medium's 'becoming.'[4] Here, then, we return full-circle to the transgressive character of the categories of existence and person alluded to at the beginning of this chapter. As a result of its transgressive nature, we must acknowledge that the self is never simply embodied in one time and place. Rather, this embodiment may be understood as part and parcel of spiritual/material processes that simultaneously involve the self's dispersal and non-locality.

Conclusion: Possessed Selves

In his book on Afro-Cuban religions, the well-known Cuban author and anthropologist Miguel Barnet argues that possession implies a 'willingness to

Conga.

embody an archetype' which occurs through a kind of conditioned reflex that
has its origins in initiation ceremonies (2001: 35). Because the 'individual is
conditioned within a social milieu and reacts to its stimuli,' he says,

> Cases in which the person possessed is a foreigner or someone who
> has not had any prior contact with these religions are rare. When this
> happens, the result is a truly grotesque and imitative performance that
> is artificial and overdone. (2001: 35)

For Barnet, successful possession in Afro-Cuban religions such as Santería is
largely a matter of convincingly reproducing the gestures and postures of the
deities in question; a reproduction essential for the attainment of a respect-
able position in the religious hierarchy. While it is unclear whether Barnet
seeks to extend these observations to the domain of *espiritismo* and its practice of possession by the dead, it remains the case that Spiritism's concept of
possession is not readily understandable in these terms.

Indio.

Within *Spiritism*, spirits are not fixed archetypes and nor are their gestures and postures able to be generalised beyond the bare essentials of features such as the age, accent or type of pidgin language-forms typical of the possessing spirit. While it may be true that during possession states certain forms of gifting are the norm – cigars and sugar cane liquor for African spirits and cigarettes and shawls for gypsies – these acts are relative to the particular configurations of each mediumistic moment. Because the configurations of any given possession event are a product of the 'selves' involved, they are to a large extent emergent and unpredictable. What I think is at stake in the kind of interpretation offered by Barnet is a potentially obfuscating understanding of 'possession' in Afro-Cuban religious and Spiritist practices. This obfuscation occurs because possession is treated as either a type of 'theatre' or – as Cutié Bressler proposes in his ethno-psychiatric study of Cuban popular religiosity – a form of dissociation in which the medium's self is ruptured and substituted by the 'ego' of another (2001: 50). Both of these stances have, in my view, been quite common to traditional theorisations of both spirit possession in particular and mediumship more broadly.

Arising from her work upon *zar* possession practices among the Hofriyati of northern Sudan, Boddy stresses the importance of taking into account, when conceptualising spirit possession, notions of the person and its social construction and determination; and, thereby, the complex relationships pertaining between what the self is and what it is not (i.e. the 'non-self'). Within *zar*, Boddy notes, 'possession is a life-long, fundamentally incurable condition, that is, however, manageable' (1988: 4–27). For Cuban Spiritism also, the spirits of the dead (*los muertos*) are not to be exorcised, but incorporated into a new form of self-knowledge involving an awareness of a dynamic, unfinished and emergent self. In contrast to *zar*, however, the spirits are not thought of as non-selves (culturally or otherwise), but as evolving extensions of a single 'self,' extended through practice, agency and space-time. Known as the 'development of the dead' (*desarrollo de los muertos*), Spiritism's learning process is one that in the best of cases leads to control, confidence and wisdom on the part of the medium. In Cuban Spiritist practices, then, possession is best understood as a mutual endeavour of *co-presence* between the dead and their mediums, rather than one of performance or dissociation. Rather than beginning with an abstract notion of an existing 'self' which then gets determined or socialised relative to its environment, we should – in some ethnographic circumstances, at least – be seeking to theorise the effects of a particular *ontology* of the self which *guides* persons in their becoming one thing rather than another.

EMBODIMENT AND THE METAPHYSICS OF VIRGIN BIRTH IN SOUTH INDIA

A Case Study

Gillian Goslinga

Introduction

Although the temple of the Pandimunisvarar of Madurai sits on the old Sivagangai Road seven kilometres northeast of this Tamil city, its pull is felt as far as bus stop number 42 in the Madurai's downtown bus depot, at the heart and opposite side of the city.[1] On every Tuesday and Friday of the week, but especially on the first and last Fridays of auspicious Tamil months, an additional fleet of number 42 buses wind their way through the Lotus City, over the Vaigai River bridge, through the modern suburb of Annanagar, and then career along the large city reservoir to drop passengers at one of Pandi's temple gates. On these days, travellers on their way to work are crowded out by throngs of Pandi's devotees. Most come from the surrounding region and most from the predominant local Thevar caste, though Pandisami, as the god is affectionately called, is known to draw devotees from all castes, high and low, vegetarian and non-vegetarian, and from all religious creeds, though mostly Hindus.

There will typically be more women than men on bus 42 on those days and more babies and toddlers on laps and in arms than usual. Dressed in their finest clothes, these babies are *Pandi koDutta pappa* – babies given by Pandi. They almost always bear the god's name – Panditunai, Thangapandi, Muttu Pandi, Pandiselvi, and so on – and the visit to the temple is often to fulfil the vow of a child's first tonsure. The Pandimunisvarar of Madurai is most famous in the region for this gift of children.[2]

As bus 42 winds its way through town to Pandi's temple boundary stone, the eyes of certain women turn glassy and inward, tears quietly stream down others' faces, jaws clench, and bodies tremble. Some women barely control huge, involuntary yawns or drawn-out belches. When the bus passes the boundary stone itself, abruptly and dramatically, women are struck backward as if bent by a strong and sudden gust of wind. Others swoon or start to dance vigorously. On especially auspicious days, one bus after another will fill with ululations and screams and dancing women as they come within reach of the temple – Pandi's *Kooyil* ('abode'). These god-dancers (*saami aaDi*) are the women whom Pandi has 'caught' (*piDi*). This force will also bring out in other women troublesome spirits (*peey*) whom are danced as well. God and spirit possession are Pandi Kooyil's idioms of cure. Much like Shiva to whom he is likened, Pandisami, it could be said, is a purveyor and administrator of souls, of the living and the dead.[3] One could also say, more provocatively, that his temple is a site of assisted reproduction.

To call Pandi Kooyil a site of assisted reproduction admittedly jars the modern imagination; 'fertility cult' might seem more appropriate, especially given the idioms of god- and spirit-possession (see, Maity, 1989). Without engaging the contentious history of so-called 'virgin birth' beliefs in anthropology or the equally contentious history of a secular modernity's relationship with its Others, it is nevertheless the overarching aim of this chapter to contest the ways in which Eurocentric social theory typically relegates the 'other-than-human' (Hallowell, 1960) to the cognitive domain of the cultural – in this case the religious *beliefs* of Pandi's devotees. Contrasted with the presumed certainty of biogenetic facts of reproduction, this relegation dematerialises not only Pandi's reproductive efficacy but also Pandi himself. That Pandi is a material presence and agent in the lives of women often in lifelong relationship with him is an absolute fact of their experience as well as of their family's. Pandi regularly visits in dreams or 'directly' in visions (*neeraadi*); he descends (*iranku*, also 'to alight') on these women with a physicality that makes their bodies weep, laugh, scream, tremble, and dance vigorously; once their mouths are 'opened,' he speaks and gives oracles through them to kin and strangers both; he guides courses of action, warning of danger and opportunity; he endows many of these women with healing powers to cure fright, fevers, black magic, and possessions by lost souls or evil spirits, often for remuneration if he has granted permission. And, of course, Pandi cures 'childlessness' (*kuLandai illaammal*), often by becoming a woman's lover. As one woman explained to me:

Vengidu: I light an incense stick for him and burn camphor, and pray with a sincere heart. Then at night when he comes, we play and laugh [a

euphemism for sex]. He comes at eleven, leaves at three. Like a husband. Like a real man, face, body, and all. Not a shadow or a silhouette.[4]
GG: How do you feel the next day?
Vengidu: It's good. We've been in the family way, no? It feels like that. Good. I don't know any ache or pain. Like when I go to the temple. My body feels strong for six months! I can do a lot of work.

Many of my informants reported such nightly visitations which are striking for their orgasmic intensity.[5] These visits often timed with pregnancies, leading one Dalit woman – who had been in relationship with Pandi for more than twenty years – to joke during our interview:

> My first husband, you know what he said to me? 'How is it that you give birth to children when I haven't been with you in the family way?' I'd answer: 'Go ask Pandi! I don't know how to answer that!' I gave birth to six children fighting with my husband all along!

By taking Pandisami (or 'the Sami') as a reality of women's experiences, this chapter seeks to interrupt inherited paradigms for interpreting possession or so-called 'virgin birth' beliefs and so produce a different kind of encounter between my reader and such events.[6] In doing so, I join a small but growing group of scholars studying possession on the same terms as their subjects, with all the caveats of translation and proper contextualisation that such a project might entail (see, Caldwell, 1999; Clammer, Poirier and Schwimmer, 2004: 3–22; Smith, 2006; Turner, E. 1993: 9–12). One common issue that seems to come up is the tension between the academic mandate for theory, often laden with Euro-American conceits – e.g. what is a person? a body? the ontology of Being? – and the sheer heterogeneity and complexity of the phenomena under consideration.

I do not explicitly take up this important methodological issue, except by resisting 'the generalising impulse of the sociological imagination' (Chakrabarty, 1997: 42) and the ways in which this imagination embeds in practices of 'reading' phenomena *during* fieldwork, glossing-over important ethnographic details that might complicate totalising explanations. In my own unfolding participation with this South Indian god and his devotees, I found again and again that the *sense* of Pandi's interventions – of his cures and his 'possessions' – could not be divorced from these details or the singularities of specific persons in specific circumstances. This is why I give in the main section of the chapter a reading of one exemplar narrative of Pandi-assisted conception, to make visible the semiotic-material agencies concretely at play when a particular someone identifies a particular child as a *Pandi koDutta pappa*, a baby given by Pandi.

Rajathiammal's Story

The story is of the conception of Rajathiammal, Pandi Kooyil's chief priest (*periya poojari*) in the present generation. Rajathiammal inherited this post much to everyone's surprise in 1991 at the age of 32, when her father died and his spiritual energies transferred to her instead of a favoured male cousin in a series of 'possession' fits and vivid initiatory dreams. (In one such dream, for example, Pandi wrote symbols on her tongue after which she was able to divine.) Rajathiammal is admittedly exceptional, but, in effect, all children of Pandi are considered exceptional. The god's distinguishing attributes – his prescience, his righteousness, his fearlessness – are widely acknowledged to incarnate in them. As children, they are rarely struck as to do so would be to strike Pandi himself and so anger him.

I juxtapose Rajathiammal's own telling of her birth story with the elaborated one told to me by her mother, Pandiammal, the morning that Pandiammal learned of the death of her youngest son, Rajathiammal's half brother. This specificity matters for I will be reconstituting Pandi's materiality, so to speak, through narratives that were told by specific persons with specific agendas in the telling. This is not to say that Pandi has no existence outside these stories or that he is constituted through the storytelling, but that Pandi's agency in the lives of devotees is also a committed hermeneutics. It is always an agency experienced from a situated *somewhere*.

What interests me are the semiotics brought to bear in these tellings. These I characterise as 'prosaic' because the details brought together to make meaning are at once mundane and temporally literal – such as the timing of hearing a temple bell chime or of catching a whiff of jasmine scent with some-thing said or thought.[7] Such timings and propinquities, correspondences of form or conduct, are what sign for Pandi (and other South Indian gods and goddesses); they constitute his signatures in the world. Again and again, what I found these signs to mean or rather to account for, as will become clear in what follows, is a moral reckoning of a person's circumstances *in a given moment of their lives* and set against a canvas much larger than the one we typi-cally grant individuals (e.g. the span of a life, their personal identity or social location) or spirit- or god-possession (e.g. its duration as event, its meaning as a social practice). Properly accounted for, such signs and their corresponding moral reckonings brought about – manifested – auspicious outcomes such as individual and social wellbeing (*sooham*), prosperity, success or the birth of a certain special child.

The Mark of Ram

When Rajathiammal declared that Lord Ram was the god to whom she owed her life, I was more than surprised. I had heard from devotees both close to and critical of the priestess that her father had for a very long time been childless and had remarried 'four or five' times to secure progeny; an obvious irony since as head *poojari* he presumably had Pandi's ear. I had assumed from the many times she referred to herself as Pandi's favourite daughter and addressed Pandi as 'Father' that this god had been responsible for her birth. That her father's *arul* ('spiritual energies') had passed to her at his death only fed my assumption. But as Rajathiammal clarified, Pandi had told the priest through a god-dancer that he did not have the right (*urimai*) to give him a child. He then sent the priest to do *pooja* in Ramesvaram on the Tamil coast because Lord Ram, an avatar of Vishnu enshrined there, held this right. Ramesvaram is an India-wide pilgrimage destination where, among other things, a class of Brahmins ritually removes *naga dosham*, a residual karmic effect diagnosed astrologically that is known to thwart conception in couples. It was shortly after this visit that Rajathiammal's mother conceived. But what confirmed Rajathiammal's divine provenance would be a pronounced discoloration and slight indentation on her forehead at birth that perfectly coincided with the forehead markings of Ram devotees. This 'natural form' (*svaroopa*) of Ram caused villagers to line up outside her mother's home to receive the baby's auspicious sight (*darshan*) in the months following her birth.

In all subsequent tellings of her birth story, Rajathiammal emphasised this mark. The only other mention was that her parents had had to divorce when she was three because – in a reversal of what we take to be the flow of descent – her father's rapidly deteriorating health after her birth was traced to a boomerang effect from an astrological fault (*dosham*) in her birth chart that meant that one parent would die if they remained together.[8] The coincidence of Rajathiammal's arrival in the world with her father's sudden poor health signed for a hidden and deep kinship between father and daughter – corroborated by the astrology reading – in which her life-force pulled from his, much like the Mark of Ram signed for her underlying kinship with the avatar of Vishnu.

The Mark of Ram, though, did not become a true portent until Rajathiammal, in the week after her father's death, revived a man 'slapped by the Muni' (*Muni aDi*) whom villagers had brought to her, near-dead, in the middle of the night.[9] As these healing feats repeated and her divination speech (*kuri parkkiradu*) proved true, Rajathiammal's fame spread. (She also began to perform successfully the annual *pooja*, a difficult ritual that entails the sacrifice of a goat and the pulling together of vast resources.) Rajathiammal freely shared these three stories with temple devotees during consultations; curiously these narratives marginalised her mother while strongly reinforcing a father-daughter kinship beyond biological descent. They also legitimated, and prosaically so, Rajathiammal as her father's *rightful* heir and one *chosen* for spiritual service, not only by the local god Pandi but also by the nationally recognised god, Lord Ram.

Rajathiammal certainly showed her sagacity when she told these stories; as a woman, her hold on her post of chief temple priest was always tenuous. But all three stories did rest on concrete evidence: the Mark of Ram on her forehead had been witnessed by the village; her father's illness was traced to an astrological flaw in her chart; the resuscitation of the dying man had been public. Thus, they authenticated her spiritual pedigree. And while I am well aware of the egregious politics behind Hindu revivalism in India at this time, I cannot help but note with irony that over the course of Rajathiammal's tenure as chief priest, Pandi Kooyil catapulted twice into national fame: once on the occasion of its first *Kumbabishekam* (Brahmanical consecration) in 2000 and then in 2003–4 as a successful defender of the religious right to perform animal sacrifices, when it became the exemplar of the enduring backwardness of village ritual practices during a short-lived enforcement of the 1950 Tamilnadu 'Animals and Birds Sacrifice Prohibition Act.' Rajathiammal's birth did augur well for the temple.

Rajathiammal dances Pandi, attended by devotees and kinswomen.

The Flowering Vine

Rajathiammal's mother, in her telling of her daughter's birth, did not contest her daughter's special gifts, but she gave them an altogether different genealogy – one that celebrated the lineage of women to whom Rajathiammal belonged. Her narrative strung together like flowers on a vine events and details that revealed these women's moral purity and integrity, and the ways in which they had been vital partners in Pandi's work (*veelai*) to bring about Rajathiammal's auspicious birth.[10] As mentioned above, the morning I interviewed Pandiammal, she had come to her daughter's home for solace in the wake of the loss of her youngest son, the only child who was not in spiritual service to Pandi. Her grief was palpable as she asked me, 'Shall I tell everything? Do you have cassette enough [to record it]? There are many steps (*paDi*) to this story.'

Pandiammal surprised me just as her daughter had. The Mark of Ram was but an insignificant and closing detail in a tale that began in her mother's generation and in Burma where her parents' parents – sweet makers from Thevar castes – had emigrated in the early 1900s. As Rajathiammal's mother, I had expected from Pandiammal a narrative that would prominently feature her reproductive body since her husband had had 'four or five' childless marriages before theirs. As we shall see, her body was indeed a terrain of struggle with respect to Rajathiammal's conception, but not the one of a culturally inflected biology.[11] As I later worked on the transcript, I realised that Pandiammal told the story in all its steps not so much for the benefit of my tape recorder but *to* the household that had divorced her. Through this long telling she reclaimed her worth, reminding everyone listening, including her daughter Rajathiammal, who almost immediately retreated to an adjacent room, that both she and her mother also held Pandi's grace (*arul*). Articulating the deep kinships between grandmother, mother and daughter, she fleshed out the concatenation of events – the timings, propinquities and turning points – that spelled out first her mother's then her own *moral* labours in the making of Rajathiammal.

The first step in the story was the revelation in Burma that Pandiammal's mother had been 'caught' by Pandi. One common symptom of possession in South India is a series of miscarriages that can sometimes be traced to ghosts (*peey*), malicious spirits (*pisasu*) or the displeasure of ancestral or lineage deities (*kula deyvam*). Pandi combines attributes of all three, making him particularly difficult to diagnose until the 'mouth is opened' and he speaks.

GG: Really? Your mother was caught?
PA: Yes, there were seven children...As soon as we were born, he would

kill us.[12] My mother did not know that he was on her. This was [Pandi's] doing. Then my mother was month-to-month [again]. And the goat went blind.[13]

GG: It must have been hard.

PA: Yes. What did my mother do? She went to the temple in that town and said, 'I'll put my *thaali* [wedding necklace] in the offering box if my goat regains its sight.' *Tak!* Just like that, the sight returned!

All seven children were subsequently returned by Pandi, Pandiammal explained – the eldest in Burma and the remaining six back in Madurai when the family relocated to Tamilnadu at Pandi's urging (speaking through her mother) ahead of the Japanese invasion of Burma. What is striking about this step in Pandiammal's narrative are the seven miscarriages. That it took seven *and* then a promissory goat to go blind for her mother to take the drastic remedial action of pledging her wedding *thaali* – a Tamil woman's most meaningful belonging (Reynolds, 1980: 35–60) – shows both her mother's desperation and fierce independence. From Pandi's perspective – if, indeed, we grant him one – the promissory note of the goat from such a proud woman would be insufficient penance for so wilful a disavowal of his possible presence. Pandi made the goat go blind and upped the ante. How much was this child worth to her? How willing was she to give up her very identity as a married woman since to remove the *thaali* would declare her a widow? How capable was she of genuine self-sacrifice and faith?

In this first step, Pandiammal painted a portrait of her mother's moral fortitude in the face of misfortune and of Pandi's challenge; a challenge her mother passed with flying colours. No sooner had the goat regained its sight than the baby was born. Pandiammal next described the facility with which a Burmese midwife was procured, the ease of the birth and the health of the baby; all indications that a shift had happened. But it would be at the baby's consecration at the local temple when Pandiammal's mother surrendered her *thaali* in fulfilment of her vow that Pandi would 'open the mouth.' The provocation was a fundamental confusion – Pandiammal's mother surrendered the *thaali* to the wrong deity; an error which the customary offerings of sweet rice (*pongal*) and sacrificial goat (the one that had regained its sight) immediately registered in their behaviour.

PA: I told you the goat got its sight back, didn't I? So my mother took off her *thaali* and put it in the offering box. She made *pongal* and offered the goat…But the *pongal* would not boil over and the goat would not twitch – the goat was just standing there! It wouldn't twitch. The rice wouldn't boil over. '*Yeppaa*! Pandi! What *Paa*!' my mother screamed. She ululated. As soon as she did, the goat shook and the *pongal* boiled over. Pandi said: '*Dey*! *Dey*! *Dey*! Give my name! Why have you come here to offer this goat? I'll strike you!' Like that, the child was made good. With this one child they returned to our home village [in Tamilnadu] before the bombs were dropped like our Sami had warned [through her mother]. My mother was like Rajathiammal…Seven children were lost – killed, right? 'I will give you those seven children back,' Pandisami said. One was born over there, six over here. He gave.

The 'opening of the mouth' is a significant turn in the life of a woman 'caught' by Pandi. Once Pandi speaks, the order of things reorganises and the economy of bodily symptoms evolves, though his *arul* – the force with which he descends on a woman – can still be hard to bear physically. This *arul* is the same force that makes a pot of sweet rice and a goat behave as auspicious ritual objects must during an offering. If *arul* is present, sweet rice will boil just right and the foam rise just so, with grace and vigour, while a sacrificial goat's spine will involuntarily tremble (making the hairs rise on end along it) at the precise moment of its consecration for sacrifice. The absence of these studied behaviours connotes something morally askew in the offering, in which case a goat sacrifice should not proceed as it would be a sin to kill the animal.

Pandiammal's mention of these details served to corroborate her claim that her mother was 'like Rajathiammal' – an equally chosen and arduously tested partner to Pandi. The piercing ululation (its quality a measure of the sincerity of Pandi's possession) and the *arul vaakku* (literally, 'graced speech') that had correctly announced Pandi as the rightful progenitor of the child and later warned the family of the Japanese bombing of Burma, also confirmed her mother as a genuine god-dancer. With these details, Pandiammal was authenticating her mother's spiritual pedigree; a pedigree that would prove instrumental in facilitating her very unusual marriage to Rajathiammal's father – a man from a lower caste and of dubious reputation because of his 'four or five' prior marriages.[14]

PA: All these [prior] weddings were the doing of elders. But this one was Pandisami's doing…In those days, we were in Thirupparankundram [west of Madurai; Pandi Kooyil sits to the east]. There was no acquaintance between him and us. None whatsoever! At the crack of dawn one day, he went to bathe the Sami. He was just sitting there when a woman dancer came running up to him and said…'I have caught and tied a cow for you in the western corner. How many weddings have you tied without asking me? Hey? How many? I have destroyed them all! Now marry the cow that I caught for you like I am telling you!'[15] He [Rajathiammal's father] replied, 'I want heirs [*varisu*]...Alright, you go to the west and catch that cow for me! Where should I look?' 'I will bring her here to you myself,' said the Sami.

Pandiammal went on to narrate how shortly after this *arul vaakku*, a man from her village went to Pandi Kooyil and visited the priest Veeramalai for a divination reading. Veeramalai immediately inquired about prospective brides since the man hailed from the western corner as prophesied. This man agreed to look on his behalf and upon his return spoke to relatives of Pandiammal's who were his neighbours. These relatives immediately brought the matter up with her parents and Pandiammal's mother – at once recognising the string of serendipities that had brought the priest's need to her attention – was quick to pledge her daughter, sight unseen. Her obligation was moral.

> PA: My mother said right away, 'Pandisami killed seven children. Seven children he returned. The priest should not go without a girl! I shall give [my daughter]. Tell him that I will go meet him. He has first preference.'

True to character, her mother at once set out by horse carriage with a few kinswomen to seal the arrangement. When the priest addressed her at once as *akka* ('older sister') – thereby invoking the celebrated South Indian exchange between a brother and a sister of children in marriage – Pandiammal's mother instantly reciprocated by calling him 'little brother' (*tambi*). The spontaneity of their affection for each other reinforced the sentiment both shared that this marriage was right. 'This was Pandi's work,' Pandiammal repeatedly insisted. It had to be. So quick a marriage agreement violated all the usual protocols, including 'seeing the girl at the well' where possible bride and groom have an opportunity to decide for themselves on a proposed alliance.

Responsible for the good marriage of his daughter, her father, however, was not so quick to consent and thereby triggered the fourth and equally dramatic step in Pandiammal's tale. The ensuing family drama involved another deity, Pandiammal's village goddess. This is not an uncommon dimension of Pandi-assisted conceptions, as tutelary and other gods and Pandi often debate rights in a child; as had been the case with Pandi deferring to Lord Ram in Rajathiammal's conception. But the woman who would bear this special child was to be Pandi's contribution, for, as we shall see later, the priest Veeramalai required a special woman to remedy his chronic childlessness. Pandiammal's father, inquiring about the priest's character in surrounding villages, quickly learned about this childlessness and the many marriages. He was advised not to give his daughter to the priest and went to see him.

> PA: So my father went to see the priest and said, 'We need to ask the mother's brother first. Then we will come and tell you if you can tie with her. Please have patience and wait a little.' But what happened was that as my father spoke over *there*, over *here* at our house, my body went stiff like this [she demonstrates] and my mouth clamped shut.
> Servant: The Sami!
> GG: Your age then?
> PA: I was maybe seventeen…This [Rajathiammal] was born at twenty-one…Like this, my eyes were popping out of my head. [Chuckles] I was struck dumb mute. My mother, she was threshing wheat to give the first measure to the Sami, but he descended on her and threw the grain away, shouting: 'I don't want this first measure! You have gone and taken away the girl! He [the priest] will be without the girl. Why should I want this measure? What is its meaning now?' I sat dumb mute, speechless, even after my mother ordered me to go inside the house and cook. I sat with my head bowed. I couldn't move! When my father spoke over there, this very big disturbance happened over here, at my house.

As with the goat suddenly losing its sight, to be struck 'dumb mute' marks in the idiom of god-possession a terrible wrong (*tappu*). And indeed, Pandiammal's father's undoing of the wedding agreement, unbeknownst to him and however well-intentioned, was a moral wrong since it seriously hindered the circumstances needed to bring about Rajathiammal's auspicious birth. This wrong *instantly* registered on the bodies of Pandiammal and her mother – much as her mother's confusion about deities in Burma had *instantly* registered on the bodies of the sacrificial goat and *pongal* offering. Like divining rods dowsing hidden, but vital underlying realities, the women's bodies became the visible signatures of an underlying moral order as yet unknown. When Pandiammal's father returned home, all hell broke loose. He scolded Pandiammal's mother for giving their daughter away to a man who kept wives 'just for six months.' Then, after everyone had gone to sleep:

> PA: That night, at one o'clock, a dream touched my mother's eyes. It was Pandisami!…My mother snaked and rolled on the floor all the way from her room to the kitchen. She ululated loudly and woke us all.

'What!? *Dey*!' the Sami grabbed my father and shouted, 'You beggar! Come here! Come *here*! Seven children I killed and seven children I gave back. Seven children! All this [house, things, children], *I* gave. If before dawn you don't say yes to this marriage, I will throw you up so high you will fly!' The Sami *was* throwing things around!
GG: Really? It happened like that?
PA: The Sami said, 'This house, everything, I will take back, you watch! I will put you out to fly!' Then, our village Sami came.
GG: Which Sami? Your lineage god?
PA: Yes, Manthaiyammal. She came and said: 'You say you will take this girl but there is no proper accommodations where you plan to take her. How, after taking my granddaughter, will you look after her? Tell me! They are not ready for her. There is not even electricity there!' They were not ready for me. Manthaiyammal made Pandisami promise there would be every comfort for me at the temple. Only when Pandi promised by putting out the camphor flame [by hand], it was agreed.

Though the marriage was sanctified that evening, it did take nearly three years for Pandiammal to marry and go live with her husband. The night her fate was decided, a battle of wills had raged among adults and gods alike, but the stakes were those of reciprocity, moral obligation and righteousness. Pandi furiously reminded those present that he was the ultimate authority of the household, its true patriarch, the source of all its abundance and wellbeing. The village goddess firmly defended her granddaughter's right to a lifestyle commensurate to that of her natal village; Thirupparankundram was prosperous, Pandi Kooyil in those days a hamlet in a thick forest.

Interestingly, god and goddess aligned respectively with wife and husband, crossing genders. But equally interesting is the fact that 'other-than-humans' (Hallowell, 1960) and humans did not exactly coincide in their coupled positions. For, unlike Pandiammal's father, the goddess did not dispute the marriage while Pandi, when he refused the first measure of grain earlier in the day, had doubted that Pandiammal's mother would abide by her moral debt to him. These slight gaps complicate – in my view, ought to refute – academic interpretations of possession as purely psychosocially caused or culturally determined. Such interpretations not only miss these meaningful gaps, they also take as self-evident that spirits and humans would perfectly coincide in singular human bodies, betraying the foundational way our intellectual tradition takes the bounded biological body to be the ontological seat for the unity of persons. This coincidence of self and body, though, is not evident in South Asia (Smith, 2006: 585, makes a similar point). At the same time, and while descriptively true, the idioms of 'dividuality,' 'permeability' or 'fluidity' that dominate theoretical discussions of the category of the person in South Asia do not fully capture the complexities of transactions between gods and humans – not least those of being mounted by a god or spirit. They still privilege the human as the exclusive locus and agency of meaning (see, Marriott, 1976; Busby, 1997; Daniel, 1984).

For example, though Pandiammal seemed to have had little to say in the drama of that fateful evening, to think so would miss the way her very flesh had been the *first* to register 'over here' her father's betrayal of her mother's covenant with the priest 'over there.' This sympathetic reaction marked her as powerfully in tune with the situation's underlying moral realities and therefore as someone of great virtue and innocence. She was special, too, and her flesh was witness. For, not any young woman would do for the childless priest and not any woman would do to give birth to the extra-ordinary Rajathiammal. To ascribe to the liberal humanist view of 'humans' as fundamentally equal and on principle interchangeable units would miss the crux of Pandiammal's tale – humans are *not* qualitatively equivalent to each other, nor are they always the masters of their own bodies or destinies. That Pandiammal held within her person a special purity was again powerfully articulated in the final step of her story when her very being redeemed the impurities in her husband's character – which proved to be more wayward than anybody knew.

> PA: [after the place was made ready for me,] just like that the *thaali* was tied and I went there to live. My mother presented him [Veeramalai] with a goat for Pandi. But what this man did was to give it to some other god, this other guardian deity!
> GG: Why did he do that?
> PA: He had a contract to fish in the lake. To get good fish returns, he gave the goat over there!...I had washed my hair only once since coming here.[16] Three months passed like that. I did not know I was month-to-month [pregnant]! Pandisami turned my memory inside out.
> Servant and GG: Really?
> PA: Yes, he completely changed my memory. I was lying down, crying, thinking about how he [Veeramalai] had given the goat away. He also took all my jewellery, my gold jewels, from the bureau and lost them all in card games. I didn't know that he had. Little by little everything was lost. Because of the goat that Pandi had not been given.
> GG: Because of the goat?
> PA: Yes, the Sami was thinking like this: 'I brought the girl here for

him, didn't I? And he didn't even offer me the goat!' That's what the
Sami was thinking.
GG: How could you not know you were pregnant?
PA: [Pandi] made the knowledge disappear from my mind. In my
memory there was nothing. Blank. I had no memory, *sakti*! I did not
remember when I last washed my hair...Like that, I was lying down
thinking I wasn't feeling well. He [Veeramalai] had pawned my jewels,
lost some, lost three measures of rice – all playing cards. My father had
said no to this man, hadn't he? But they had tied me to him anyhow.
I cried, lying there thinking of these things!...There was a woman who
told *kuri* here. My husband went to consult her about what was going
on, about all his bad luck. He complained to her that 'This girl is lying
down all the time. I have lost all my rice. Since the girl has come,
nothing is going right!' She told him [through *arul vaakku*]: 'The goat
that was given to me you went and gave somewhere else, didn't you?
I am the one doing all this to you. This is my work. The child that is
sleeping in her stomach I put it there! But I will take that child back,
too.'
GG: He said it like that?
PA: Yes, only then did we come to know that I was pregnant. Like that,
he spoke. I thought I had an illness the strength of a diamond, but
I was only month-to-month. My mother asked me, 'Since you came
here, how many times did you wash your head?' I told her just once.
We got the goat back. [It had not been sacrificed yet.] The Sami said [to
Veeramalai], 'Go bathe and take Rs.1.25 *kaaNikkai* [offering or fine]
from the hand of this young virgin (*kanni*). Sit at the card game and
I will give everything back to you.' That day he won everything back.
Even the goat he got back. After everything came back, she was born,
with the Mark of Ram on her forehead.

In the moral reckoning of this last step of her story, the dissolute behaviour of Pandi's very own priest – lacking in integrity, ungrateful, selfish,
greedy, and immature – directly threatened the life of Rajathiammal *in utero*,
Pandi's would-be heir, and his own. There was more than poetic justice in
Pandi's suggested 'remedy' (*parikaaram*) that he take a fine from his young
wife's hand. For, in contrast, Pandiammal – guileless and pure – possessed
the virtue that had secured her very special child's life and safe-passage into
this world. She had proven to be indispensable, as had her mother before
her. This was no mere self-promotion as she told her tale in the household
that had divorced her, but a cogent and compelling exposition of all the

prosaic concatenations that, like flowers blooming on a healthy vine, spoke through their outcomes – with their fruits – of their intrinsic righteousness. This is perhaps what Hindus understand by *dharma,* the righteousness that holds the world together in goodness. But, whereas Pandiammal reckoned the righteousness of her daughter's god-given conception all the way back to her mother and included in her narrative a whole range of signs, agents and circumstances, Rajathiammal, her daughter, almost cruelly, privatised her birth story to the three details – the Mark of Ram, the divorce, the spiritual and healing energies she inherited from her father – that related her exclusively to Pandi through her father, the wayward priest.

Conclusion

I have in this chapter taken the Pandimunisvarar of Madurai on the same terms as my informants to say something about the hermeneutics of so-called 'virgin birth' in South India and the semiotic-materiality of a South Indian god. My close reading of Rajathiammal's conception story is an exemplar of the compendia of Pandi-assisted conception narratives I collected during my fieldwork. All stories behind a claim of *Pandi koDutta pappa* (a child given by Pandi) harbour in their singularities their own prosaic thickets of moral reckonings in which Pandi's work, his *veelai,* is revealed. But for this work to be *seen* there must be someone to register the concatenation of events and signs that are his signatures; there must be someone to read this prose and to speak its import. In this case study, that witness – that *seer* – was Pandiammal, who told her story on the morning fate took the only child that had always and only belonged to her.

In presenting her narrative, I have also sought to problematise several of the metaphysical presuppositions that often uncritically undergird modernity's knowledge about the world – of the biological body as the sole locus of procreation, of persons and bodies as sovereign autonomous agents and of a world at large devoid of moral intelligence. I have also wanted to make room for an other-than-human to matter, a god whose business – not unlike that of Shiva's – is the unenviable task of administering wayward human souls.

TA(L)KING POSSESSION

Exchanging Words and Worlds among Charismatic Christians

Simon Coleman

Introduction

In the late 1980s, I found myself standing in the kitchen of an elder of Uppsala Pentecostal church. By then, I had been living in Uppsala for a few months, carrying out fieldwork in his church as well as in a charismatic ministry, called the 'Word of Life' (*Livets Ord*), which had been founded about five years earlier on the outskirts of the city.[1] We were discussing the Word of Life and its parallels to and differences from 'classic' Pentecostalism, its apparent attraction for a number of Christians in the town, including some Pentecostals, and its controversial leadership style. The elder, a knowledgeable man, was deeply versed in the history of his own movement. He began to talk about the new group's founder, Ulf Ekman, a former priest in the Swedish Church who had imbibed much 'Prosperity Theology' during a year at Kenneth Hagin's Bible School in Tulsa, USA.[2] After some remarks on Ekman's personal history, the elder added a somewhat conclusive statement which struck me forcefully: 'Ekman is a shaman.'

I think it unlikely that the elder was deploying the word 'shaman' because he knew that he was talking to an anthropologist of religion. In fact, I was to find it cropping up in other contexts at the time, such as local newspaper articles that were tracking the progress of the new preacher. As used by the elder and by journalists, the term had a number of resonances: the image of the 'shaman' not only contrasted with that of 'pastor' (adding a hint of the primitive and the exotic), but also resonated with an increasingly national moral panic that the Word of Life was 'brainwashing' Swedish youth into unthinking ecstasy. It also hinted at the reports of extreme 'spiritual' manifestations occurring at the group – outbreaks of hysterical laughter, miraculous healings, aggressive glossolalia (speaking in tongues), and so on. The term was thus one of both distinction and a kind of dismissal, a placing of Ekman in a category definitively marked 'non-Pentecostal' (even if broadly similar accusations had been made of the early Pentecostal movement in Sweden some seven or eight decades earlier).

Within anthropology, the notion of the 'shaman' tends to imply a figure who gains power through travelling and making contact and communicating with the spirit-world. As such, the shaman is not quite the same as a person who is merely possessed by a spirit, who exercises less control over the relationship and its social effects (see, Lewis, 2003). It seems to me that the elder's remark was initially intriguing not only because of its clear expression of distaste, but also because it raised questions of both agency and legitimacy in relation to the exercise of spiritual power: Who might be in control of the revival apparently taking place at the Word of Life, and to what end? How might one deploy a Pentecostal or even a 'commonsensical' gift of 'discernment' in determining the 'genuineness' or otherwise of what might be occurring (see, Luhrmann, 2007: 83–102)?

In fact, these ambiguities over the moral valency of the spirit(s) frequently permeate not only much Pentecostal and charismatic discourse, but also much of the literature on spirit possession (e.g. Lambek, 1980: 319). One aim of this chapter, therefore, is to examine charismatic practices in the light of anthropological writings on possession; not, as in the case of the elder, to suggest politically loaded distinctions between forms of spiritual power, but to see how some of the themes in the possession literature relating to the form and authority of communication, authenticity and the construction of the self can illuminate a study of the workings of the Spirit within a ministry such as the Word of Life. In the process, I want to argue that charismatic 'possession' gains power not despite of, but precisely because it plays on deep ambiguities relating to its meaning, interpretation and source. The kind of Christianity practised at the Word of Life is often characterised as dependent on clarity of meaning and purpose – indeed, such clarity is, as we shall see, something of a fetish of charismatic discourse (Coleman, 2006: 42–4). However, I see charismatic 'possession' as playing on decidedly grey ideological areas relating to such issues as the borders between the self and others, between spontaneity and iteration and between possessing and being possessed.

At the centre of charismatic 'possession' practices, as with so much evangelical activity, is the deployment of language – particularly words expressed orally or at least playing on the relationship between the written and the spoken. Examples include speaking in tongues, quoting strategically from the

Bible or even repeating the words of others; they may form personal anec-
dotes, biblical narratives or a mixture of the two. In doing so, they frequently
raise questions concerning the authorship and voicing of words, the responsibility for utterances and speaking as a physical act as well as a means of
communication.

A further dimension of such charismatic practices involves what one
might call 'meta-possession' – i.e. an account of a possession event that itself
takes on performative power, producing the very forms of spiritual presence
that it purports merely to describe (see, Coleman, 2006: 39–61). Common
in evangelical circles, this practice echoes a wider narrative strategy within
the group of recounting what has happened in another place and/or time
but suggesting that the circumstances described relate directly to the present
situation. The original template of this approach might be said to be the use
of parables from the Bible, but it can also apply to a situation where a speaker
describes a powerful movement of the Spirit, prompting listeners themselves
to respond to the Spirit, thereby subverting the distinction between story
and event.

In focussing on inspired language as communicator of meaning but also
as bodily expression – an 'object' possessed by a speaker and one that can
be exchanged with and therefore possessed by others – I address broader
concerns within linguistic anthropology around the expression of authenticity and spontaneity in utterance (Keane, 2007). I also analyse such charismatic 'inspiration' as a key mediator between notions of personal 'possession'
and the construction of transnationally-orientated charismatic publics. I
argue that such 'talking possession' reveals key dimensions of the relationships not only between believers and the Holy Spirit, but also between (often
dispersed) believers. A focus on the interchangeability and iterability (i.e.
the ability to be repeated) of 'spontaneous' tongues, narratives, testimonies,
and preaching 'in the Spirit' among believers (both pastors and 'lay') indicates how verbal 'possession' is also a kind of gift, and moreover one whose
exchange reveals much about the apparent permeability of the charismatic
person. To 'talk' possession thus has at least two interrelated meanings: it
can imply description of events of being possessed by the Spirit, but also the
speaking out of inspired words, directed towards a person or persons, so that
'talking' ideally becomes 'taking' possession of the spiritual state of another.

As the elder's disparaging use of the word 'shaman' implies, these practices
have often been controversial in Christian as well as lay circles in Sweden.
This is not only because they involve the unabashed and highly public
expression of religious conviction in contexts that are seen as relatively secu-
larised. I want to argue further that they play on questions – ambiguities

– relating to the material world, language and mediation, as well as forms of consumption that imply not only an alternative way of practising religion in contemporary Sweden, but also another way of being 'modern' members of a global as well as national society. I shall make my case by first sketching charismatic notions of the working of the Holy Spirit, showing how they relate to notions of the body as well as to the status of language. This sketch is then juxtaposed with salient themes derived from the anthropology of spirit possession. Both of these sections frame my tracing of instances of 'charismatic possession' derived from fieldwork within the Word of Life, illustrating their significance as central, constituting practices of supporting the ministry and its ambitious aims.

The Spirit, the Person and the Body

Charismatic Christians see themselves as inspired by the Holy Spirit. In line with Pentecostal theology in general, the Spirit is seen as both dwelling *within* the person and working *through* that person in the exercise of the Christian life. A commonly expressed trope is derived from Paul's First Letter to the Corinthians, particularly the point at which the apostle famously calls the human body 'a temple of the Holy Spirit' (chapter 6, verse 19). While such a view is often interpreted by Christians of all denominations as involving the necessity to keep the body pure as a suitably holy container of the Spirit, in 'Prosperity' circles such as the Word of Life another dimension is also emphasised: that of the self as potentially unlimited container of Spirit, a sense that the inner-space of the self that can receive the Spirit is unbound, in contrast to the physical limits of the body. Thus a more conventional, boundary-reinforcing evocation of purity is counterbalanced by a complementary image of power, of sanctified excess, of being utterly 'open' to the promptings and 'in-fillings' of Spirit, which are conceptualised as free gifts, potentially available to all who make themselves appropriate recipients and receptacles for God's generosity.

The Holy Spirit not only forms part of the Holy Trinity alongside God the Father and Jesus the Son, but also helps to constitute a tripartite division of the believing person as made up of Spirit, Mind/Soul and Body. Again, common Christian imagery is given a particular kind of focus. Lecture notes given to me by a student at the Word of Life Bible School express this idea with a kind of graphic literalism, in a way that converts Paul's words into a visual image: her sketch is of a schematic representation of a temple that doubles as a body. Within the diagram, the arrows – moving from top to bottom – refer to Spirit ('Anden'), Soul ('Själen') and Body ('Kroppen'), respectively.

According to her labelling, 'The Spirit (the holiest of all)' is in the place where the altar is conventionally located; 'The Soul (the holy)' is in the main part of the church; and 'The Body (the vestibule)' is on the outside. The image shows the body of the Church but also the Church as body, and moreover one made up of a clear spiritual hierarchy that can also be expressed in spatial terms: the body is on the periphery, the soul/mind is further in, while the Spirit is at the very core of being a Christian person. This is not, then, a depiction of incarnation – of the blending of the divine and the human – but rather of the relative values given to different and differentiated parts of the self. The highest worth is placed on that aspect of the self which is most open to communication with an external, divine presence. In practice, for Word of Life Christians, there is nonetheless almost a physical sense of the Spirit as located 'in' the stomach region, significantly not in the head or the heart, but in the very centre of the person.

Charismatic (and Pentecostal) theology and practice lay stress on the notion that the presence and movement of the Spirit is often evidenced by the character of spoken language located in testimonies, sermons, songs, prayers, glossolalia, an inner voice, and sometimes even an apparently everyday conversation. Speaking inspired words in these contexts accomplishes much: it creates communication as event, as located within and indexed to a particular situation, such as a private prayer, a form of public worship, a testimony, and so on. More ambiguously, it relates the speech act to a given person, whose claim over the ownership, legitimacy and authority of the words may vary according to circumstances.[3] Most importantly, however, it implies/claims the possibility of a lack of mediation – material, mental or otherwise

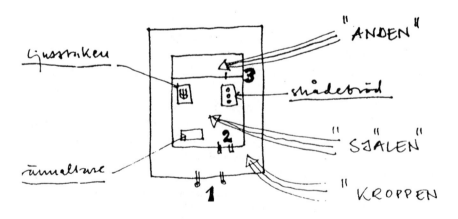

The body as temple.

– between the person and the Spirit, despite the fact that the medium of language is being used.

The student's lecture notes on the workings of the Holy Spirit note that one is to 'receive in the Spirit and receive in faith…God is Spirit and he talks to Spirit, your Spirit,' while 'it's the person's Spirit which is born-again. And one interprets that so that it's the Spirit alone that communicates with God, really.' And she draws again on the notion of communication in another image sketched into her notes, this time in the form of an arrow directed from God into the very Spirit of the person which is depicted as being located at the centre of a series of concentric circles that make up the totality of the self (see, Coleman, 2010: 186–202). Significantly, however, the student completes her diagram by drawing another arrow, reaching from the Spirit outwards beyond the body into the world beyond. Communication here turns into a kind of exchange, as 'inspiration' is followed by an externalisation of spiritual power – or perhaps this is better put by saying that the person becomes a new centre, able to initiate and direct movements of the Spirit.

To recall the imagery of the gift, the power 'received' from God is stored in the Spirit but, like the 'objects' implicated in all gift economies, cannot be allowed to remain static (Coleman, 2004: 421–42). The system only works if the recipient becomes a donor of inspiration, who feels empowered to act in and on the world as a whole. Such external actions are frequently seen as ideally without limit, just as the inner person can take in a boundless quantity of 'Spirit.' The inspired believer should ideally feel confident enough to missionise at any time, to become a world-leader in business or politics as well as in a ministry, and so on. There is an echo here of a Hegelian depiction

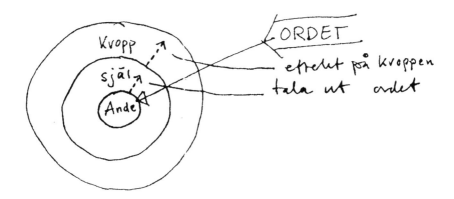

The person made up of concentric circles, with the Spirit in the centre of the self.

of objectification as a dual process by means of which a subject externalises itself in a creative act of differentiation and in turn appropriates this externalisation through 'sublation' (Engelke, 2007: 26). Successful action in and on the world acts back to reinforce the sense of a powerful self, who can then go on to further action. Especially in the early years of the ministry, a phrase on the lips of many Word of Lifers has been 'I feel in my Spirit (*Jag känner i min Ande*) that…' followed by a statement of the way things *ought* to be. The simplicity of the words masks a complex invocation of agency. 'Feeling' in the Spirit is not an appeal to emotion, but a means of bypassing the mind and plugging into the legitimacy provided by the divine; it is thus an avoidance of mental mediation, and yet to be effected it must be expressed in words, indexed to a particular situation.

These, at times literal, sketches of Word of Life notions of Spirit bear significant comparison with work done elsewhere. Thus, Rabelo, Mota and Almeida, writing of poor Pentecostal women in Salvador, Brazil, talk of inspired worship as involving the super-position of voices so that the worship space becomes totally filled by divine presence, which also makes of each body a 'dwelling' (2009: 1). Such presence is, again, complexly expressed through language – a semiotic form that is nonetheless constantly breaking out of its semantic boundaries, in tongues, in the chaos of multiple voices and in the ambiguity of whether to attribute its source to the person or to God. The cultivation of an open disposition to the sacred involves bodily liberation of the self from all 'worldly' matters, including the embarrassment of being used by the Holy Spirit – laughing, crying, shouting, jumping – thus demonstrating a measure of subjection of the body and the will to divine order. One of the (from a worldly perspective) paradoxes of such a disposition is that making the self an apparently passive instrument of God provides access to spiritual gifts, to a socially acknowledged set of abilities such as healing, interpretation and revelation (Rabelo, Mota and Almeida, 2009: 7). At the same time, it balances precariously on a thin interpretative and moral line: the surrender of the self that is required for the body to be a dwelling for the Holy Spirit comes perilously close to the total loss of control that prevents witnessing God's work, and which signifies out-and-out 'possession;' an alternative state of being that may come, of course, from the Devil.

Sánchez's discussion of the mystical foundations of squatting among contemporary Venezuelan Pentecostals displays a further dimension of the complexities of agency and mediation involved in allowing the Spirit to dwell in the self (2008: 267–305). As in Sweden and Brazil, we see the drive towards obliterating the gap between God and human, so that representation of the divine becomes a kind of presencing. Part of the process becomes a form of double-possession, however, even as 'the squatters speak of themselves as "vessels" to be filled by Spirit' (2008: 270). The Spirit seizes the squatters as they illegally seize urban space, engaging in acts of external appropriation of worldly, urban space. These believers provide particularly stark illustrations of what Sánchez calls 'Pentecostalism's peculiar spatio-temporal drive' (2008: 272). This drive is also evidenced in the huge projection screens found in Pentecostal churches all over the world (certainly that of the Word of Life), enabling services to incorporate heterogeneous landscapes caught in rapid succession. As Sánchez puts it in an example he witnesses, the voiceover 'manages to suture the Holy Spirit to the moving eye of the camera, generating the impression of a disembodied supernatural agency smoothly yet relentlessly taking over the whole of the planet from above' (2008: 272). At the same time, the ubiquity of the Spirit becomes localised in individual selves, as during worship the hands of believers are raised aloft like 'vibrating antennas, thus ready to receive the gift of the Holy Spirit descending among them right from the stage' (2008: 300).

There is much about charismatic practice in Sweden – the economic and political circumstances, ideas about gender relations, assumptions about the governance of the church, and so on – that has little or nothing to do with these believers in Brazil and Venezuela. And yet in each case the role of the person as complex mediator of the presence of the Spirit is invoked, a role that itself provokes questions of how the outer world relates to the inner. In the process, the exact responsibility for agency becomes a significant question, as do the appropriate limits and legitimacy of such agency: at what point does the surrendered self lose too much control? Can a Spirit-inspired believer really justify seizing all of 'the world's' resources, regardless of the law? We might regard these questions as exploring the complicated boundaries and affinities between legitimate 'possession' and lack of 'self-possession' (in the sense of the social etiquette and expectations of everyday life). We see also the problem of how the Spirit's presence and movement are to be represented in ways that transcend the limits of normal representation. Speaking in tongues expresses a glide away from semantic moorings, just as the images provided on film flit across global landscapes, unfettered by any single location.

Spirits Compared

How does what I have said so far compare with the extensive literature on spirit possession, which apparently takes us far from Pentecostal or charismatic forms of Christianity? Here, I want to examine three points of significant intersection – 'communication,' 'selfhood' and 'authenticity.' Each of these points of significant intersection also plays (in culturally specific ways) on ambiguities associated with mediation, morality and legitimacy that I have hinted at above.

I start with the issue of communication. As Lambek puts it, possession can be viewed as a system of communication based on a minimal triad of three 'persons;' host, spirit and intermediary (1980: 318). For Lambek, an important aspect of such a communication triad is that – as well as sustaining a relationship with an outside intermediary – it maintains a separation between host and spirit. By delivering messages through a third party, the spirit shields its host from being implicated as an accessory to the generation of spirit messages. Although she lays emphasis on looking closely at what is said during possession episodes, Placido agrees that, on one level, spirit possession can be seen as a kind of ventriloquism in which mediums acquire a voice more powerful than their own as humans (2001: 207). Beyond formulaic, repeated formulae the spirits can address the needs of specific individuals (2001: 217).

In both of these examples, the distinction between host and Spirit is key, whereas in the charismatic examples we have seen it is this distinction itself that is interestingly problematic. The message of the divine 'speaks' through the person, and yet, as we shall see, it speaks more powerfully through some persons than others, indicating a kind of indexicality of the Spirit related to the qualities of the host. Furthermore, in charismatic contexts, what may be communicated may simply be the act of connection itself; as tongues, for example, indicate the presence of the Spirit but not necessarily any semantic content, unless 'interpretation' of the message follows. Very significantly, also, the Pentecostal and charismatic notion of Spirit implies not simply the dwelling of the Spirit in the person, but an ontological connection between the Spirit located in the person and the Holy Spirit as a whole. The person is possessed by and receives inspired messages because s/he possesses – at a certain level *is* – Spirit.

Spirit possession usually implies not only the sending of messages, but the construction of a particular form of self. For instance, Boddy links possession in the Sudan with fundamental and problematic questions of identity and selfhood, with zar possession becoming a lifelong, 'incurable' condition that is manageable (1988: 4–27). The resultant self is not a fixed entity but a process, and also one that cannot be viewed in conventional Western terms as an autonomous individual. Thus, in a later comparative piece Boddy argues that:

> To the extent that someone is perpetually influenced by *multiple* foreign or historically antecedent spirits...she contains and embodies alternative dividualities – two composite and divisible 'persons' respectively

produced via protean relationships with spirits and other human selves.
(1998: 257)

Such a view may seem to place such possession impossibly far from a Swedish
charismatic ministry, and yet as LiPuma argues in the same volume, we
should mistrust the simplistic and ideologically loaded notion that the West
constructs 'individuals' while others construct 'dividuals' or relational persons
(1998: 56). Persons everywhere can be seen to grow transactionally both
as the beneficiary of other people's actions and as depending on others for
knowledge about themselves (1998: 60). In the Melanesian context the corollary to the involvement of persons in exchange is the relationship between
these persons and the things that flow between them (1998: 68). In fact, this
image of personhood does not seem impossibly far from a charismatic depiction of the Spirit as gift, moving from God to the person but also, as we shall
see, mediated by fellow believers who themselves contain – and transmit –
spiritually loaded language.

Such language can come in different forms. We have already seen Placido's
reference to both more and less formulaic uses of words by the spirits (2001:
207–24). Lambek adds that certain kinds of iterations may prompt questions of seriousness and conviction, of the relation of the performance to
the intention of the performer (2007: 69, 75). In charismatic contexts, these
questions of iteration, formulation and intention take on particular inflec-
tions, as believers speak the words of the Spirit, the Bible or even a powerful
and inspired preacher. Where the sincerity of and commitment to the
present event of worship (or mission) are seen as paramount, the sense that
the person might be a mere mouthpiece for the words of an external force
might seem to be deeply problematic. Similarly, Shoaps points to the chronic
tension between textual and spontaneous elements of Pentecostal communication (2002: 34–7); in other words, between routinised, formulaic religious
language and that which appears to come spontaneously and authentically
from the inner person (see, Coleman, forthcoming). We might ask what kind
of 'self' is being constructed through the transactions and mediations of the
Spirit under such circumstances? In fact, I want to argue that this is indeed
an issue that provides both opportunities and problematic questions for
believers engaging in charismatic practices, as – to borrow vocabulary from
Lambek – 'conviction' develops out of 'confiction' (2007: 74).[4] In this problematic we see how what Johnson and Keller call 'the work of possession(s)'
involves both possession and being possessed; how charismatic subjectivity
can be made through practices of inspired, linguistic consumption as well as
production (2006: 112).

In the next section I trace these ambiguities relating to communication, selfhood and authenticity by looking at specific examples of the workings of the Spirit at the Word of Life. I trace the deployment of language to the mediation of the Spirit, but also look at how both language and inspiration blur boundaries as much as they erect them; asserting 'excess' as well as 'purity,' challenging 'selves' as much as empowering them. In order to do so, I try to look at Spirit working, as narrated both by powerful leaders and by ordinary, sometimes deeply ambivalent, members of the ministry.

The Spirit from Above and Below

It is a spring evening in the late 1980s, around the time that I had my conversation about Ulf Ekman in the kitchen of the elder of the Pentecostal church. This time, however, I am attending an evening meeting at the Word of Life itself, listening to a young pastor recount a recent journey that he took to the United States with 'Ulf' and some other members of the ministry.[5] His description is also a testimony, framed by the prayers of the congregation. It is also a distinctly *charismatically* inflected discussion of a journey. We learn very little about the actual places visited, about beautiful landscapes or cultural attractions, but rather the narrative landscape is filled with congregations visited, famous preachers encountered and miracles experienced. At this time, the Word of Life had only been in existence for some five years or so, and Ekman was poised on the cusp of a career that would gain him recognition as an internationally renowned figure within 'Prosperity' circles. The following describes one of the early encounters on the trip:

> The American pastor had never heard Ulf, he'd only heard about him. He introduced Ulf as a powerful man of God, an apostle who goes up and down the whole of Europe. And it just opened up in the Spirit immediately and everybody just sat there hungrily and sucked in what God had laid down in Ulf...We have much to give them – especially this Spirit of conquering, the Spirit of aggressiveness and really taking in new territories for Jesus.

The preacher is referring here to his head pastor, a man who is known to almost all of those present, but he is also investing Ekman with a dimension of distance – depicting him in the way that others might view him when seeing him for the first time. Ekman's power is indexed by his immediate effects: 'the Spirit' is opened up without delay, without seeming effort, even across the cultural boundaries encountered when a Swedish pastor visits an American congregation. Note that the spiritual power is 'ingested' rather than interpreted and is channelled in ways that reflect rather precisely the sketches of inspired personhood that I referred to above. The divine communicates with the Spirit of a person (here, Ekman), who passes on the power to others; in this case, amplifying its effects by broadcasting it to thousands of people simultaneously. The description also moves easily from the Spirit to broader spatial ambitions; to unsaved territories. We might claim an echo here of the spatio-spiritual ambitions of the Pentecostal squatters described by Sánchez (2008: 267–305). In a classic evangelical trope, the passage also moves easily from the third person to the collective first person. 'He' shifts to 'we,' as the direction of the message shifts to those who are listening in Sweden; just as 'there and then' become 'here and now.' Indeed, we learn that even Christians from a small country can 'give' to fellow believers in the United States, just as we learn that our role is not merely to listen to a testimony, but to act in the world. Indeed, the preacher concludes this part of his narrative by stating that 'We are more led by the Holy Spirit than we believe, yes?'

If we see the Swedish preacher here inviting his audience to emulate their head pastor, his narrative also establishes significant parallels across the wider, global landscape of inspired Prosperity ministries. Thus he talks of a later leg of the journey, when the Swedish group visits the Ohio-based ministry of Rod Parsley.[6] We are told that Parsley 'is very like our pastor when he preaches' – indeed, the parallels are apparently somewhat uncanny. Both men are said to have studied at Hagin's Bible School in the same year (without knowing each other), both have attended the seminars of another preacher, Lester Sumrall, at the same time, both have named their congregations 'The Word of Life,' and both are constructing auditoria containing 5,200 places. The pastor concludes of both men: 'Exactly the same Spirit over both – they are equally wild, both of them!' The apparent coincidences here express the valorisation of a certain kind of repetition; one that hints at the divine plan and inspiration underlying the actions of both men who are setting up ministries thousands of miles apart. The Spirit, filtered through different cultures and personalities, is still 'exactly the same.' These links between the two men are then demonstrated further in the narrative, when the Swedish party visits Lester Sumrall at South Bend, Indiana. Sumrall does Ekman the honour of coming to meet him at the airport and we hear that 'Sumrall has taken Parsley and Ulf to himself like his children...Sumrall didn't see Stefan and me – just Ulf.'

A kind of 'Pentecostal's Progress,' this narrative provides a multi-layered account of the legitimacy of the Swedish leader of the Word of Life and, by implication, of the ministry's members who are gathered to hear the stories of Ekman's success in the evangelical Promised Land of the United States.

Success in preaching is accompanied by divine forms of parallelism and then by a genealogical connection with an earlier generation of preachers, represented by the venerable Lester Sumrall. It is also an account of Ekman as mediator (travelling master?) of Spirit – derived from God, refracted to multiple others and generically applicable. Furthermore, the telling of the story of the journey reinserts it into a Swedish context in a number of ways. The young preacher is not Ekman; he is a man who has metonymic links with Ekman through accompanying him on the journey, but is also using the story of Ekman's spiritual power to create his own sermon, and one that begins and ends with prayers in the Spirit. The account is also a means of moving from the third to the first person, which involves the turning of the responsibility for taking spiritual territories on to the audience; a *story* of possession that *leads* to possession in the sense of personal inspiration and spatio-spiritual expansion – what I am calling here 'meta-possession.'

A combination of mimesis and ontology – emulating a powerful leader and appealing to the presence of common Spirit – is being recounted here in a narrative, but it is also a story about words as mediators of divine messages. Indeed, verbal exercises may explicitly be used to bring the Spirit into play through iterations that are forms of emulation of powerful leaders. Thus on an occasion when Sumrall himself comes to the Word of Life he begins his sermon with a form of 'positive confession' in which all of the congregation are to take part (Coleman, forthcoming). Sumrall orders the congregation: 'Say "I am blessed!" [The crowd responds with 'I am blessed.'] Say "I am blessed!" [Crowd responds.] Say it again! "I am blessed!" Hallelujah! Praise God! Tell your neighbour. Say "I am blessed!"'

We see here how Sumrall converts his audience from listeners to speakers/ actors, as evident also in the young preacher's account of Ekman's actions in the USA, where the description of Ekman is converted into the way 'we' are led by the Spirit. This time, the words of the inspired preacher are taken over by the audience, as each individual appropriates the words taken from the stage and puts them into practice by addressing them to another person – just as phrases from Ekman's tongues are sometimes echoed by believers. Tellingly, each person becomes blessed by broadcasting their own blessed state to another; externalising – but also constituting – an internal state through words borrowed from a powerful source. The original words are repeated four times, indicating the cumulative effect of performative and inspired language. Here, then, iteration – the borrowing of words – implies no lack of authenticity (see, Lambek 2007: 65–81). This suggests a transactional model of charismatic personhood, where the power to build up the self is mediated not only through language in disembodied terms, but also by the speaking of language to another. To speak words is to locate them in the self, but to direct them to another is immediately to move them 'on,' to ensure that they remain as mobile as the Spirit is meant to be.

What I have said so far indicates the passage of the spirit 'from above' – not only the ways in which spiritual power can come from leading preachers but also an idealised depiction of how spiritual power is assimilated to the self. It is also important, however, to examine the workings of the Spirit from the viewpoint of ordinary believers. If we do so, we often see a rather more nuanced orientation to the Spirit; or at least a sense of the construction of the inspired person as indeed a process – a work in progress – where ambiguities lie not only in the autonomy of the self, but also the ability of the self authentically to sustain the power of the Spirit.

Certainly, some informal discourse recounted to me in interviews and conversations echoes what we have seen so far. As one Bible School student put it – moving to Uppsala because she felt she recognised aspects of Ulf Ekman in herself – 'I went in feeling I didn't want to discuss, just to receive.' Her statement pithily encapsulated a sense of self as pure receptacle. Another informant – an older woman who had previously spent many decades in the local Pentecostal Church – described her changing subjectivity by indicating the complex workings of the Spirit in relation to various media of communication. Thus, she talked of how her and her husband's 'journey' into the group began with the reading of *Set My People Free!* by Ulf Ekman's father-in-law, Sten Nilsson (1989). While the book refers to the liberation of the Jewish people, it also becomes a paradigm of her personal liberation into a new and inspired life. 'We read Nilsson's book...Here one could see the Spirit-world for the first time. It became so living for us – we just read and read about what we had in Jesus Christ, what authority we had.' Here, the reading of an inspired text prompts a reinterpretation of *the* text. Visiting the group seems to have the same effect. 'It made God's Word and the Bible so living... Ulf Ekman...presented God's Word and his teaching...God's Word must be understood directly through the Holy Spirit.' Referring to the new way she is reading and hearing words from the Bible, she then concludes: 'One takes God's Word in one's Spirit; one doesn't just *listen*, one takes it *in*.'

In this view, merely to listen implies a problematic form of mediation, whereas to 'take in' bypasses body and soul and reaches straight into the Spirit. The building up of an inspired self involves a certain reduction of the person as a whole – a disciplining of the non-spiritual self that is exercised through practices of speaking as well as hearing, reaching out to others as well as cultivating the self. The 'irrelevance' of the physical becomes evident in the way she describes her experiences of services. 'I became so built up; I could be there three hours and not be tired at all.' It is also evident in practices that to an outsider might not seem spiritual at all, such as her gaining the courage to buy a bicycle and cycle around her local area; a modest marking of territory, if hardly as ambitious as squatting. A younger woman put such disciplining to me more starkly. 'One shouldn't worry about one's old person, yeah? Kill the old person.' To become 'born-again' implies the demise of a previous model of self. Or, as a young lawyer put it at a talk given to Word of Life students: 'When you meet a person, you're not just meeting a person...I am meeting a person who has a Spirit...There's a spiritual battle for his life.'

Some of these statements perhaps seem ironic, as the directness of the Holy Spirit is only experienced after, in a sense through, the sermons and texts of powerful preachers. Even personality – arguably the most idiosyncratic dimension of self – can be subjected to spiritual exchange or, at least, the drawing on a common source; as we saw with the same 'Spirit' inhabiting both Ekman and Parsley. In a similar vein, here are the words of a young member of the Bible School talking of how she learned to view herself: '[They] prophesied over me and said I would become Sandy Brown number two...And I began to identify myself then with becoming a world evangelist like Sandy Brown.' This linking of the self with a hero of the movement is hardly surprising, but what is interesting is how the person is linked with a specific preacher and then made the recipient of performative language designed to fulfil such a prophecy.

At times, the disciplines and claims involved in living up to a life domi-nated by such a notion of Spirit can become problematic. One dimension of such ambivalence emerges from the closeness of the imagery of the Spirit to other more troubling forms of 'in-filling.' We saw how Rabelo, Mota and Almeida referred to the closeness between being a dwelling for the Holy Spirit and the total surrender that implies demonic possession (2009: 7); and there is no doubt that a powerful demonology underlies the politics of much discernment at the Word of Life. Those who are spiritually powerful may also attract 'attacks' – manifested in doubts and threats to health, etc. – from the Devil who is scared of their power. One Bible School student described how – upon resisting certain elements of Word of Life practice – she encountered a spiritually defined attack on her sense of self. '[Leaders] have questioned my spiritual maturity, they have got the idea that I have critical demons, and that I speak directly from Satan.' Strikingly, her ability to speak in an unmediated, direct way appears undiminished, but the origins and authority of the communication are questioned (see, Engelke, 2007). The legitimacy of 'spiritually-derived' communications has also sometimes been questioned in more overt ways, albeit in contexts where the effects of demons are harder to invoke. Thus, in the late 1980s Ulf Ekman had to make an announcement from the pulpit, preventing members of the ministry and Bible School students from going to specific others and saying things like 'I feel in my Spirit that we will be married.' In such cases, the legitimacy and ambition of the message of the 'felt Spirit' conflicted both with the intentions of other Spirit-filled Christians and with the advice of the ministry's leadership.

Generally, however, the legitimacy of the Spirit is not challenged in public contexts, especially when such critique would be seen as 'negative confession' – powerful words that might rebound on the speaker – even if the link between authority and authenticity is sometimes questioned more privately by those who harbour doubts about elements of the group's theology. One young congregation member noted of the teachers at the ministry:

> One says as a teacher that 'It's not me you should listen to, it's God's voice, it's God who is speaking,' so that one makes oneself so humble in that way, but it means that one is even more, oh, a spirit-filled teacher, right?

Here, the ventriloquism involved in being 'filled' by the Spirit – combined with the assumed ontological link between Spirit and self – becomes problematic, as it seems difficult to know how to 'discern' (and challenge) the legitimacy or otherwise of spiritually powerful others. Furthermore, this questioning of legitimacy can even be applied to the self. As the same informant put it:

> I am a Spirit and I have a soul and I live in a body. And it becomes a very fragmented picture of humanity...I began to search for myself in all this. Who am I? Am I just an empty shell?...I gained a schizophrenic sense of who I was.

We see how the hierarchy of the elements that make up the self – with the body as mere 'vestibule' – become deeply troubling for this person as she attempts to negotiate the self-objectification involved in the discipline of the Spirit. This, then, is a form of charismatic 'dividuality' that is no longer seen as a positive experience; where the permeability of the self becomes an alienating threat rather than permitting an accumulation of spiritual power. Notably, this person also talked of how the language of the group (e.g. spiritual admonitions and lines from sermons) stayed with her – dictated to her inner thoughts, like an unwanted tune that one cannot get out of one's head – even at times when she wished it would go away. The boundary between possessing and being possessed was being transgressed in a way that no longer felt comfortable, and such internally directed 'talking' became an unwanted form of 'taking.'

Concluding Remarks

I have talked of the Spirit rather than of spirits, and of a form of possession that seeks ultimately to create a global charismatic landscape, peopled by believers who can recognise the generic, ideally ubiquitous powers of the Holy Spirit in each other. The disciplining of the self that is necessary for such ideas to take purchase can from one perspective be seen as leading to dividualised avenues of empowerment, and from another as an inauthentic, Procrustean reducing of the elements of personhood into a notion of Spirit that denies the value of the local and the idiosyncratic.

In either case, the person becomes a product of transactions between language, movement and worship, each of which can act as a suitably transparent or, at least, 'living' medium for the workings of the Spirit. Such transactions are always potentially capable of occurring. The forms of possession described here are not merely to be staged in designated places, among particular people at particular times; part of the disciplining of the self involves always being open to the workings of a Spirit that is always within – and does not merely fall upon – the self. Furthermore, the inner landscape of the Spirit-filled person – one that can never actually be completely filled with enough inspiration – ideally corresponds with more material forms of possession in the outer world. Here, the believer is ultimately permitted to appropriate everything – riches, power, space, souls – without a limiting horizon to his or her ambition.

As I have described it, then, charismatic Spirit indeed comes close to a Hegelian account of Spirit as 'universal currency' – a medium bridging heterogeneous dimensions of life (Sánchez, 2008: 281). In doing so, it presents an alternative vision of modernity in the context of Sweden, where divisions between public and private religion, immaterial and material manifestations of faith and even between believing persons are broken down in the name of a 'living' faith. We might wonder whether the accusation of shamanism – of presenting a version of religion that is anachronistic in the modern world – itself mistakes the power of the Spirit to survive, even to flourish, in the contemporary world.

PART III

POSSESSION AND INVOCATION IN LATE-MODERN CONTEXTS

The term 'late-modern' signals a belief that contemporary urban-industrial society is constituted by the radicalisation of the *same* kinds of processes (e.g. individualisation, detraditionalisation and pluralisation) responsible for the emergence and consolidation of modern urban-industrial society as it has occurred over the course of the last 150 years in the North and 80–100 years in the South. As late-modern society is – at least, to a meaningful extent – in continuity with what has gone before, contemporary socio-cultural trans-formations of the urban-industrial landscape comprise less a fundamental break with established processes of modernity than a series of variations on the modern theme. Relative to what has gone before, contemporary socio-cultural transformation is, then, more a difference in degree than a difference in kind. Each of the three chapters which make up the final part of our book conveys something of the late-modern, urban-industrial context as both in continuity with and a radicalisation of what has gone before.

Treating the Brazilian new religion of Santo Daime, Dawson's chapter tracks developments in the movement's spirit possession repertoire against the back-drop of its insertion within and subsequent domination by an urban-professional ethos constituted by a typically modern preoccupation with self-development. At the same time, this modern preoccupation with self-fulfilment plays out within a progressively late-modern context characterised by – among other things – an increasingly individualistic, instrumental and expressive attitude. In combination, this typically late-modern range of concerns has resulted in the gradual modification of Santo Daime's – already highly diverse and fluid – spirit possession repertoire. Here, traditional components are either incremen-tally replaced or remodelled, while novel beliefs and practices are introduced by way of appropriation from other sources – particularly Afro-Brazilian ones – or creative manufacture. In addition, Dawson's treatment of Santo Daime shows its hybrid ritual repertoire to furnish room for many of the classical types of spirit possession and to demand of its mediums a technical mastery of both their craft and the ritual space they inhabit.

Staemmler's chapter engages the cultural phenomenon of Japanese comic books and cartoons known collectively as *manga*. Focussing upon the highly successful and long-running manga of *Shaman King*, Staemmler offers insight into both traditional Japanese spirit possession repertoires and their contemporary reworking along popular cultural lines. Here, the author identifies a number of socio-cultural – and typically late-modern – dynamics which impact upon *Shaman King's* representation of spirit possession. Set against the backdrop of tradition's declining influence and the increased accessibility of globally diffused practices and beliefs, *Shaman King* is shown to be a highly variegated phenomenon which arises on the back of socio-cultural pluralisation, hybridism and invention. *Shaman King's* reworking, if not reinvention, of established Japanese possession practices is shown by Staemmler to centre upon its characters' appropriation of supernatural powers which elevate them to the kind of extra-ordinary status traditionally reserved for the spirits. As with a number of the possession repertoires so far treated, *Shaman King's* mediation of human – spirit interaction rests ultimately upon its empowerment of individual agency and all that ensues from it.

The book's final chapter draws upon extensive fieldwork with practitioners of modern Witchcraft – known also as Wicca – and Paganism in Australia. While Ezzy's chapter focuses mainly upon an ethnographically informed reading of the contemporary Pagan possession rite of Baphomet, the Wiccan ritual of Drawing Down the Moon and Heathen seidr (neo-shamanic) practices are also mentioned. Typical of much late-modern non-mainstream spirituality, the possession repertoires engaged by Ezzy are shown to be highly inventive, hybrid and self-valorising. At the same time, they are infused by an immanentist concern to celebrate the 'pleasures of this life' as expressed through natural processes in general and human physicality in particular. Characteristic of their magical orientation, Pagan possession repertoires are deeply pragmatic affairs whose principal concern is that of engendering self-development through the harnessing of supernatural energies which course through nature and, by extension, the human body. Ezzy shows Pagan possession practices to be informed by a worldview which treats good and evil not as mutually exclusive categories but as part of the same ontological continuum. As a result, Pagan possession repertoires afford their practitioners opportunity not only to celebrate what is good about themselves but also to explore the darker side – 'shadow self' – of their nature.

SPIRIT, SELF AND SOCIETY IN THE BRAZILIAN NEW RELIGION OF SANTO DAIME

Andrew Dawson

This chapter explores the growing popularity of spirit possession within the Brazilian new religion of Santo Daime.[1] The following material opens by introducing Santo Daime and plotting the historical trajectory of spirit possession, most commonly termed 'incorporation' (*incorporação*) by members. In so doing, we move from Santo Daime's beginnings in 1930s' Brazil to its present-day status as a member of the non-mainstream global religious scene. Subsequent to detailing the contemporary spirit possession repertoire of Santo Daime, the chapter offers a typology comprising the most prominent kinds of incorporation practised by Santo Daime members – known popularly as *daimistas*. My treatment of spirit possession in Santo Daime closes by identifying the most likely factors behind the increasing popularity of certain kinds of incorporation relative to more traditional forms of spirit-orientated activity.

The Historical Trajectory of Spirit Possession in Santo Daime

Santo Daime emerged in the Amazonian state of Acre among the mixed-race, semi-rural subsistence community led by Raimundo Irineu Serra (1892–1971). Known commonly as 'Master Irineu,' Irineu Serra is held by many to be the reincarnation of the spirit of Jesus. Based at the community of *Alto Santo*, Santo Daime emerged as a recognisably distinct religious entity in the late-1930s. Subsequent to Irineu Serra's death, a breakaway organisation known as Cefluris – the Eclectic Centre of the Universal Flowing Light Raimundo Irineu Serra – was founded by Sebastião Mota de Melo (1920–90) and his followers. Known as 'Padrinho Sebastião,' Mota de Melo is believed to be the reincarnation of the spirit of John the Baptist. Headquartered at *Céu do Mapiá* in the state of Amazonas, Cefluris is now led by Alfredo Gregório de Melo and Alex Polari – regarded as the respective reincarnations of Solomon and David. On the back of the organisational expansion of Cefluris, Santo Daime reached Brazil's major conurbations (e.g. Rio de Janeiro and São Paulo) in the early 1980s before spreading to Europe, North America and Australasia (Couto, 2004: 385–411).

Santo Daime is the oldest and most geographically dispersed of Brazil's ayahuasca religions – the other two being Barquinha and the Vegetable Union. When applied to these religions, the generic term ayahuasca denotes the combination of the vine *Banisteriopsis caapi* and the leaves of the shrub *Psychotria viridis* (Dawson, 2007: 67–98). Ayahuasca is a psychotropic substance traditionally consumed by indigenous inhabitants of the Amazon which passed to non-indigenous cultures through its use among mixed-race communities and rubber-tappers in the late-nineteenth and early-twentieth centuries. Called 'Daime' by *daimistas*, ayahuasca is regarded as an 'entheogen;' that is, an agent whose properties facilitate ('catalyse') the interaction of humankind with supernatural agents or forces (Polari, 1999). By virtue of Daime's psychotropic effects, ritual participation in Santo Daime entails learning to work (*trabalhar*) with an altered state of consciousness.

The trajectory of spirit possession in Santo Daime has three main phases. The first phase comprises the period of Irineu Serra's leadership from the time of the religion's birth to its founder's death in 1971. Before the founding of Santo Daime and throughout his time as its leader, Irineu Serra had a reputation as a healer (*curandeiro*) whose powers resided both in his knowledge of folk medicine and his ability to work with the spirits. Although the earlier years of Irineu's life and Santo Daime's history remain open to a degree of conjecture, there is wide-spread agreement upon the formative influence of what Furuya calls 'afro-amazonian' religiosity – here, a mixture of Afro-Brazilian, popular Catholic and indigenous components (1994: 27). Together, these variegated ingredients combined to produce a religious-cultural worldview infused by the everyday interaction with and ritualised appropriation of a relatively diverse range of spiritual agencies (Galvão, 1955; Maués and Villacorta, 2004: 11–58). A combination of oral history, narrative analysis and anthropological investigation evidences the centrality of spirit-orientated activity to the early religious repertoire of Santo Daime (Goulart, 2004; Labate and Pacheco, 2004: 303–344). Although engagement with the spirits of deceased human beings probably occurred, available (but, self-interested) evidence indicates that interaction with nature spirits was the most important form of spirit-orientated activity undertaken by the early *daimista* community. In keeping with existing forms of popular healing (*curandeir-ismo*), then, early *daimista* activities involved, among other things, regular consultation with spirit guides (regarding the cause of a particular illness or run of bad luck, for example), practical engagement with spirits (e.g. in the case of spirit infestation) and co-optation of spirit intervention (e.g. to treat illness or ward off spirit assault).

From the late-1940s onwards, the religious repertoire of Santo Daime was progressively modified as a result of Irineu Serra's increasing attraction to traditional European esotericism (e.g. Theosophy, Anthroposophy and Rosicrucianism) as mediated through the publications of the Esoteric Circle of the Communion of Thought – *Círculo Esotérico da Comunhão do Pensamento* (Moura da Silva, 2006: 225–40). Among other things, traditional esotericism concerns itself with interior states of mind, experiences and dispositions which are awakened through access to particular forms of knowledge and practice. These interior realities are nurtured through a range of disciplines and techniques (e.g. meditation, introspection and regression) and provide access to further truths located deep within the self (Faivre, 1986: 156–63). Although Irineu Serra eventually severed formal relations with the Esoteric Circle, by the time of his death, the influence of European esotericism had played a significant role in reforming the religious repertoire of Santo Daime. As a result, the spirit-orientated activity which had once been so important to Santo Daime was marginalised, if not denigrated, thanks to the introduction of many of the rationalised and individualistic practices of traditional esotericism. Rather than encouraging personal wellbeing through the ritualised interaction with spirits, the Santo Daime repertoire now promoted the nurturing of the 'higher self' through the harnessing of impersonal cosmic energies. Although never officially repudiating the existence of spirits, by the time of Irineu Serra's death in 1971, Santo Daime embodied, at most, a kind of nominal spiritism in which spirits existed in theory but not in formal ritual practice.

Like Irineu Serra, Sebastião Mota de Melo enjoyed an established reputation as a *curandeiro*. Unlike Master Irineu, however, and somewhat indicative of his different background, the popular spiritism within which Sebastião Mota de Melo was raised had little, if anything, by way of Afro-Brazilian influence. By the time of his conversion to Santo Daime in the mid-1960s, Sebastião was a practising medium in the Brazilian Kardecist tradition – for which the disembodied spirits of deceased human beings constitutes the sole supernatural reference point (Cavalcanti, 1983).[2] Although acting as medium for some of the most exemplary spirits of Brazilian Kardecism (e.g. Bezerra

The star-shaped central table was introduced to Santo Daime by Sebastião.

de Menezes and Antônio Jorge), Sebastião continued to employ many of the symbolic components of the popular spiritism of *caboclo* (peasant) culture; which, by implication, involved recognition of the supernatural agency of certain animals. In addition to both his late-comer and exogamous status, Sebastião's still explicit association with spirit-orientated activity impeded his campaign for the leadership of Santo Daime subsequent to Irineu Serra's death. Upon failing to gain control of the movement, Sebastião split from the originating *daimista* community of Alto Santo and, taking a sizeable tranche of established practitioners with him, founded a separate branch of Santo Daime known today as Cefluris. As 'Santo Daime Cefluris' is the primary focus of what follows, unless otherwise stated the following use of the term Santo Daime refers to this organisation.

By the mid-1970s, the community of Padrinho Sebastião had re-established Kardecist-informed mediumistic activity as a formal component of the Santo Daime ritual repertoire. It did not, though, replace the esoteric framework which had become so important to Irineu Serra but rather integrated the two paradigms within a single, and self-consciously eclectic, worldview. Consequently, and while esoteric concerns with developing the 'higher self' remained to the fore, interaction with individual spiritual agents – understood now as the disembodied spirits of deceased humans – represented an increasingly legitimate mode of *daimista* activity. As indicated above, the supernatural agency of certain animals was likewise acknowledged. Interaction with these animal spirits, however, was and continues to be regarded both with a degree of suspicion and as likely to result in some form of illness or bad luck (Arruda, Lapietra and Santana, 2006: 146). Although the growing influx of new age backpackers brought with it the adoption of a progressive number of alternative spiritual practices and beliefs, in terms of spirit-orientated activity the increasing appropriation of ritual components from Umbanda had most impact upon the subsequent direction of the *daimista* repertoire.

The origins of Umbanda are commonly dated to the 1920s during which the religion emerged from the fusion of elements drawn from Brazilian Kardecism and popular Afro-Brazilian religiosity (Brown, D. D. 1994). Umbanda complements Brazilian Kardecism's traditional concentration upon the spirits of deceased Caucasians with a focus upon other kinds of spirits, the most important of which are those of deceased Amerindians (*caboclos*) and African slaves (*pretos-velhos*). In addition to having spread throughout the Amazonian region by the 1960s, at the time of their appropriation by Cefluris, Umbanda practices were establishing themselves among sectors of the (overwhelmingly white) urban-industrial middle-classes. Indeed, it was the growing import of urban middle-class members within the now expanding movement of Cefluris that most influenced the ingression of Umbanda practices within the increasingly hybrid repertoire of Santo Daime. By the time of Sebastião's death in 1990, Umbanda-inspired possession rituals were being practised by nascent *daimista* communities throughout Brazil. It should be noted, though, that Umbanda-inspired possession rituals were not at this time considered part of the official *daimista* calendar, they were not conducted in the 'church' (*igreja*) and nor was the appearance of Umbanda spirits sanctioned outside of strictly delimited ritual contexts. All of this was to change, however, under the dual leadership of Alfredo Gregório de Melo (Sebastião's son) and Alex Polari (former political prisoner and founder of one Santo Daime's most important churches, *Céu da Montanha*, in the state of Rio de Janeiro).

Subsequent to Sebastião's death and the progressive influence of urban professionals across the ever-expanding Cefluris movement, beliefs and practices appropriated from Umbanda made their way increasingly from the ritual margins toward the repertorial core of Santo Daime (Guimarães, 1992;

Junior, 2007). For approximately two decades, the incorporation of spirits appropriated from Umbanda practice have taken place in the church of Céu do Mapiá at a number of semi-official rituals, the most important of which are those of Saint Michael (*São Miguel*) and the White Table (*Mesa Branca*) which occur respectively on the 7th and 27th of each month. Complementing the traditional practices of Concentration, Dance, *Feitio* and the Mass, the addition of these two rituals to the cultic repertoire of Céu do Mapiá and growing numbers of other churches represents a fundamental modification of the Santo Daime religion. Explicitly intended as cultic arenas for incorporation, the formalisation of these two new rituals not only cements spirit possession within the *daimista* worldview but does so in a way which valorises Umbanda-inspired practices relative to the longer established, but lower profile, motifs of Brazilian Kardecism. Although of a more *ad hoc* and unofficial nature, I have also seen spirit-orientated activity occur at the long-established *daimista* rituals of Concentration, Dance and the Mass. In addition to the spirits of Brazilian Kardecism and Umbanda, and indicative of its progressive appeal to the urban middle-classes (e.g. Prandi, 1991), a growing number of churches today practice the incorporation of supernatural agents venerated in the traditional Afro-Brazilian religion of Candomblé. In keeping with the Candomblé worldview, these supernatural agents are usually referred to as 'gods.' In practice, however, the incorporated agents perform the same cultic functions as their Umbanda ('spirit') counterparts.

The Daimista Possession Repertoire

The evolution of the *daimista* possession repertoire is characterised by the appropriation of successive spirit discourses of a variegated and often contrasting kind. Catalysed by rapid geographical and demographic shift, the trajectory of spirit possession has been further accelerated by Santo Daime's progressive insertion within the alternative cultic milieu populated by the urban middle-classes and suffused by the increasingly vertiginous dynamics of contemporary spirituality (Dawson, 2007). Occurring within the relatively compressed historical framework of sixty years, Santo Daime has evolved from the afro-amazonian cultic repertoire of a small band of impoverished, mixed-race peasants to become a globally diffused new era religion practised by the predominantly white, urban middle-classes. In between, Santo Daime has embraced traditional European esotericism, Kardecist Spiritism, New Age spirituality, and Umbanda. In respect of its contemporary repertoire, Santo Daime is currently evolving thanks to the growing use of possession motifs drawn from the traditional Afro-Brazilian religion of Candomblé. The various 'spirit idioms' (Crapanzano, 1977: 11) of Japanese new religions

– popular in Brazil for a number of decades – are likewise proving influential sources of spirit-orientated practical knowledge. As yet on a small scale, extra-terrestrial discourse and attendant channelling motifs are also beginning to crop up.

Engaging spirit possession on the Pacific atoll of Nukulaelae, Niko Besnier employs Bakhtin's notion of 'heteroglossia' to describe the spirit discourse of Nukulaelae as a variegated phenomenon comprising multiple voices which articulate often contrasting if not incompatible experiences (1996: 75–98). In comparison with the spirit discourse of Nukulaelae, and a great many other narratives for that matter, the spirit idiom of Santo Daime might well be termed 'hyper-heteroglossic.' Hybrid by birth and self-consciously eclectic in tenor, the Santo Daime repertoire allows for the articulation of a wide range of spirit-orientated experience. For example, and indicative of tradi-tional Afro-Brazilian influences, some *daimistas* describe possession as an event involving suppression of the conscious self and an inability to remember anything from the point of actual possession to the moment of 'despatch.' Others, however, adopt a typically Kardecist line to describe themselves as remaining conscious throughout the possession episode. Here, some regard their subjective presence as integral to directing the possessing spirit; whereas others talk of the self as an interested but passive third-party looking on to what the spirit is doing through their body. The *daimista* spirit idiom also permits the expression of possession as an ecstatic process involving the dislo-cation of the self from its physical moorings. Employing esoteric notions of astral flight, some *daimistas* talk of disembodied trips across the globe or of visiting different historical periods to interact with other (usually famous) personalities. Indigenous shamanistic and popular folk motifs of soul-flight are likewise employed to describe disincarnate journeys to assorted spiritual realms populated by supernatural agents of both human and non-human provenance. Others, however, eschew both enstatic and ecstatic conceptuali-sations of spirit-orientated activity. Instead, notions of expanded conscious-ness or broadened spiritual vision are employed to articulate interaction with the world of spirits. In a similar vein, some *daimistas* describe the spirits with whom they interact as astral counterparts of the variegated aspects of the material self.

It is important to note that not all of the above modes of expressing spirit possession in Santo Daime are treated as mutually exclusive. Indeed, it is commonplace for some *daimistas* to employ a number of motifs to describe a single possession episode. Others, however, apply different motifs to articu-late what they regard as different kinds of spirit possession. It should also be noted that not every member of Santo Daime regards the incorporation of external spiritual agents as a necessary expression of *daimista* religiosity. While the regularity of possession rituals and the incidence of individual possession events have increased markedly in recent years, there remain large numbers of practising *daimistas* who do not incorporate spirits. Although spirit possession is accepted by the majority of these individuals as an entirely licit component of the Santo Daime repertoire, the practice of incorporation is not something they engage in on a personal level. As with the foundational community of Alto Santo, these individuals may be regarded as 'nominal spiritists.' While not gainsaying the legitimacy of the possession motifs mentioned above, nor regarding their own practices as incompatible with the prevailing spirit idiom, those who choose not to incorporate spirits express themselves religiously by employing alternative components – of a predominantly esoteric provenance – from the Santo Daime repertoire.

The pantheon of spirits lauded by Santo Daime is as hybrid and fluid as the religious repertoire through which it is manifested. As with most of the other spiritist religions in Brazil, Santo Daime acknowledges the existence of a Creator deity whose absolute status and generative cosmological activity sets the metaphysical backdrop against which spirit possession plays out. Likewise in keeping with established spiritist religions, the god of Santo Daime, called 'Father' (*Pai*), is an altogether otiose divinity who remains distant from everyday belief and cultic practice. The highest and most powerful spirits of Santo Daime are inherited principally from popular Catholic and esoteric paradigms. In addition to the popular Catholic trinity of Jesus, Mary and Joseph, the archangels Michael, Gabriel and George feature prominently in *daimista* hymnody. The spirits of other biblical characters (e.g. John the Baptist and Solomon) and heavenly beings (e.g. Cosmo and Damien) are also praised. Except for a few instances I have come across, spirits from the higher echelons of the *daimista* cosmos tend not to be incorporated. Where they do appear in material form, the extensional syntax of reincarnation rather than the punctual language of possession is employed.

The ritual workload of incorporation is overwhelmingly borne by spirits appropriated from Brazilian Kardecism and Umbanda. Antônio Jorge, Doctor Fritz and José Bezerra de Menezes are the most famous figures of Brazilian Spiritism regularly called upon during rituals of incorporation (see, Santos, 2004). From the multitudinous range of the Umbanda spectrum, the mainstream spirits of deceased indigenes (*caboclos*), black slaves (*pretos velhos*) and children (*herês*) appear most frequently and are complemented by representatives of the oriental lines (*linhas do oriente* – e.g. gypsies, cowboys and European aristocrats) and street people (*povo da rua*). Although calling upon the supernatural agency of the *orixás* (Umbanda spirits regarded as gods in

A grotto dedicated to the *pretos velhos*.

their original context of Candomblé), these beings have not traditionally been incorporated within mainstream Santo Daime. The ritual incorporation of *orixás* is, however, on the increase. At the lower end of the spiritual hierarchy, spirits in want of charity are known variously as 'suffering,' 'disorientated' and 'inferior.' Incorporated by trained mediums as part of ritualised possession practices, these spirits also act in extra-cultic contexts attaching themselves to (*encostar*, literally 'to lean on') the spiritually unwary, ill-prepared or careless – causing illness, bad luck and other unwelcome effects. Although by no means shared by every community, the term *atuação* (literally, 'action' or 'performance') is sometimes employed to distinguish involuntary possession from voluntary incorporation (*incorporação*).

As with Kardecist Spiritism, the official narrative of Santo Daime regards everyone as having mediumistic tendencies. Consequently, and irrespective of age, spiritual maturity and formal training, every human being is prone to some form of interaction with the spirit-world. For many, however, this interaction is so subtle and our experience of the spiritual domain so dulled that it goes unnoticed at a conscious level. This is unfortunate because a lack of awareness of the manner in and extent to which the spirit-world impacts upon the material sphere at best undermines human freedom (here, self-determination) and at worst leaves the unwary open to spiritual assault. Even for those without the aptitude or desire to become a practising medium, some degree of training in respect of managing spirit-interaction is highly recommended. For those with a greater receptivity to and desire of inter-acting with the spirit-world, formal training is something of a necessity. To this end, communities affiliated to Santo Daime are expected to offer regular mediumistic training.

The requisites of successful mediumship in Santo Daime are varied in nature. Among the many issues and technicalities which need to be mastered in the cause of successful mediumistic activity, the following are worthy of note. First, and perhaps most importantly of all, the individual must learn to control the physical side-effects of incorporating an otherwise disincarnate spirit (e.g. shaking, expostulating and gesticulating). In addition to inducing and managing the possession event, the individual must also learn to iden-tify and express appropriately the particular type of spirit by which s/he is being possessed. Given that different kinds of spirit execute different ritual tasks, a medium's ability to communicate the type of spirit incorporated is a vital part of her performative repertoire. As each of the various rituals of the Santo Daime calendar performs a very specific function, it is likewise important for those incorporating spirits to know in what contexts and at what juncture a particular type of possession is permitted. Although spirit possession of most kinds is actively encouraged in the rituals of *Mesa Branca* and *São Miguel*, only limited types of possession are qualifiedly permitted in some (e.g. Concentration and Dance), while other rituals have tradition-ally tolerated no kind of possession at all (e.g. Mass and *Feitio*). As with the increasing incorporation of *orixás*, however, the growing popularity of possession within Santo Daime is progressively relativising traditional strictures in respect of both the types of spirit incorporated and the ritual contexts in which they appear.

As *daimista* rituals are tightly regimented events, a particular kind of incor-poration must also occur at the correct point and for the proper duration. The incorporation of the wrong kind of spirit at an inappropriate moment both interrupts the spiritual current generated by the ritual in question and risks public censure – sometimes administered during the ritual itself – from those in authority. At the same time, the medium must also pay close atten-tion to existing social hierarchies. For, in addition to influencing the number and cosmological status of the spirits one regularly incorporates, social standing may also determine the pecking order in which individuals get to incorporate. In the same vein, *daimista* ritual space is a highly differentiated arena with participants occupying a specific place relative to their sex, age, marital status, and seniority (some communities also use height as an additional determinant).[3] Consequently, the medium has a responsibility not only to incorporate the right kind of spirit at the right moment, but also to ensure that enactment of the possession event does not lead to assigned spatial boundaries being transgressed.

A Typology of Spirit Possession in Santo Daime

In view of the above, and prior to offering my typology of voluntary sprit possession in Santo Daime, two points might be made by way of preliminary comment. First, spirit possession in Santo Daime exists as both a symbolic and practical expression of the psychotropic experience engendered by the ritual consumption of *Daime*. In effect, the ritualised consumption of *Daime* and the subjective management of its attendant effects furnish a cultic-discursive template which correlates strongly with the practical-symbolic characteristics of possession experienced as an 'altered state of consciousness.' Resisting the rhetorical charm of designating spirit possession in Santo Daime *an altered state of an already altered state of consciousness*, albeit more mundanely, spirit possession may be classified as one among a number of forms of altered states of consciousness at play across the *daimista* movement. Second, the possession repertoire of Santo Daime furnishes both practical and symbolic space for each of the classic types – e.g. shamanism, mediumship, possession, and trance – traditionally discussed in relation to spirit-orientated activity. As indicated above, intentional interface with the spirits stretches from the nominal spiritism of those who participate in spirit-orientated rituals but who do not incorporate – through those who claim to visit, look upon, and/ or dialogue with the spirit-world without actually claiming to be inhabited by spirits – to those who actively induce and manage a full-blown possession event. Setting aside the uneven appearance and equivocal use of vocabulary across the *daimista* movement (i.e. *xamanismo, mediunidade, incorporação/ atuação*, and *transe*), each of the practical-symbolic experiences they express correlates with one or more of the classic types. Unlike certain other religious-cultural contexts, though, Santo Daime does not tend to regard the practical-symbolic experiences idealised by these types as necessarily different in kind or mutually exclusive of each other.

Given the practical-symbolic overlap, uneven appearance, equivocal expression, and vertiginous evolution of the different forms of spirit possession across the Santo Daime movement, any typology of possession – no matter how 'ideal' in the Weberian sense – promises to be both a messy and provisional affair. Holding this point in mind, and in view of this chapter's principal concerns, I wish to eschew (here, at least) employing the spectrum of classic types mentioned in the book's Introduction. Instead, I offer a typology of voluntary incorporation which is informed by the nature and degree of interaction exhibited by the mode of possession in question and its relationship to the ritual context of enactment. The two types of voluntary incorporation to be examined here, I label 'individual' and 'interactive.'

Individual Possession

'Individual possession' is so termed because the person being possessed is the principal locus of spirit-orientated activity. There are two kinds of individual possession – 'private possession' and 'expressive possession.' 'Private possession' is the most traditional form of incorporation practised by the Santo Daime religion and tends to appear most frequently within the movement's older communities. Most commonly involving discrete interactions with less evolved (e.g. 'suffering,' 'disorientated' and 'inferior') spirits, this form of incorporation accords with established *daimista* notions of 'trial' (*prova*) and 'firmness' (*firmeza*). In view of the exacting psychophysical effects of consuming *Daime*, in tandem with the numerous strictures regulating ritual participation, *daimistas* must remain firm – disciplined, resolute and focussed – in the face of the trials provoked. In combination with the prevailing spirit idiom, these values engender a two-fold rationale for private possession. First, the act of incorporating spirits is seen as an additional trial to that provoked by the psychotropic effects of *Daime* and the generic demands of ritual participation. Consequently, private possession likewise demands firmness which, in turn, entails restraint on the part of the possessed. A general rule of thumb regarding this form of possession – whence I take the term 'private' – is that the act of incorporation should be conducted in such a way as not to distract others from remaining firm in the face of their own particular trials. Second, private possession comprises an act of charity in which the lower spirits incorporated are prayed with, instructed in the ways of *Daime* and exhorted to accept their allotted path. As with the merit earned by staying firm in the face of trial, the performance of charity towards the incorporated spirit is held to generate credit or 'karma' which is subsequently drawn upon in this life or a future incarnation. Although each of these elements tends to be present in most explanations of private possession, differences in emphasis exist within each community and across the movement as a whole.

'Expressive possession' is the most recent form of incorporation to establish itself in Santo Daime and is rapidly on the way to becoming the most popular. Although typologically distinct by virtue of its outward expression, in actuality expressive possession is a modified form of private possession.

Perhaps because of its relative novelty within the Santo Daime tradition, expressive possession lacks a well defined ritual function. Unlike both private and interactive forms, expressive possession overwhelmingly involves the incorporation of higher spirits appropriated from Umbanda. Though not always the case, the higher spirits incorporated tend to be the spirit guides of the possessed individual. Given their prevalence across the Santo Daime movement, this means that expressive possession usually involves the incorporation of *caboclo* and *preto velho* spirits; although the appearance of other kinds of spirits (e.g. *orixás*, children, cowboys, and aristocrats) is on the rise. The continuing racial stigma attached to blackness, coupled with the exoticism of the idealised Amerindian, however, entails the preponderance of *caboclo* over *preto velho* spirits. Consequently, the sounds and gestures most associated with expressive possession are those of *caboclo* spirits.

Expressive possession is so designated because of its demonstrative and theatrical character. Similar in form to charismatic modes of worship (though less ostentatious than neo-Pentecostal forms), expressive possession appears to have no obvious ritual function other than the dramatic externalisation of the incorporating spirit's presence. Clearly, the onset of the sounds and gestures associated with expressive possession serve to indicate the arrival of the spirits subsequent to having been called at the appropriate juncture by the relevant tranche of hymns. Once present, however, the spirits do little more than reassert their incorporated condition through their respective stereotypical noises and stylised gesticulations. Perhaps in view of its relative novelty, expressive possession lacks the kinds of ritual rationales offered in respect of private and interactive forms of incorporation. When asked to explain the purpose of expressive possession, the responses offered by *daimistas* most commonly include reference to: the spirit serving to protect against the unwarranted appearance of inferior spirits; the spirit's desire to enjoy the trappings of physical sensation (e.g. singing, dancing and *Daime*); the edifying benefits which the spirit's presence brings to its host; and the externalisation of particular aspects of the higher self.

Interactive Possession

In contrast to individual possession, interactive possession is predicated upon ritualised interface with other human beings. Practised only by trained mediums, 'interactive possession' is thereby more restricted in scope than individualised forms of incorporation. By no means mutually exclusive, and in no order of priority, interactive possession has three principal modes of cultic expression. First, it exists as a form of charity enacted towards lesser spirits, the majority of whom are the suffering souls of deceased human beings. Here, the medium works upon lesser spirits whom she has incorporated or upon spirits in possession of others who may or may not be trained mediums. On occasion a skilled medium may relieve a less experienced colleague or untrained *daimista* by assuming responsibility for a troublesome spirit by transferring it to her body. The possessed medium then works with other mediums – possibly incorporating higher spirits for assistance – who help to instruct (*doutrinar*), enlighten (*iluminar*), reassure, and guide the incorporated spirit to the end of easing its pains and aiding its passage to the spirit-world. The administering of *Daime* to the troubled spirit is commonplace in work of this nature.

Interactive possession might also be practised as an act of charity towards one's fellow *daimistas*. Here, mediums possessed by higher spirits move among their peers to distribute astral energy by way of the 'pass' (*passe*) and other forms of gesture. A traditional practice of Kardecist Spiritism, the pass involves the incorporating medium passing her hands around the head, limbs and torso of another person. In so doing, the medium helps to reinforce or recalibrate the vibrational field of the pass's recipient. Third, interactive possession exists in oracular form. Restricted to the most senior mediums, this mode of interactive possession intends the edification of ritual participants through the impartation of wisdom, instruction or admonition. Although oracular possession tends to employ the traditional supernatural agents of Kardecist Spiritism, the spirits of deceased *daimista* celebrities, including Sebastião himself, are occasionally incorporated by members of Santo Daime's higher echelons. As with private possession, interactive possession (in all its forms) constitutes an act of charity said to earn cosmic merit ('karma') for its practitioners. Unlike private possession, however, the most popular forms of interactive possession – those involving the incorporation of lesser spirits and the administration of the pass – tend to be practised almost exclusively by women. While the rationale for the virtual female monopoly of these interactive forms of possession varies across the movement, as with both Kardecist Spiritism and Umbanda, its recurring motif alludes to the greater receptivity of women to the spirits.

The Incorporization of the Daimista Ritual Repertoire

More diverse than Brazil's other ayahuasca religions – Barquinha and the Vegetable Union – the demographic profile of Santo Daime is nevertheless overwhelmingly white, urban middle-class in nature; a far cry from the mixed-race, subsistence life-style of its Amazonian origins. Refashioning the movement in its own image, this, now dominant, urban middle-class constituency is the principal driving force behind the increasing popularity of incorporation relative to other components of Santo Daime's traditional ritual repertoire. Of vital importance, however, is the fact that the contemporary urban-professional membership of Santo Daime is principally drawn from what I have elsewhere termed Brazil's 'new era spectrum' (Dawson, 2007).[4] The new era spectrum comprises a fluid nexus of relationships involving a highly diverse array of beliefs and practices which articulate a range of dynamics typical of late-modern, urban-industrial existence.[5] By virtue of its late-modern ethos, the new era spectrum embodies a typically individualised, pluralistic, consumerist, and technologised worldview (see, Bauman, 2005; Beck, 2002; Canclini, 1995: 41–65). In effect, the *incorporization* of the contemporary *daimista* ritual repertoire is undertaken relative to a range of characteristics typical of the new era spectrum.

In respect of the particular characteristics of the new era spectrum through which these typically late-modern dynamics are mediated, the most relevant for our purposes are: a *holistic* worldview in which a universal force underlies and unites every individual component of existence – such that particular beliefs and practices are but relative (and, thereby, interchangeable) expressions of the cosmic whole; an *individualistic* emphasis upon the self as the ultimate arbiter of religious authority and the primary agent of spiritual transformation; an *instrumentalised* religiosity driven by the goal of absolute self-realisation – to which end an eclectic range of spiritual knowledge and mystical techniques is employed; an *expressive* demeanour through which inner states of being are externalised by verbal and practical means tending toward the dramatic; a *meritocratic-egalitarianism* which is both inherently suspicious of religious hierarchy and expectant of just rewards for efforts expended; and, an *immanentist* spirituality which – alongside the avowal of transcendent transformations and rewards (e.g. reincarnation and cosmic merit) – valorises the pragmatic implications of self-realisation (e.g. psychological and material wellbeing).

Together, these factors combine to engender a religious worldview in which the individual has the right, if not the duty, to pursue her absolute self-realisation through any available means and at any possible opportunity. Such is the self-orientated nature of this pursuit that prevailing narratives and customary practices are evaluated relative to their perceived support for or hindrance of individual fulfilment. As a consequence, the traditional *daimista* repertoire and its established components are reviewed, revised and, at times, rejected with a view to their optimal facilitation of individual expression. Subjected to the unremitting assertion of the late-modern self, Santo Daime's traditional spirit possession repertoire is undergoing change in three important respects: first, interactive possession is becoming increasingly popular; second, the practice of private possession is being progressively replaced by its expressive counterpart; and third, Umbanda-inspired discourse and practice is rapidly gaining ground relative to traditional repertorial components.

Although established *daimista* discourse acknowledges that all humans have mediumistic tendencies, in actuality Santo Daime ritual practice has traditionally managed both how and by whom particular forms of mediumship are enacted. Whereas the traditional ritual repertoire of Santo Daime has made the practice of private possession available to every *daimista* this has not been the case with interactive forms of possession. First, the regulatory strictures surrounding *daimista* cultic practice have traditionally limited the performative space afforded to interactive possession. Given its restricted window of ritual opportunity, the cultic enactment of interactive possession is limited and, by virtue of its performative status, subject to rationing by way of selection, training and authorisation to practise. Second, because the hierarchization of ritual space in Santo Daime traditionally reflects prevailing social hierarchies, the most prestigious roles of the cultic repertoire have tended to be occupied by those perceived to enjoy the greatest amounts of social-capital. Third, as noted above, the most popular forms of interactive possession are almost exclusively enacted by women. In combination, these dynamics entail that the relatively limited performance of interactive possession is restricted to a small band of ritual elite and their sponsored acolytes, the overwhelming majority of whom are female. Whether resulting from hierarchy or gender stereotyping, Santo Daime's rationing of interactive possession flies in the face of the aforementioned (new era) preoccupations of contemporary urban-professional *daimistas*.

Within some urban-professional *daimista* communities, the tensions generated by the rationing of interactive possession have been solved by relaxing traditional restrictions upon both the context and manner of its enactment. As a result, interactive possession is democratised as rituals dedicated solely to its performance are staged for any member, irrespective of status, to practise their mediumship. Commonly termed *giras* (a word borrowed from Afro-Brazilian traditions), these rituals are not governed by the same regulations which apply to official Santo Daime cultic practice. As such, standard requirements in respect of, for example, uniform (*farda*), divisions of the sexes and sundry other modes of participation (e.g. standing, sitting and entering/exiting ritual space) do not apply. Consequently, and as borne out by the theatrically expansive use of ritual space and employment of Afro-Brazilian cultic paraphernalia (e.g. dresses, headwear, pipes/cigars, necklaces, and walking-sticks), the expressive latitude which these rituals furnish participants is significantly greater than that afforded by traditional *daimista* works.

For a growing number of *daimista* communities, however, such has become the importance attached to interactive possession that its ritual valorisation has resulted in a wholesale rejection of all traditional restrictions upon its practice. This, in turn, has given rise to a move away from the organisational auspices of Santo Daime. For other communities wishing to remain loyal to the established *daimista* repertoire, events dedicated solely to interactive possession are regarded as standing outside of the formal cultic calendar and thereby practised in addition to official rituals such as Concentration, Dance and the Mass. As evidenced by ongoing changes to private possession, however, even within these groups – not to mention the many other communities without such para-liturgical practices – the typical (new era) preoccupations of contemporary urban-professional *daimistas* continue to impact upon the traditional spirit-orientated repertoire.

Most common within older (i.e. non-urban professional) communities of Santo Daime, private possession has a thoroughgoingly inward focus. Indeed, such is the *intra*personal nature of private possession that the merit acquired through its practice is held to be vitiated by external manifestations likely to distract one's neighbour or attract the attention of others. In view of the aforementioned preoccupations of urban-professional *daimistas*, however, the inward focus of private possession is increasingly giving way to the outward orientation of expressive possession. Although various factors contribute to what might be termed the *expressivization* of individual possession – not least changes to the ritual functions of trial and charity – one important dynamic is worthy of note. In tandem with established strictures regulating how and by whom interactive possession might be practised, the means by which the average urban-professional *daimista* might both assert her spiritual status and practise his mediumship are further restricted by traditional demands in respect of the inward focus and inconspicuous enactment of individual possession. Although by no means immune to pressure for change, the elite status and ensuing cultic protection enjoyed by interactive possession imbues it with a somewhat heightened degree of resistance. In comparison with interactive possession, however, the greater accessibility of individual possession to the average *daimista* renders it a more fruitful pressure point for repertorial transformation. Relatively more amenable to ritual reformulation than its interactive counterpart, individual possession is thereby subjected to incremental modification as it is remodelled along expressive rather than private lines.

The growth of Umbanda discourse and practice relative to established components of the traditional *daimista* repertoire results from the latter's inability to furnish sufficient practical-symbolic means to mediate the new era preoccupations of the now dominant urban middle-classes. Although evidence of *umbandist* forms of spirit-orientated activity within Santo Daime dates back to the early-1980s (Polari, 1999: 109–17), it was not until the movement fully established itself in the traditional urban-indus-trial heartlands of Umbanda that the umbandization of its ritual repertoire commenced in earnest. It was at the beginning of this period of geograph-ical transition that the term *umbandaime* was coined to describe the fusion of Umbanda and Santo Daime. Commencing in the late-1980s with the staging of para-liturgical rituals inspired by *umbandist* possession practices, the umbandization of the *daimista* repertoire was firmly secured by the late-1990s via the inclusion of the rituals of Saint Michael and the White Table within the cultic repertoire of Santo Daime's mother community, Céu do Mapiá. Today, the majority of *daimistas* regard both the spirits and practices appropriated from Umbanda as integral parts of the Santo Daime religion.

It would be mistaken, however, to regard the umbandization of Santo Daime as the wholesale adoption of Umbanda discourse and practice. Rather, the umbandization of Santo Daime is a process inspired by rather than slavishly replicating Umbanda possession practices. Orchestrated by aforementioned characteristics of the new era spectrum, selected elements of *umbandist* discourse and practice have been wrested from their traditional religious contexts and relocated to the *daimista* repertoire. Excised from its original ritual domain and isolated from its customary frame of reference, selected *umbandist* discourse and practice is rendered wholly amenable to being remoulded, reintegrated and re-operationalised relative to the prevailing preoccupations of white, urban-professional *daimistas*. Whereas the practice of possession in Umbanda has traditionally revolved around the quest for cure (predominantly among the poor) or edification (chiefly among the not-so-poor), this is not the case in Santo Daime. Relocated to the *daimista* ritual repertoire, the therapeutic and instructive emphases of *umbandist* possession practices are subsumed within a broader set of concerns centred upon the self-assertive and expressive preoccupations of the late-modern individual. Although centred upon the ritualised incorporation of *umbandist* spirits, expressive possession is not a form of spirit-orientated activity traditionally found in Umbanda, just as interactive possession is of a very different ilk than its *umbandist* counterpart. Despite the ostensible centrality of Umbanda spirits, each is a thoroughgoingly *daimista* phenomenon which articulates typically new era preoccupations centred upon the late-modern self. Whilst much of the cast, dialogue and performance of incorporation appears distinctly *umbandist*, its orchestrating ritual direction and attendant dramatic thrust is pure Santo Daime.

A drum (*tambor*) traditionally used in Umbanda and now commonplace in Santo Daime.

Ongoing changes in the spirit possession repertoire of Santo Daime are wholly symptomatic of the demographic shift undergone by the movement over the course of the last two decades. This demographic shift has fundamentally altered the socio-cultural context in which much of its ritual activity is undertaken. Refracting a very different set of socio-cultural dynamics, the *daimista* ritual repertoire asserts its contemporary relevance by articulating the practical-symbolic demands of a now dominant urban-professional membership imbued with a characteristically late-modern worldview. As Santo Daime continues to establish itself in various parts of the urban-industrialised world, both its ritual repertoire in general and its spirit-orientated practices in particular undergo further transformation. Although these transformations continue to reflect the characteristically late-modern preoccupations of their urban-professional constituencies, they nevertheless articulate an increasingly variegated range of socio-cultural contexts. The future of Santo Daime, along with its spirit possession practices, promises to be progressively diverse.

IMAGINING SPIRIT POSSESSION

Mixing Traditions and Current Trends in the Japanese Manga *Shaman King*

Birgit Staemmler

Spirit Possession in Japan

Japanese comic books (*manga*) have recently become well-known outside of Japan and translated into a number of different languages. Many of these manga were first published in monthly magazines and later as independent books in Japanese and other languages, as animated movies and video or computer games. Fan items such as trading-card games, toys and T-shirts are produced as manga and their characters gain popularity. *Shaman King* by Hiroyuki Takei is one of these highly successful Japanese comic books (1998–2004). I have chosen *Shaman King* to illustrate spirit possession in Japan because it touches upon various aspects of and images about spirit possession in Japan. Additionally, its immense success is bound to have impacted strongly upon the images of shamanism and spirit possession held by its consumers, many of whom are young Japanese males who are unlikely to juxtapose *Shaman King*'s image of spirit possession with one that is more academically founded.

The main concerns of this chapter lie with the images and contexts of spirit possession and shamanism depicted in *Shaman King*. Thus, after a brief introduction of spirit possession in Japan and *Shaman King*, I analyse its general images of shamanism, spirit possession and possessing spirits against the backdrop of traditional Japanese beliefs and practices. Next, I turn to the representation of specifically Japanese aspects, that is Japanese practitioners of spirit possession and the image of Japan conjured by *Shaman King*. Although shamans and other religious specialists from various parts of the world are portrayed in *Shaman King*, I restrict my analysis to Japanese examples. It may do well to note here that my approach is not that of comparative literature or manga studies, but that of anthropology.

As Japan was never dominated by one religion to the total exclusion of all others, institutionalised as well as folk religious forms of Shinto, Buddhism, Taoism, Confucianism, Shugendô, and Christianity have coexisted over the centuries, each occupying its own particular niche. Japan has a long tradition of belief in spirit possession – both solicited and unsolicited – as Carmen Blacker's *Catalpa Bow* (1986), first published in 1975 yet until today the standard work in English, illustrates. Solicited spirit possession in Japan usually involves female spirit mediums. The first examples date back to myths and legends recorded early in the eighth century (see, Naumann, 1988: 32–7, 83–8; Staemmler, 2009: 47–55). More recent examples of solicited spirit possession are *itako* – blind women in northern Japan who are trained as spirit mediums and serve their clients by voluntarily inducing spirit possession to act as mouthpieces for spirits of deceased family members. There are also individual men and women who undergo an initiatory process similar to that described for Siberian shamans. They are referred to by various local terms as they develop into local practitioners conducting personal and seasonal rituals – including those of spirit possession – for a small group of followers (Satô, 1981: 149–86). In the prefecture of Okinawa female shamans called *yuta* similarly undergo an initiation process after which they serve their local clients with shamanic and divinatory rituals (Blacker, 1986: 114).

Famous examples of unsolicited spirit possession may be found in medieval literature which tells of people whose illnesses were finally diagnosed as caused by malevolent or envious spirits. Rituals of appeasement and exorcism by varying religious specialists were required to remedy such spirit possession (e.g. Bargen, 1997: 76–108; Morris, 1970: 260–1). In early-modern Japan unsolicited spirit possession most frequently involved various types of possessing animals, most prominently foxes, snakes and badgers, who for various reasons took possession of individuals causing them to become inexplicably ill or continuously unlucky until the possessing spirits were appeased, subjugated or exorcised. This kind of spirit possession was often closely associated with accusations of witchcraft, as certain families – often those slightly more prosperous than their neighbours – were accused of purposefully keeping and manipulating possessing animals (Ishizuka, 1959: 20–74, 117–35). Although belief in ecstasy – i.e. the temporary absence of a soul from its body – is rare in Japan, it is found in Shugendô, the Japanese order of mountain asceticism. Shugendô centres around the belief that ascetic exercises practised in sacred mountains provide the practitioner – the *shugenja* or *yamabushi* – with supernatural powers with which to heal, conduct exorcisms or issue protective amulets. Although initially an individual practitioner's religious exercise, Shugendô has over time developed into a widespread religious institution (Blacker, 1986: 164–207; Rotermund, 1967; Staemmler, 1999: 78–97).

In 1873, practices related to faith healing and spirit possession were declared 'superstitions' and forbidden by law. Spiritualism as practised in the United States and England, however, became very popular in the late-nineteenth and early-twentieth centuries, although urbanisation and industrialisation soared and Western sciences and bio-medicine became dominant. Many of the new religions that developed in Japan from the mid-nineteenth century onwards include belief in spirit possession by virtue of their founder's initiatory experience. Some of these new religions even accept spirit possession as part of their ritual repertoires (Davis, 1980; Staemmler, 2009). Today, Japan is one of the world's richest and technologically most advanced countries and belief in spirit possession plays but a marginal role. Yet, the 1970s witnessed a resurgence of interest in spiritual matters which gave rise to the founding or arrival of several new religions and to a movement of workshops and publications similar to the Western New Age movement (Shimazono, 1996 and 1999: 121–33). This resurgence was slowed, however, after the new religion of Aum Shinrikyô attacked part of Tokyo's underground in 1995 with the poisonous sarin gas. This event led to severe mistrust of both new religions and the spiritual movement. Yet, parallel to the publication of *Shaman King*, a veritable 'spiritual boom' began during which individual diviners and other spiritually gifted people seek supernatural assistance to publicly advise people – via magazines and television – on problematic aspects of their lives (Tsujimura, 2008: 219–26).

Shaman King

Shaman King may be classified as a 'story manga,' in that it develops its plot over many (here, 285) chapters rather than consisting of brief unconnected episodes. It is a *shônen manga* in that it is written for boys rather than girls, young adults or men. *Shaman King* is an adventure or action manga set in modern urban Japan.[1] *Shaman King* was drawn and written by Hiroyuki Takei (born in 1972) who had made his debut as series author with *Butsu Zone* (2007) after having received the Tezuka prize for his short *Itako no Anna* in 1994. First published between 1998 and 2004 as a series in the currently most successful weekly boys' manga magazine *Shônen Jump* – in 2003, for example, *Shônen Jump* sold 3.2 million copies per week (Shimizu, 2004: 23) – *Shaman King* was published as a series of 32 paperback books from December 1998 to January 2005 (*Wikipedia* a and b).[2] Following *Shaman King*'s rather abrupt termination in *Shônen Jump*, Takei has – between December 2007 and March 2009 – published its 'complete edition' with additions and some modifications. Translated into several languages (e.g. English, French, German, and Italian), *Shaman King* has been turned into an animated movie in 64 sequels aired by Television Tokyo from July 2001 until September 2002.[3]

Despite its length, *Shaman King*'s plot is easily summarised: Yoh Asakura is a 13 year old Japanese boy, junior high school student and aspiring shaman who enrols in the shaman fight which takes place every 500 years between shamans from all parts of the world.[4] The eventual winner of the shaman fight will be allowed to merge with the 'Great Spirit' and thereby reshape the world to his own liking. Along the way, Yoh, his friend Manta and his fiancée Anna fight and befriend several other young shamans and get involved in the ultimate fight against Hao – who is both favourite to win the fight and as influential and powerful as he is evil.

Shaman King is not the only Japanese manga with a religious topic. Triggered by Jirô Tsunoda's *Ushiro no Hyakutarô* – which in the 1970s reintroduced Western Spiritualist topics to Japan – manga with religious topics have become popular, replacing earlier trends of Science Fiction and Horror. Using a mixture of Western and more traditional Japanese religious concepts (see, Thomas, 2008: 120–42; Yamanaka, 1996: 163–75), some of these religiously informed manga seem to be based on their authors' personal interests in such things as witches, protective spirits, demon hunters, and Ouija boards. Others, however, like Makoto Ogino's *Kujaku Ô* (1985–89) – and *Shaman King* as I will show – simply use religious elements to develop setting and plot and to imbue their characters with supernatural powers (Yamanaka, 1996: 163–75).

Influential examples of manga which portray spirit possession are Masashi Kishimoto's extremely successful serial *Naruto*, whose publication in *Shônen Jump* began in 1999. The hero is a teenage aspiring *ninja* who has a fox demon sealed inside him which gives him additional power. *Naruto* is set in a fictitious country during an unspecified time which combines both modern and pre-modern elements. Kamui Fujiwara's three-volume *Seirei no Moribito* (2007–08) is based on Nahoko Uehashi's (2006) fantasy novel of the same title which was later extended to a fantasy series of ten volumes. Here, the main character is a female bodyguard who is employed to protect an aristocratic boy seemingly possessed by a malevolent water demon. The setting is a fictitious East Asian country in an unspecified pre-modern age. A third example is the first volume of Osamu Tezuka's (1928–89) semi-classic *Hi no Tori* (1967) which is set in prehistoric Japan and evolves as a potpourri of various mythical topics and persons, including the third century ruler Himiko who is often referred to as 'shamaness' (Phillipps, 1996).

Shaman King's Imagining of Spirit Possession and Shamanism

Shamanism

In *Shaman King* a shaman is defined as 'someone who connects this world and the world beyond' (1, I: 23) – officially translated into English as 'a link between the physical and the spiritual worlds' (En: 1, I: 21). A longer explanation is given in chapter four (I: 102), which is strongly influenced by neo-shamanism and hence emphasises North America's role along with an unambiguously positive image of shamans. This wide definition of shamanism allows Takei to include various characters into his story who would not classify as shamans in any narrower definition, yet also add colour to the manga. These include the necromancer Faust VIII, the pretend-vampire Dracula, the dowser Lyserg, and Tamao's use of the Ouija board. Throughout *Shaman King* shamans use neither psychotropic substances nor drums in their work. Trance – i.e. altered states of consciousness often associated with shamanism and spirit possession – is of no importance, as all characters remain fully conscious and wide awake when in a solicited state of spirit possession.[5] The notion of ecstasy in which the soul leaves the body either due to illness or to travel to the world beyond – the latter of which Eliade and other scholars regarded as shamanism's *conditio sine qua non* (Eliade, 2004) – merely serves as an explanation of why shamans can be returned to life after suffering fatal injuries (195, XXII: 143).

Shamans' social functions are briefly mentioned, but of no importance to the plot. Indeed, shamans' selection of spirit helpers and the shapes of their oversouls (see below) enable them more to fight than to heal or guide souls. Although many present-day non-scholarly works on shamanism portray shamans very positively as in harmony with nature and striving to re-establish harmony between themselves, nature and other human beings, in *Shaman King* most shamans are described as powerful, ruthless and very dangerous. Most shamans in *Shaman King* have inherited their powers, with some coming from age-old shamanic families. Shamanic illness and initiation are of no significance and shamanic training is described as consisting of physical rather than psychological or religious exercises (e.g. 11, II: 50–3). Death and rebirth – important elements in traditional shamanic initiation rites as in some religious manga (Yamanaka, 1996: 181) – also gradually develop importance in *Shaman King*. For example, Yoh is the first to undergo a one-week retreat in a pitch-dark cave named after the Japanese underworld; some of Yoh's allies are killed in battle and revived – interestingly by Christian and Buddhist shamans – with considerably greater powers; and Yoh's key antagonist, Hao, is so powerful because, having mastered the art of rebirth, he has been reborn at least twice (55, XVIII: 64).

Despite Japan's geographical proximity to Siberia, no Siberian contestants take part in the shaman fight. Neither do Okinawan, Korean nor Mongolian shamans. Instead, the fictitious North American First Nation 'Patch' is depicted as host and (almost) impartial referees of the shaman fight, thereby endowing these North American practitioners with the very special status of meta-shamans. It is in the Patch's secret ancient village – hidden beneath the remains of the Ancestral Puebloan cliff dwellings in Mesa Verde, Colorado – that the Great Spirit manifests itself once every 500 years. Intentionally paradoxical, the Patch tribe is partially portrayed as stereotypically timeless and unemotional noble savages who immediately relate to the Great Spirit. Contrariwise, however, they suffer notably in Tokyo's midsummer heat (54, VII: 10–12), sell articles of indigenous handicraft to make ends meet (38, V: 63–4) and use high-tech equipment such as pocket bells and broadcasting (31, IV: 99 and 32, IV: 115–16).

In combination, the above paragraphs attest to the influence of neo-shamanic and esoteric literature on Takei's imagining of shamanism. They also indicate that it was not shamanism as such that Takei was concerned with. Rather, Takei used shamanism as a popular catch phrase – an all-embracing term with which to encompass as many mysteriously spiritual phenomena as possible. As shown below, Takei likewise modified descriptions of Japanese religious practitioners to meet the requirements of his story.

Spirit Possession

Spirit possession features prominently in *Shaman King*. Through Manta's astonishment and gradual understanding, readers are introduced to these concepts. Because in Japanese tradition solicited spirit possession is mostly manifest in states of trance accompanied by verbal utterances and unsolicited spirit possession in illnesses and misfortunes, Takei saw the necessity of explaining his characters' more transforming types of spirit possession to his readers. Spirit possession in *Shaman King* is to be understood quite literally as a spirit entering or being inserted into a person's body or, as a more advanced technique, into a material object (see below). As no ecstasy occurs prior to spirit possession, two souls temporarily reside in the individual's body.

Several different types of spirit possession are depicted and explained. None of these require preparatory prayers or drumming; in fact, Anna trained Yoh to enter into spirit possession within seconds (12, II: 84 and 26, III: 172). Neither does spirit possession require a particular form of closure. It either ends when the shaman is exhausted – as the 'unnatural situation of two souls in one body is rather strenuous for the medium' (23, III: 111–12) – or the spirit leaves unspectacularly. Yoh only once exorcised his samurai spirit by apparently pulling him out of his chest and throwing him away shouting 'exorcism mode' (16, II: 159–60). Thus, although shamans connect this world and the world beyond and a suitable state of mind is repeatedly emphasised as a necessary condition for successful spirit possession, spirit possession is, in fact, divested of any religious context and presented as a particular kind of battle mode. It is a means of elevating both heroes' and opponents' physical powers to a non-ordinary state, just as heroes in other manga would use different levels of robots, cards or magic to acquire supernatural powers.

To keep the story moving – and in preparation for trading-card and computer games – shamans in *Shaman King* are said to gradually master ever increasing levels of solicited spirit possession. *Shaman King's* first level of solicited spirit possession is plain *hyôi gattai*, which is translated as 'integrate' in the English edition (Jp: 1, I: 47; En: 1, I: 45). *Hyôi* is a standard Japanese scholarly term for 'spirit possession,' whereas *gattai* literally means 'to join bodies' and is not commonly used in connection with spirit possession. *Hyôi* is defined in Manta's dictionary as a 'phenomenon when [someone is] possessed by a spirit' – with 'possessed' here rendered by a more colloquial term often associated with unsolicited spirit possession (1, I: 49). *Hyôi 100%* ('100 per cent integration') is the second level of spirit possession which allows a shaman to make full use of a spirit's physical power, as long as the two souls act in unison (7, I: 180–1, 187). The third level of solicited spirit possession is that of 'oversoul.' It is achieved by inserting one's spirit helper into an object symbolising its greatest power; e.g. Yoh's samurai spirit helper into his sword (29, IV: 64–7). The fictitious English word 'oversoul' is also used in the Japanese text, as there is no notion of oversoul in Japan where material objects are rarely considered possessed. In fact, it is explained that oversoul is so powerful because it is considered a 'forced condition' (29, IV: 67). Oversoul is necessary for the continuation of the series' plot and its upward spiral of power and ferociousness. Over time, oversoul develops further functions (53, VI: 171–2), subsequently being surpassed by 'oversoul with two objects' (128, XV: 63–70) and 'double oversoul' with two spirits in one object (205, XXIII: 165–7).

A shaman like Yoh achieves *hyôi* spirit possession quite physically by turning his spirit helper into a bodiless ball and pressing it through his chest into his body. This enables him to use the physical strength and techniques which the spirit owned at the time of its original body's death (see, 16, II: 162–3). On the first occasion, Manta witnessed with great astonishment that

Yoh's facial expression, voice and movements completely turned into those of the possessing samurai spirit as he now wielded the wooden memorial post like a real samurai would wield his sword (1, I: 50–1).

In both *Shaman King* and Japanese tradition, spirit possession can also be caused by a person transferring a spirit into the body of a medium. This 'mediated spirit possession' is usually employed to gain information from the possessing spirit, as the 'mediator' who handles the spirit is able to conduct a dialogue with it through the medium who – now possessed by the transferred spirit – acts as its mouthpiece. In most cases, the medium is female and the mediator in control of the ritual is a male religious practitioner, often a mountain ascetic (Staemmler, 2009: 26–8, 41–85). In *Shaman King* this communicative function is only necessary for spirits who have achieved Buddhahood, whence they are inaccessible for Yoh and his friends. Interestingly, in the most prominent instance, gender roles are reversed as it is Anna – the female *itako* (blind spirit medium) – who is able to catch the spirit of the old kung fu master with her rosary and force it into Yoh, the male shaman (16, II: 157–61). Communication then takes place only after the kung fu master inside Yoh's body has battled down the uncontrollable spirit of his disciple. Communication takes place not between human and spirit, but between two spirits who would not have been able to communicate otherwise because one of them had achieved Buddhahood and had thus entered into a different layer of the world beyond.

An entirely different type of spirit possession in *Shaman King* is the concept of unsolicited spirit possession. The term used here is *toritsukareru*, which is a common Japanese term for being possessed by a malevolent spirit, thus neither concept nor terminology is fictitious or requires much explanation. Some victims of unsolicited spirit possession are able to observe their surroundings – e.g. Lyserg (103, XII: 90) – but they have no command over their bodies and their voices and facial expressions correspond to those of the possessing spirits. Exorcism of possessing spirits is described as difficult, requiring psychological rather than physical victory over the spirit (21, III: 71–2). Traditionally, exorcism was also often accomplished by offering the spirits food and appropriate rituals.

Possessing Spirits and Oversouls

A plethora of souls and spirits is introduced in *Shaman King*, although deities – which in Japan are often the possessing entities in solicited spirit possession – play but a marginal role. The image of souls and spirits is based on common Japanese conceptions, although as parts of folk belief these are neither uniform nor static. Takei eclectically selected some of them, invented others, categorised them, and subsequently combined the result with the concept of a universal Great Spirit – the latter being alien to Japan but suitable to spirit-summoning shamans and the North American Patch referees. The ultimate aim of the shaman fight is to identify the most potent shaman who will then be able to unite with the Great Spirit, the source of all life and place to which all souls return (108, XIII: 14–15). Indicated by its name and location in Mesa Verde, the concept of a Great Spirit seems to have been stereotypically modelled on American First Nation beliefs.

Major deities traditionally revered in Japan include Shinto deities such as the Sungoddess, Buddhist deities such as Amida (Amitābha) Buddha and syncretistic mixtures of these two. Christianity was introduced to Japan in the sixteenth century and although outlawed until the late 1800s it has attracted a stable minority of the population. Natural features such as mountains, rivers and prominent rocks were believed to be inhabited by more or less powerful local deities whose attitude towards humans is ambiguous; supportive if treated well, but malevolent if neglected or maltreated. Owing to Buddhist influence, the soul of a deceased person is believed to go either to hell or acquire Buddhahood – i.e. enter Nirvana. Souls of people tied to earth by some unfulfilled desire or excessive hatred will, as vengeful spirits, attract attention to their plight by causing accidents, illnesses and misfortune.

In *Shaman King*, spirits which have achieved Buddhahood – translated into English as being 'in heaven' (10, II: 32) or to 'rest in peace' (17, II: 188) – can only be summoned by Anna. Probably because they are believed to be content and immaterial and can thus contribute little to a ferocious battle, these spirits are of minor importance in *Shaman King*. Human spirit helpers are invariably spirits bound to this world, such as Amidamaru waiting for his friend or Tokagerô longing to revenge himself. The relationship between a shaman and his spirit helper is either one of mutual friendship – as with Yoh and Amidamaru – or one of master and subordinate – as with Ren and Bason (7, I: 163–7). Spirit helpers also exist in animal form, such as Mikihisa's impressive fox and badger spirits – whose lowly counterparts, Conchi and Ponchi, serve as spirit helpers and frequent sources of embarrassment to Mikihisa's young disciple Tamao. In Mikihisa's fox spirit, Takei mixes two traditions of belief. Foxes, like badgers, were believed to be tricksters who appeared in the guise of travellers or beautiful women and fooled people out of their money or food. They were also frequently associated with unsolicited spirit possession. On the other hand, the fox deity Inari (Mikihisa's fox spirit is called 'Imari') serves as a messenger between humankind and deities (Smyers, 1999). Possibly owing to the waning importance of belief in trickster foxes, however, the difference between these and the deity Inari has become obscured. Neither of the two is related to Shugendô, to which Mikihisa and Tamao belong, and for whom *tengu* (mountain goblins) would have been more obvious spirit helpers, since *shugenja* were closely associated with *tengu* and Mikihisa is constantly wearing a mask which marks him as a *tengu*.

With the exception of evil spirits, spirits are depicted as having a physical form which is invisible to most and cannot be touched or manipulate objects unless in possession of a living human body. Although, initially, most spirits are of human or animal shape, they become larger, fiercer and gradually gigantic fighting machines as the series continues. Spirits and oversouls are thus presented as external quasi-physical beings able to fight each other by proxy of their flesh and blood owners. At the same time – and attesting to the dominance of Western bio-medicine and psychology in modern Japan – they are explained as internal psychological phenomena. As repeatedly asserted, an oversoul's power is only ever as strong as the shaman's psychological power (e.g. 131, XV: 119). Yoh's strength, then, lies in his quiet self-confidence (61, VII: 152–3), just as the demons molesting Anna stem from her own unhappy thoughts (169, XIX: 170–1).

Japanese Shamanism in *Shaman King*

Onmyôji and Shugenja

Hao Asakura, the main evil character of *Shaman King*, is modelled after Abe no Seimei (921–1005CE), a highly influential medieval *onmyôji* about whom legends became very popular after Baku Yumemakura wrote a series of novels about him in the 1990s. *Onmyôji* are practitioners of Onmyôdô – literally, the 'way of shadow and light' – which is a Japanese adaptation of Chinese divination and astronomy based on natural and celestial phenomena. Onmyôdô-based astronomy, calendar-making and divination dominated Japan's society in the Heian period (794–1185CE) (Murayama, 1980: 990–1). Yoh's grandfather, Yohmei Asakura, is also an *onmyôji*, while Yoh's father, Mikihisa – like their ancestor Yohken Asakura – is a *shugenja*. As such, Mikihisa is depicted both in typical Shugendô attire (89, X: 190 and 234, XXVII: 24) and with fighting techniques having Shugendô-related names and shapes (236, XXVII: 49–58). Described as friendly and caring (e.g. 148, XVII: 90–4 and 147, XVII: 77), the *shugenja* play no major role in *Shaman King*.

Apart from the fact that a family of hereditary *onmyôji* is unlikely to list *shugenja* among its line-preserving members, the relative importance attributed to *onmyôji* and *shugenja* in *Shaman King* cannot be explained by their relevance to shamanism or spirit possession. Whereas *shugenja* are religious practitioners quite closely corresponding to narrower definitions of shamans, *onmyôji* are not. However, after *shugenja* had initially lived secluded lives of asceticism, in the early modern era they became closely related to people's everyday lives as they lived among them and conducted rituals for them. *Onmyôji*, on the other hand, were more aloof and intriguingly mysterious. Although they controlled much of high society's everyday life in the Heian period, not much is known about them. Their divinations were based on secret manuals illegible to most Japanese, even today; whereas it is commonly known that *shugenja* undergo well-documented austerities through which they eventually master extraordinary powers, such as walking over fire, which they display openly. Nowadays, Shugendô temples are open to visitors and their formerly inaccessible sacred mountains have become popular hiking trails – reflected in Mikihisa's religious practice being described as consisting of difficult mountaineering. Despite their supernatural powers, *shugenja* are practically graspable, whereas *onmyôji* are not. Additionally, there has of late been something of an *onmyôji* boom and widespread interest in divination in Japan. For example, two thirds of the women questioned in 1996 had experience with techniques like Ouija boards (Ishii, 1997: 93); which, incidentally, Takei curiously associates with Tamao and hence Shugendô (49, VI: 104–6). When Takei gave *onmyôji* a key role in *Shaman King* he used Onmyôdô's air of mystery and contemporary popularity, thereby consolidating *Shaman King*'s attractiveness.

Itako

Yoh's fiancée Anna Kyôyama is introduced as an *itako* (blind spirit medium), which Anna herself repeatedly defines as someone who 'at any time can call and talk to any spirit anywhere, even if the spirit has acquired Buddhahood' (e.g. 25, III: 160). Her surname of 'Kyôyama' is written with the characters for Osorezan – a mountain in northern Japan which is both very close to the area in which Takei himself was brought up and intimately associated with *itako*. Anna also figured in Takei's manga *Butsu Zone* and *Itako no Anna*. She was brought up by Yoh's blind grandmother, who is a more realistic *itako* because most living *itako* are old women, as hardly any girls today choose *itako* as a profession.[6]

The image of an *itako* conjured by Anna does not coincide with that of a real *itako*, because Anna has healthy eyes and is fully trained at the tender age of 13 – when, traditionally, blind girls would have just begun their training as an *itako*. Takei counters this by asserting that Anna was 'the real thing,' whereas most *itako* only pretend to become possessed (164, XIX: 64). Real *itako* perform the ritual of *kuchiyose* in which they act as a mouthpiece for spirits and thereby enable people to talk to deceased relatives. As *itako*'s services are most often requested by bereaved parents or elderly women in charge of their family's spiritual wellbeing, most readers of *Shaman King* are unlikely to have witnessed a *kuchiyose* (Blacker, 1986: 140–63). Instead of entering a state of trance and hence spirit possession, Anna literally calls the spirit from the world beyond, but inserts it not into her own but into another shaman's or medium's body; e.g. Yoh (16, II: 156–62) or Ryu (25, III: 163–6). Anna wears a long string of pearls around her neck which is described as a 1,080-bead rosary (99, XII: 28), which she uses to evoke trance and to catch and manipulate spirits. Usually, *itako*'s rosaries would have between 108 and 300 beads and are used in combination with certain sutras to induce trance and spirit possession (Blacker, 1986: 148–9).

Ainu

Yoh's first opponent in the qualifying round is Horohoro, a friendly young Ainu from Hokkaido who places his minute spirit helper into his snowboard to achieve an oversoul which can produce snow storms and freeze his opponents. Ainu are an ethnic minority in Japan who used to live in most of Hokkaido, the northernmost of Japan's four main islands, and on the Sakhalin-peninsula. Similar to ethnic minorities in other countries, Ainu have been fought, beaten, resettled, and re-educated until most of the Ainu language and oral tradition was forgotten. In fact, Takei deemed it necessary to explain to his readers what Ainu are (33, IV: 136–7).

Similar to the presentation of the North American Patch tribe, Ainu, too, are exoticised as an all but timeless and noble people, albeit easily irascible; i.e. semi-wild. Although neo-shamanism emphasises proximity to and concern with nature, in *Shaman King* only Horohoro and the 'Icemen' – a team with shamans from western Russia, Iceland and, surprisingly, Ireland whose members have learned to cooperate with a fierce natural environment – are concerned about nature (e.g. 34, IV: 157–9 and 127, XV: 41). Horohoro's concern focuses on bears because they used to play an important role in Ainu thought and religious practice (Adami, 1991: 89–93; *Shaman King* 94, XI: 90–3). His other concern is for butterbur plants because his spirit helper is a Koropokkuru. Koropokkuru are very small and friendly beings who, according to Ainu myths, lived in the distant past close to Ainu villages seeking shelter under large butterbur leaves (Asai, 1977: 362–3). In actuality, Siberia-influenced shamanism was more prominent with the Ainu of Sakhalin, whose shamans used drums and achieved ecstasy to heal the sick or gain information from divine sources (Adami, 1991: 99–142). However, in Hokkaido – the home island of Horohoro – male shamans have long ceased to exist and the rare female *kusu* wait to be possessed by deities to enquire about reasons for illnesses (Adami, 1991: 151–3). Here, too, Takei plays on common clichés and images of the Ainu and adapts a notion vaguely associated with shamanism to suit the needs of his story.

Yoh Asakura: the Japanese Shaman

Whereas the other characters of *Shaman King* are attributed characteristics generally based on their religious speciality, the main character of Yoh is not. A kind of 'all-rounder,' Yoh is not based in any particular religious tradition, although his geographic and national affiliation is accentuated by his spirit helper, the samurai Amidamaru. Samurai, their ideal of loyalty and excellent swords, constitute one of those clichés commonly associated with Japan. Amidamaru fully complies with these stereotypes. Although Amidamaru is a human spirit rather than a nature spirit, Yoh achieves oversouls because samurai ethics teaches absolute loyalty (29, IV: 67–8). Amidamaru had not gained Buddhahood because of a promise he had failed to fulfil (2, I: 68–75) and he sacrifices his treasured sword to save his master (21, III: 68–88). When the main round of fights starts Yoh is given a second, short sword by his grandfather – all samurai in early modern Japan were allowed to carry two swords – which is identified as a semi-mythical national treasure and thus also links Yoh to Japan as a nation rather than a mere geographical area.

Yoh's mother Keiko, who plays but a marginal role, is initially introduced as a shamanic *miko* in the tradition of Himiko, yet is depicted in the robe of a shrine *miko*; i.e. a young woman working at a Shinto shrine, selling amulets and assisting the priests in their rituals (7, II: 14). Himiko was a third century ruler, described in the first written record about Japan, the *Gishi wajinden*, as mastering the 'way of the demons' (Ishihara, 1985: 49, 83 and 112). Despite studies proving the contrary (see, Naumann, 1989: 309–26), Himiko is commonly viewed as a 'shamaness.' In *Shaman King*, Himiko is said to have been able to hear the deities' voices and thereby save the people from disasters (7, II: 14). The combination of Himiko and *miko* in an explanation of shamanism ties in with the later description of Japan as a country with an ancient shamanic tradition where, in former times, people frequently sought counsel from shamans. This statement is accompanied by an image of a *torii* – a gate marking the entrance to a Shinto shrine (43, V: 157–9). *Shaman King*, thus, corroborates the cliché of a shamanic tradition in ancient Japan intimately linked to present-day Shinto. Yoh, the main character, is a laid-back, friendly teenager and the character readers identify with most. Yet, he implicitly propagates various popular and nationalistic autostereotypes about 'traditional' Japan; e.g. samurai ethics and Shinto's history as indigenous, shamanic religion.

Izumo and Tokyo: Issues of Time and Place

Two key locations within Japan are juxtaposed in *Shaman King* – urban Tokyo and spiritual Izumo. As Japan's 8.5 million metropolis, Tokyo is quite realistically depicted as an urban centre with towering skyscrapers and few green oases. Although members of the Patch tribe apparently represent an outsider's view – as they behold Tokyo as unbearably hot in summer, expensive and horribly crowded (54, VII: 12) – *Shaman King* is written by a Japanese author and thus builds on emic clichés. It is in Tokyo, as the world's most degenerate place, that the shaman fight is to be held. As a fan has carefully documented, Funbari ga Oka – the area in which Yoh and Anna live – is modelled after Hinbari ga Oka, which is one of many suburban centres on the outskirts of Tokyo (Tomoe, http://cabin.jp). An area like many others, Funbari ga Oka is likely to resemble the home areas of many *Shaman King* readers. The associative step between a realistic, familiar setting and the fictitious plot and characters is thereby further facilitated.

The opposite of Tokyo is Izumo, Yoh's home region. Izumo is depicted as wide and close to both nature and Japan's mythical roots and spiritual origins (48, VI: 83–5). Here, is the mythical entrance to the mythical world-beyond in which Yoh undergoes his one-week retreat (48, VI: 75–88). Ryu's training, Yoh's grandfather's *onmyô* divination and the sealed manual describing Hao's techniques are all located in Izumo. Tokyo's concreted-in river inhabited by domestic swans (1, I: 20) is contrasted with Izumo's unpredictable river Hii, which is walled-in by immense rocks and inhabited by spirits of ancient settlers and formerly a ferocious eight-headed mythical serpent (102, XII: 73–4). The deity Ôkuninushi is both the main deity of the Grand Shrine of Izumo – whose building complex resembles the Asakura house – and regarded as the deity governing the underworld (Antoni, 2005: 11); rendering plausible the fact that Yoh underwent his one-week retreat in the netherworld accessed in Izumo.

In actuality, Izumo is a rural region adjacent to the Japanese Sea and quite distant from Japan's urban centres. Izumo is also home to the Grand Shrine of Izumo, which has rivalled – since the late-1800s – the official religious centre of the Grand Shrine of Ise. Ise is dedicated to the Sungoddess who is the highest deity of the Shinto pantheon and alleged ancestress of the imperial family. According to Japanese myths, it was in Izumo that the Sungoddess's violent, impulsive and mischievous brother, Susanoo, fought the giant eight-headed serpent and extracted a sword from one of its tails. This sword was to become one of the imperial regalia (Aston, 1972: 52–3; Chamberlain, 1981: 71–3). In *Shaman King*, this same sword becomes Ryu's new weapon, while the eight-headed serpent determines the name and shape of his high-level oversoul (133, XV: 166), thereby closely associating the outcast Ryu with the outcast deity, Susanoo.

It was through the nationalist scholar Hirata Atsutane (1776–1843) and Lafcadio Hearn (1850–1904) – a writer and journalist whose view of Japan was as romanticised as it was influential – that Izumo became widely known as 'a synonym for pure, authentic and genuine Japan' (Antoni, 2005: 12). Contrasted with the refined and official Ise or urban-industrialised Tokyo, Izumo is thus associated with authentic religious experience. Thus, although the *itako*'s Osorezan or Shugendô's sacred mountains might be more appropriate places of origin for Japanese shamanism, for the kind of shamanism Takei portrays in *Shaman King*, Izumo is the ideal location.

Conclusion

Like other manga published in *Shônen Jump*, *Shaman King* was produced under considerable pressure for weekly mass consumption rather than being created as an exclusive piece of literary art. It naturally contains many elements typical of a serial *shônen manga*, such as chapters of about 20 pages each, colloquial language, extensive fight scenes, and a hero who has to use his supernatural powers to save the world. Characters in *Shaman King* may be divided into 'goodies' and 'baddies,' although – unlike American comics but typical of Japanese manga – they have the potential for development (e.g. Ryu or Tao Ren) (Shimizu, 2004: 24–5). Yoh and his friends emphasise socially accepted values such as friendship – both among humans and between humans and spirits – peace of mind and the avoidance of violence, which in a *shônen manga* is reduced to beating one's enemies without actually killing them (see, Maderdonner, 1986: 42). While the important positive characters are teenage boys – like most of the comic's readers – many of their opponents are adult men. Parents, girls and women are largely marginal characters.

Shaman King – including its new complete edition – has been translated into several languages. Trading-card and video games are based on it, and innumerable fan articles and fan sites also give testimony to its popularity. Anna even became mascot of the website of Mutsu's police department (Mutsu being the town nearest to Osorezan where *itako* figure most prominently); an indication that Anna is regarded as sufficiently popular to be acceptable as an *itako* despite the obvious discrepancies between her and real *itako*.

As most Japanese do not consider themselves religious (Ishii, 1997: 169), the attraction of manga related to religion may seem astonishing, unless one bears in mind the keen interest in spiritual and religious matters that exist beyond the confines of established religion (Tsujimura, 2008: 216–29). As the history of manga shows, many successful manga have drawn on topics of current general concern such as competition with the West, technological progress and new spiritualities (Berndt, 1995: 15–74; Maderdonner, 1986: 1–94). Takei likewise picked up a popular trend – the new spiritualities movement described by Shimazono (1996 and 1999: 121–33) – appropriated its beliefs and practices and used them as literary tropes to inform his work. However, Takei avoided straightforward association with the – still negatively connoted – New Age by rooting these imported elements firmly in Japanese myths and accepted versions of religious history and by combining them with traditional Japanese religious phenomena such as *itako, onmyôji, shugenja*, and solicited/unsolicited spirit possession. Also, spirit possession in *Shaman King* is presented not as a religious topic but as a straightforward narrative device which serves to empower the characters with supernatural faculties.

Due to the constitutional separation of religion and state, there is no religious education in Japanese public schools. Consequently, the definitions and extensive explanations of shamanism and spirit possession given in the first few chapters of *Shaman King* are necessary, since readers cannot be expected to have clear concepts of things such as these. As *Shaman King* is a successful boys' comic, its influence on its readers is likely to be considerable, especially because they have no pre-existing understanding of shamanism with which *Shaman King*'s representation must compete; just as their notions of *itako, shugenja, onmyôji*, and spirit possession are likely to be vague. Albeit neither illegitimate nor unusual for manga, Takei implicitly draws on various stereotypes – e.g. the noble savage, samurai ethics, Himiko as shamaness, and Shinto as an unchanging religious undercurrent – which consolidate in the mind of the readers existing popular myths of Japanese identity. Since *shônen manga* often draw on fictitious beings, supernatural powers and parallel worlds, many readers of *Shaman King* may well also perceive shamanism as fictitious. At the same time, they are likely to absorb and accept, if unconsciously, the concrete images of more familiar concepts and stereotypes.

Quoting the fantasy critic David Hartwell, Napier points out that reading fantasy literature promises an escape from reality (1996: 6). With *Shaman King* this escape is twofold. First, as a manga, *Shaman King* has images as well as text and is thereby quick and easy to read. As students entering junior high school have only learned half of the nearly 2,000 Chinese characters in general use in Japanese, it also facilitates learning by providing readings for all Chinese characters. High school and junior high school students are expected to study very hard in preparation for upcoming entrance examinations. The suspense-packed 200 page paperback editions of manga such as *Shaman King* offer an efficient means of being absorbed by another world within the limited amount of free time left between school, cram-school and homework.

Second, despite their relative material affluence, many boys grow up in Japan without – at least, in their eyes – a particularly exciting life or attractive prospects for the future. Albeit temporarily and rather fantastically, identification with Yoh and other manga characters both provides these boys with the excitement they seek and meets these desires in a socially acceptable manner (see, Napier, 1996: 6). Responding to a desire for adventure and excellence, *Shaman King* provides contact with spirits and other supernatural beings about which vague notions have survived urban-industrial modernisation and through whose embodiment individuals are apparently endowed with quite alluring supernatural powers. Influenced by Osamu Tezuka's humanism (see, Berndt, 1995: 53), Takei's *Shaman King* strongly emphasises the importance of friendship combined with mutual assistance and respect. Such values may be particularly appealing in a highly competitive environment, because they indicate that there are – in reality as well as fiction – more important things than academic success. The international success of *Shaman King* indicates that its provision of a culturally specific escape into a fantasy world is both acceptable to and appreciated by young readers in many countries of the modern, industrialised world.

THE ONTOLOGY OF GOOD AND EVIL

Spirit Possession in Contemporary Witchcraft and Paganism

Douglas Ezzy

Introduction

The circle is cast: incense, water mixed with salt and the sacred knife are carried round the circle and inscribe the boundary of our sacred rite. The quarters are called: East, North, West, and South. We then chant the 'Witches Rune' (Valiente, 2000), holding hands and whirling in a circle. I dance with three other people in a medium-sized outbuilding in a leafy suburb in eastern Australia. Two of us are visitors. The other two are accomplished Wiccan practitioners. It is dark outside, and the wine we drank earlier enhances the effect of the thick incense, the chanting and the dancing to put me in a slightly altered state of consciousness. Eventually, we stop dancing and the priestess nods to her priest. He kneels before her and 'draws down the moon' invoking the presence of the Goddess (Adler, 2006). The priestess 'opens' herself up, inviting the Goddess, represented by the moon, to enter her body. Her arms are held out, tilted slightly upwards, her long hair flows gently over her dark blue robe and she stares into the distance, entranced. The words she speaks are the words of the Goddess, reciting 'The Charge of the Goddess' (Valiente, 2000). She recalls the names the Goddess has been called in various cultures, and speaks of meeting in secret under a full moon to dance, sing and celebrate. At the heart of the verse is an injunction to enjoy the pleasures of this life, and to revere the beauty of the earth, for 'all acts of love and pleasure are my rituals' (Valiente, 2000: 55). In closing we are reminded that the mystery is to be found 'within' ourselves. After chanting some popular Pagan verses, the ritual ends with a farewell to the quarters and the circle is opened. We return to the house and 'ground' ourselves with a hearty meal.

Contemporary Paganisms are profoundly 'this worldly' religions, similar to their religious forebears of classical Greek and Roman Paganisms and many contemporary indigenous religions. Pagans tend to reject the dualisms of natural/supernatural or body/spirit. This life, this body, is sacred. Nature is spiritual. For this reason Paganisms are often called 'nature religions.' The pleasure of this life is understood as basically good. The body, sexual desire, the reality of death, and the darkness of our fears are all sacred gateways to inner knowledge. The possession trance I have just described, affirming and relatively non-confrontational as it was, provides an emotionally powerful embodied experience of precisely this understanding. In many ways, the ritual of Drawing Down the Moon is emblematic of Paganism more generally. Contemporary Pagans tend to be relatively uninterested in what people believe. They are more concerned to work with their feelings, aiming to transform their embodied experience.

Contemporary Pagan possession rituals are embodied performances that transform the ritualists' understandings of themselves and their place in the world. Stoller argues that spirit possession is an embodied phenomenon and not simply about meanings (1995). He describes the spirit possession of the Hauka in post-colonial West Africa, arguing that we need 'to think about spirit possession as a set of embodied practices with serious social, cultural and political consequences.' When the spirit enters social space through the ritual performance it transforms mediums 'both physically and symbolically' (1995: 7). Drawing Down the Moon transforms participants' embodied experience of pleasure and sexuality into a sacred moment. This starkly contrasts with the dominant culture that sees sexual pleasure as either antagonistic to spirituality or reduces sexual pleasure to the carnal and secular (Benjamin, 1988).

Contemporary Witchcraft and Paganism are now established new religious movements in urban-industrialised countries. In Australia they are collectively similar in size to Scientology, the Church of the Latter Day Saints and small Christian denominations such as the Brethren. At the 2006 Australian Census approximately 0.13 per cent of the Australian population nominated Paganism, Witchcraft or a Nature Religion as their religion. They include a diverse range of ages and backgrounds, but tend to be more popular among women and people with higher levels of education (Berger and Ezzy, 2007). In the late-1990s a large number of young people started identifying as Witches and Pagans, reflecting the wide availability of information about these phenomena in books and on the Internet.

This chapter examines possession through a detailed account of 'Faunalia,' a Pagan festival in which one ritualist is possessed by Baphomet, a somewhat controversial Pagan deity. The participants at this festival tend to be older (it is an adults-only event), but are otherwise similar to the broader Pagan community. Drawing Down the Moon is a relatively common possession rite among contemporary Witches. As the account above suggests, the tone of the ritual is celebratory, focusing on positive and affirming symbols. Baphomet is a more marginal figure associated with 'darker' and more challenging facets of contemporary Paganism. Both point to the embodied and transformative focus of possession rites that link to a more general concern with authenticity and self development (Greenwood, 2000; Taylor, 2007).

Possession Rituals in Contemporary Paganisms

Contemporary Paganisms – a deliberately plural umbrella term – include a variety of religious traditions such as Wicca or Witchcraft (the tradition that informs the opening account of Drawing Down the Moon), Druidry and Heathenry (Harvey, 1997). All tend to follow a ritual calendar linked to the seasons of the sun and the moon, although there are important variations between the traditions. Witches follow a set of rituals developed by Gerald Gardner and Doreen Valiente with circle casting at its centre. Witches work with a broad range of deities including Greek, Roman, Egyptian, Celtic, and others (Hutton, 1999). Druids typically follow a similar circle casting, but are more orientated toward deities of the Celtic tradition. Heathenry draws on the Norse deities and traditions such as those described in the medieval texts of the Eddas. Heathens do not typically cast a circle, creating sacred space through other ritual means such as rhythmic chanting and drumming (Harvey, 1997).

Blain provides a detailed academic ethnographic account of the shamanic 'seidr' practices of contemporary Heathens (2002). She is particularly concerned to examine the performed nature of these experiences and to interrogate their epistemological status. Blain draws on postmodernist theory to reject simplistic dichotomous understandings of truth, arguing instead that ethnographers should examine the trance experience as 'experienced by participants from within their own spiritual world-views, as partial truths, as community construction where "community" includes more than the visible human participants.' Blain examines the trance experience's 'discursive construction, its specificity, its embeddedness and its political dimensions' (2002: 27).

Blain's approach is similar to the hermeneutic approach to the study of religion beautifully articulated by Flood (1999). Flood develops an argument for a dialogical hermeneutical approach to the study of religion: 'dialogism with its links to hermeneutics and narrativism…is suspicious of claims to objectivity and truth, but is fundamentally grounded in communication and acknowledges a self-in-relation' (1999: 10). Applied to the study of possession and trance, this approach sidesteps the issue of the truth or falsity of the experience as a false dichotomy. As Edith Turner has said, 'It is true that I once had an experience of religion, after which I didn't see the point of disbelieving other people's experiences' (1992: xiii). Instead, the focus of the research is on what the symbolic system and the embodied performance of the possession trance communicates to participants. Within this approach, the interesting thing from an academic point of view is to examine how the symbols and experiences of the religious tradition shape participants' practice and self-understandings, and relate to broader cultural processes.

Blain provides a long and detailed account of a number of seidr (shamanic) trance experiences (2002). Groups of Heathens drum, sing and participate in guided meditations into the nine worlds of Heathen mythology. In some instances the seidworker sits with a veil over their head, enters a deep trance and is approached by other participants with questions seeking guidance on various issues that concern them. Blain provides a succinct summary of the trance journey of the seidworker Raudhildr that beautifully illustrates the nature of these trances.

> She made a journey to visit the Maurnir, who (according to her and Diana) are female giants. The Maurnir dwell in a cave, and she went there, naively she says, because she thought it would be interesting. She was attempting to journey to all of the denizens of the Nine Worlds. They were there, and saw her, and asked why she was there. The Maurnir have much wisdom, and she asked (again naively, she says) if they would teach her, if she could learn from them, share in their wisdom. They said no, they couldn't teach her, but if she wished she could become part of the wisdom. She agreed that this would be a good thing. So they ate her. They threw aside the bones, as they ate. Her bones were lying on the cavern floor, when Loki appeared and started dancing and singing, calling to the goddesses and gods to put her back together, which they eventually did. So Loki was dancing a shaman dance. When she was together again, she thanked him and asked him why he'd done this. He said 'once, you gave me a drink' (as an offering in a ritual). (2002: 23)

This experience was terrifying, as would be expected. However, beyond the death and dismemberment theme that characterises many shamanic initiation experiences, I want to point to the broader theme of the understanding of good and evil contained in this account. In Heathen mythology both the giants and Loki are ambivalent figures. While the Gods of Valhalla often fight the giants, the Gods also fall in love with and marry some giants and seek wisdom from them. Similarly, Loki is an ambivalent figure, both a close companion of Odin and one who is not entirely to be trusted. Are Loki and the giants evil? While there are parallels between Loki and Satan, the comparison is misguided because polytheistic Pagan theology does not have a dualistic understanding of good and evil. One of the key differences between Paganism and Christianity and post-Christian cultures is their understanding of good and evil as it relates to deity, self, the other, and the world. Whatever else deities are, they are also symbolic representations of aspects of self, other and the world. I argue that one of the things contemporary Heathens and Pagans who enter into trance are doing is developing a more complex and ambivalent emotional and performed response to those parts of self and other that have been traditionally understood as evil.

How people make sense of and respond to evil is a product of their more general worldview or ontology. Nussbaum differentiates, on the one hand, a Platonic and Kantian worldview, in which 'the good' is singular and integrated, and can be discovered by careful rational thought and practised by active human agents. On the other hand, she suggests that Greek tragedy and Aristotelian thought see human morality as sometimes shaped by powers beyond human control in which 'the good' is not always possible for humans who are both agents and passive recipients of consequences of large processes (1986). The difference in ontology identified by Nussbaum is closely related to the understanding of good and evil characteristic of Pagan and Christian or post-Christian cultures.

Classical philosophers and Pagans did not think of the Gods as embodying pure or unmixed good or evil. Rather the Gods were capricious 'sometimes benevolent, sometimes hostile,' symbolic of natural forces and processes that were largely indifferent to humans (Pagels, 1995: 120). Most classical and contemporary Paganisms are closer to the Aristotelian understanding of good and evil described by Nussbaum. In contrast, many Christians understand good and evil through the lens of a Platonic or Kantian worldview: God and 'the good' are unified and they understand their enemies to be inspired by 'spiritual forces of evil in heavenly places' (Ephesians, chapter 6, verse 12). God is on their side and their suffering and experience of 'evil' is attributed to the activities of Satan. In her analysis of the understandings of Satan that developed at the time of the conversion of the Roman Empire from Paganism to Christianity, Pagels argues that what divided Classical Pagans from Christians was not so much the monotheism of Christianity, but their understanding of evil (1995). Quoting from the early Platonic philosopher Celsus, she notes that:

> For all the 'impious errors' the Christians commit, Celsus says, they show their greatest ignorance in 'making up a being opposed to God, and calling him "devil," or, in the Hebrew language, "Satan."' (1995: 143)

Baphomet, the deity central to the possession rite described below, reverses this process. Baphomet is a deity with heavy Satanic symbolic resonances, and the Baphomet rite reinterprets these resonances as sacred and positive, sacralising, for example, sexual desire and relinquishing the fear associated with it.

In summary, so far I have argued that a more complex and ambivalent understanding of good and evil is one of the central differences between contemporary Paganism and the Christian and post-Christian culture in which it is most often situated. Sexual desire, bodies and the 'animal nature' of humanity are re-interpreted within this framework. Possession rituals such as Drawing Down the Moon in contemporary Witchcraft are a moment of performed and embodied transformation in the experience of these aspects of the self. I now turn to a more detailed account of the Baphomet possession rite.

Faunalia: A Pagan Festival of the Goat God

'Faunalia' is a pseudonym for an annual Pagan festival that took place over a number of years in a rural location in south-eastern Australia. I attended the festival in 2003 and 2005. In 2005, about 80 people attended, mostly good friends, although there was a good representation of 'newbies.' I interviewed 27 participants, including 12 that I interviewed both before and after the 2005 festival.[1] The remainder of this chapter focuses on one interview with a key ritualist. The other interviews provide essential context and background, although they are rarely quoted.

Faunalia is somewhat controversial among Australian Pagans because of its adults-only rituals and its reputation for being wild and emotionally intense. The festival lasts over five days, with a short one or two hour opening rite on the first night and a relaxed dance party on the last night. The two main rituals on the Friday and Saturday nights start at approximately 11.00pm and last most of the night. The disquiet about Faunalia is perhaps fuelled by the festival organisers' aim to reclaim the early-modern Witches' sabbat as a positive Pagan ritual. 'Wildthorn,' the co-creator of the festival along with 'Phoebe' (both pseudonyms), described his intentions this way:

> I wanted to create a rite that would challenge people's prejudices. There
> was a certain element of shit-stirring and iconoclasm. At first it was just
> gonna [going to] be a mere Pagan revel with just a few elements drawn
> from the sabbat. It would be evocative and Pagan and ecstatic. A lot of
> modern Paganism is way too sanitised and inoffensive and not chal-
> lenging to the status quo. I wanted to have an experience that was an
> emotional experience that was moving and wonderful and magical. So
> I got some ideas from the legend [of the Witches' sabbat]. I'll use that
> bit, but not that bit.

Wildthorn's explicit aim is to make the ritual 'challenging of the status quo.'
The transformation of the place of sexual desire within a sacred understanding
of good and evil is at the heart of this challenge. The Baphomet possession
rite reorientates participants' embodied responses to sexual desire from either
evil or secular, to sacred.

Baphomet is the deity at the heart of Faunalia and is invoked on the
Saturday night ritual. The Baphomet ritual has remained central to Faunalia,
while the other rituals have changed over the years. The Knights Templar
were accused of blasphemously kissing Baphomet's behind (Cohn, 1970:
3–16). The deity bears some similarity to the devil card in the Rider Waite
version of the Tarot deck, but is best know from Eliphas Levi's representation. Levi was a nineteenth-century occultist who described Baphomet as the
'sabbatic goat' (Jackson and Howard, 2003). It is this connection between
Baphomet and the myth of the early modern Witches' sabbat that intrigued
Wildthorn and Phoebe.

A number of Witches have argued that the Christian inquisitors who developed the early-modern myth of the Witches' sabbat discovered an ancient
fertility religion that has continued to the present time (Hutton, 1999).
Ginsburg presents a subtler version of the thesis, arguing that European
shamanistic folk practices were reinterpreted by Christian inquisitors as
evidence of the existence of a Witches' sabbat (1992). Ginsburg contends
that although the Witches' sabbats were a fantasy, they were based on a
systematic Christian misinterpretation and diabolistic reinterpretation of a
pre-existing set of folk beliefs and practices. While there has been considerable academic criticism (e.g. Hutton, 1999), the idea that the practices of the
Witches' sabbat described an ancient and ongoing Pagan religious practice
is taken up in a number of practitioner texts on contemporary Paganism.
Whatever the historical veracity, it clearly has powerful symbolic resonances
for contemporary Pagans.

Where the Christian inquisitors sought moral self-development through the repression of the body and its pleasures, participants at Faunalia seek moral self-development through the celebration of their bodies and its pleasures. Baphomet represents precisely those aspects of what it is to be human that many people fear. The Christian inquisitors feared the bestial this-worldly aspects of human nature. Sex, dancing and other pleasures of the flesh were sinful. The Baphomet rite takes these pleasures – including their symbolic representation in Baphomet – and embraces them as valued aspects of what it is to be human. The ritual sacralises bodies, sensuality, dancing, and eroticism, along with fear, the animal nature of humanity and intense emotional experiences. These are all sacred aspects of Baphomet. Put another way, participants say that the ritual allows them to explore their shadow selves (a Jungian term described below), finding courage to face their fears, rediscover their repressed sexual selves and develop new embodied self-understandings.

Baphomet is an incarnation of hybridity, liminality and animalistic sexual desire. Both male and female, I use the pronoun 'hir' to refer to Baphomet. Human and beast, goat and bird, creator and destroyer, Baphomet represents alterity, ambiguity, ambivalence, and the Jungian 'shadow self' – a concept that often informs contemporary Pagan thinking. Baphomet is intriguing, terrifying and seductive, all at the same time. Baphomet is not a commonly invoked deity in Pagan ritual.

Karen, a forty-two year old married Witch noted emphatically: 'We don't worship Baphomet. We simply honour the energy. It's a very different concept.' Worship, particularly of monotheistic deities such as Yahweh, God and Allah, typically involves obedience. In contrast, honouring suggests respect, but not devoted obedience. Classical accounts of rituals in honour of Dionysus or Bacchus suggest a similar understanding (Dalby, 2003; Otto, W. 1965). The deity was honoured, but the aim of the rite was for devotees to develop a respectful relationship with, rather than a subservient obedience to, the deity. The relationship between participants and the deity honoured in a ritual tends to be much more complex and ambivalent in these non-mono-theistic religions. While a deity may be honoured, ritualists are not necessarily required to love everything this deity might represent nor obey everything the deity might suggest they do. Pike provides an excellent broader ethnographic discussion of the role of ritual and liminality in a similar Pagan festival in the United States (2001). For the remainder of this chapter I focus on the trance experience at the heart of the Baphomet ritual.

Baphomet and Pagan Trance

The Baphomet rite was first performed at a different Pagan festival, before the beginning of Faunalia. Wildthorn wrote the ritual and Phoebe and several other local Pagans joined together to perform the ritual. In this first performance, Phoebe played a relatively minor role at the beginning of the ritual; another participant played the Baphomet role.

> Phoebe: Baphomet [the ritual that was performed at the Pagan Festival] blew my mind [laughs]. It was an amazing experience. We had a big cauldron burning and were dancing around it. The ritual started. I zoned out. I'd done my bit [in the ritual], I guess. And there was an issue before I left about going skyclad [naked] or not with Dean [Phoebe's husband who does not attend Faunalia]. And at that stage I hadn't gone skyclad at all. And I thought, well, look, you know, whatever happens, happens. But I remember leaving here and saying to my husband, 'There is no way I'm going naked. There is no way!' [laughs]. So he was fine. He was really fine with me going and he was secure, I guess. But, Doug, [laughs], when the revelry started, it was me that ran up to the central fire and I literally ripped my dress off and threw it into that fire. And I didn't take my undies off I guess, but that was enough, that's all I needed for that moment. I did not sleep for two days. So I was awake for two days, walking around the woods, the forest. I saw fairies. You know, I'd go off with my cigarettes and, and I'd sit on my own throughout the day many times for two days. I couldn't settle.

As Phoebe's account above suggests, one of the central issues that most Baphomet initiates confront is that of their sexual desire. Nudity is common in the Baphomet rites, most of the participants were naked for most of the several hours of the 2005 Baphomet rite. The ritual is also very erotic. After the more scripted early segments, the Baphomet rite transforms into a free-form revelry marked by dancing, kissing, flirting, and trance. These experiences were profoundly confronting for Phoebe. Phoebe recounted a painful story of her disrupted and abusive childhood. As a teenager she ran away from home and married at a very young age into a violent and ultimately failed relationship. One of Phoebe's dominant childhood influences was an understanding of sex and sexuality focused on fear and repression.

> Phoebe: I couldn't have sex with my [first] husband [laughs] until I got rid of a bloody family photo that I had on a dresser in my room. My father would come home and if we were watching telly and some

of the soapies [and] a kiss exchanged, he'd turn it off, we all had to go
to bed [laughs]…So Baphomet was about accepting everything about
myself. At the first Pagan Festival it was the first time I experienced a
passionate kiss with another woman. And that blew me away. And for
months I was ringing up friends of mine that were gay, saying 'What
the fuck's going on here.' I remember coming home and telling Dean.
Oh, it blew me away. And the end result after many months of working
with that was that [I realised I had to] accept myself. If I had a different
upbringing, I definitely would have embraced bisexuality. I find women
very, very appealing energetically. As I do men. So Baphomet was about
accepting the sexual me. Accepting the balanced me, the male and
female.

After the experience of the power of this first ritual, and a somewhat ambivalent reception of the ritual by some people at the Pagan Festival, Wildthorn
and Phoebe decided to start Faunalia with the Baphomet ritual at its heart.
Phoebe always played the Baphomet role at Faunalia between 2000, when
it began, and 2005, when I interviewed her. Her costume includes a pair
of black feathered wings and a beautifully handcrafted goat-head mask that
she wears or 'adorns.' The first Baphomet ritual at Faunalia was at the top of
a hill, where the ritualists waited. Fairy light candles marked the path that
the participants walked from their camp accommodation up to the hilltop
accompanied by hand held drums. There was a very large bonfire and a heavy
mist settled over the site. I asked Phoebe if she could remember this ritual.

Phoebe: Very much. The fairy lights. I remember the mist coming in,
rolling in, seeing this enormous fire. [I was] really excited, but also
very, very focussed, getting ready. I take things very seriously when it
comes to that, and if I'm going to be drinking this energy, then my
role [is that] when I touch, everyone gets a touch, everyone gets a taste,
everyone drinks.
Doug: So you're at the ritual site, the bonfire's going and you can hear
them walking up with the drums going.
Phoebe: Everything inside – the beats were like my heart. It's almost
like I was able to feel everyone's excitement, everyone's – not only
the excitement, but the anticipation of it all. I was no longer I. I was
something so great that it blew my mind. Did it blow every inch of me?
It totally did. It's similar to channelling, I guess, [when] you're deceased
loved ones, but it's not. There's no words.

Most participants reported similarly intense emotional responses to the Baphomet rite. The emotional power of the Baphomet rite derives to a significant extent from the carefully crafted liminality and alterity of the ritual (Turner, V. 1969). The liminal state is the in-between moment of transition between ordinary states. The entire Faunalia festival is a liminal event, described by Phoebe as a 'world between worlds.' 'Alterity' derives from the Latin for 'otherness' and refers to the unusual and radically 'not normal' nature of the rituals, practices, clothing, and events of Faunalia. It is the power of these ritual processes at Faunalia that generates the altered states of consciousness, including trance and possession. The festival food is vegetarian and the organisers discourage the use of alcohol, although a small number of people imbibe moderately during the party on the last night. I am unaware of the use of any psychotropic substances during the event. The carefully crafted ritual environment is more than sufficient to produce greatly heightened and altered states of consciousness. One of the most important contributions to

A Baphomet banner from Faunalia.[2]

the success of Faunalia is the extensive and careful preparation that goes into
the performance of rituals.

In 2005, the ritual site was some 200 metres from the main camp build-
ings. It was an area about 30 metres across that was enclosed in a temporary
hessian wall erected for this ritual. There was a huge central bonfire with
several peripheral fire pots. The hessian walls were hung with various banners
of pentagrams and flaming cauldrons. All of the 80 participants dressed in
special costumes including long flowing cloaks. Many had extensive make-
up. One had leopard spots all over her body, another two were completely
covered in white ochre. The anticipation and ritual procession also contribute
to a temporal liminality. The ritual itself followed the format typical of
most Witchcraft rituals: a circle was cast, deities were honoured and a cup
of wine was passed among participants (Greenwood, 2000; Hutton, 1999;
Pike, 2001). However, Faunalia is different because of the complex nature of
Baphomet and the highly charged erotic, ecstatic experience and intensity of
emotional responses to the ritual.

> Doug: Any outstanding memories in that first ritual with Baphomet?
> Phoebe: Everything. [laughs] The craziness, the chaos, the sitting and
> appreciating, but also confusion. Appreciating the sensual aspects of
> people being sensual with each other. As I'd take that mask off I sit,
> and that helps me ground, of course, and I just sit like that, and
> I watch, and observe. And the energy is spiralling, and spiralling,
> and spiralling. And watching people. It was very animalistic. It was
> very primal. It was a world between worlds. Looking in the trees and
> you've got faces looking back at you, you've got energies that are not
> of this world. I don't have the words. The feelings, the excitement,
> I can see it, you know, I can see it. I'm looking at you but I can see
> it. It – oh [sighs]…It was a world between. We were taken back in
> time to our ancestors. We had energies there that were old, and had
> danced the dance thousands of times before. We were honouring
> ourselves as this generation, but we were also honouring way back
> when [short laugh].

Faunalia participants aim to engage embodied, felt, powerful emotions.
Crites has noted that ritually re-enacted sacred stories

> seem to be allusive expressions of stories that cannot be fully and directly
> told, because they live, so to speak, in the arms and legs and bellies of
> the celebrants. These stories lie too deep in the consciousness of the

people to be directly told: they form consciousness rather than being among the objects of which it is directly aware. (1971: 295)

The rituals described here operate in this realm. They drive 'something deeply into the bone' (Grimes, 2000: 124). While participants may talk about their experiences, particularly in the group debriefing sessions, much of what is significant is not articulated linguistically, but felt, danced and performed, understood as the 'energy' of the rite. Ritual debriefings occur on the day following a ritual and can last two or three hours as participants take turns to reflect on their response to the rite. People will sometimes choose not to talk about their experiences, while others who have difficulty articulating how they are feeling may say that they are still 'processing' their responses. One important concept participants use to articulate their experiences is the Jungian idea of 'the shadow.'

> Phoebe: [Baphomet is] sexual and chaotic. Baphomet's everything. Baphomet's all the fears, Baphomet's all the okays. Baphomet is every-thing. Baphomet is the chaos. Baphomet's the light in the chaos. Baphomet's the darkness in the chaos. Baphomet's the all. And yet he's the nothing. He's the voice. I don't have words. There was pain, a lot of pain this year. [Baphomet was] very compassionate. Hey [laughs]. [Baphomet's] the healer. He's the confronter and confronts you. But this year it was more healing. Look at the shit we bury. Look at our feelings. And bring them up, vomit them out, just chuck it out. Don't hang on to it anymore.

The organisers of Faunalia recommend Robert Johnson's book *Owning Your Own Shadow: Understanding the Dark Side of the Psyche* as useful background reading. Johnson defines the shadow as 'that part of us we fail to see or know' (1991: 4). Most commonly, the shadow is understood as emotions, such as fears, obsessions and projections that shape people's behaviour without their conscious awareness. Baphomet is a potent symbolic representation of the shadow self. However, the shadow is not all negative. Johnson provides an examination of how falling in love can be a manifestation of the shadow when an individual unconsciously projects all that is good in themselves onto another person whom they idealise and 'love.' During interviews a few people discussed, without prompting, the concept of 'the shadow' and expressed a desire to 'work with' this aspect of themselves at Faunalia. The aim of 'shadow work' is to bring these unconscious processes to conscious awareness so that they can be integrated into the conscious self. Drawing on Jessica Benjamin's psychoanalytic analysis of 'acting' as an 'intermediate position between unconscious and conscious' (1998: 12), I argue that the ritual 'acting' at Faunalia allows participants to 'work' with their shadow selves through embodied performance, even though their experiences may not be entirely articulated linguistically as part of the cognitive, conscious self. Trance and possession are a particularly intense form of 'shadow work.'

The concept of 'shadow work' has some parallels, and significant differences, to Csordas' account of the 'demonic crisis' among charismatic Christians (1994). Csordas uses the term 'demonic crisis' to refer to events that occur during charismatic Christian healing rituals where the ritual leaders discern individuals who are demon possessed and go on to cast the demons out of that person. While demons are often associated with various sins, there are also demons associated with 'insecurity, depression, rebellion, and inter-personal problems' (Csordas, 1994: 181). Csordas argues that the demons are a 'cultural objectification' of thoughts, behaviours or emotions that the Christian experiences as problematic. Both Baphomet, and the demons of charismatic Christianity, are symbolic resources that facilitate experiences within a ritual context. However, unlike the charismatic Christians – who seek release and deliverance from their demons – the participants at Faunalia pursue a dialogical engagement with the somewhat demonic Baphomet, and release from the oppressive fear of Baphomet and the fear of the emotions and experiences Baphomet represents. This does not mean that participants come to like or would choose to engage in what Baphomet represents (although at least one participant sees hir as a guardian angel). If Baphomet represents a sexually active self, this does not require that the participant engage in sex; indeed, some participants choose to remain celibate at Faunalia. Rather, it means that participants work toward release from their fear of their sexual selves.

> Phoebe: I was raised from strict Roman Catholic. And until I adorned the [Baphomet] mask myself six years ago, there was still a lot of frag-ments of Catholicism there. [When I put on the mask I thought] here I am, now I'm Satan. The mask [was] the next step for me to pretty much cut the ties of Catholicism. Baphomet/Dionysus is the god form, but the Catholics chose to represent [hir as] Satan in the Bible and in their teachings. [Baphomet helped me realise] I'm actually a good person, and it's okay. There's no burning pits of hell.

Baphomet is an embodied, performed representation of the shadow self. For Phoebe, and for most participants at Faunalia, the Baphomet ritual enacts a transformative process that reorientates embodied responses to aspects of the self previously understood as evil and Satanic. While Baphomet is complex and endlessly reinterpreted, Phoebe explicitly mentions the pleasure of sex and a bisexual orientation as aspects of her own self that she previously understood as evil, to which she now has a transformed embodied orientation.

Phoebe's description of her developing experience of being possessed by Baphomet can also be read as a description of her ongoing transformation in self-understanding.

> Phoebe: I think the intensity of the energy [of Baphomet] scared me. The first maybe three years I would work with the energy for almost three months before the event. I'd talk. I'd meditate. I'd find myself doing housework and talking to Baphomet.
> Doug: Yep.
> Phoebe: And I would say: 'You have 75 per cent' [laughs] 'but I want this much.' And it's not even Phoebe, it's the mother, the wife. The monogamous one. [laughs]
> Doug: Yep.
> Phoebe: I was fearful of the fact that – what if? And a lot of that fear, not only did it come from me, but also [from other people who were] really scared, what if? What if?...It would have been – oh, not quite 75 per cent, but I think it was 80 or 85, and I had the 15 per cent the first time. I don't know all the history on Baphomet and that's okay. I understand the energy. And that to me is important. And I'd meditated. So I'd go to bed during the day. I'd lie down. I'd say things like, 'You're old. I know that you're primitive, I know that you're primal.' I'd go through some of the chants in Baphomet. But I continuously have had that energy with me for almost three months. This year [was different] it was a matter of reading a poem and the picture. And that was it. And it was only a couple of weeks. And all I found myself doing this time was just reciting it. And the more I recited it, the more I could feel the energy building up. This year I think I gave myself 100 per cent. Even last year there was still just 5 per cent. Over the years I've gotten more comfortable with the energy. I was the empty glass that was going to carry the energy.

Phoebe's account of her responses to the 'energy' of Baphomet can be understood as another way of talking about her embodied emotional responses to those aspects of her self that Baphomet represents. In order to understand this I draw on the psychoanalytic theory of Benjamin who argues that relationships exist within a dialectic of control and independence (1988). The self is neither completely controlled by nor completely independent of 'the other.' 'True independence means sustaining the essential tension of these contradictory impulses; that is, both asserting the self and recognizing the other' (Benjamin, 1988: 53). When the other is completely controlled, their independence is destroyed. However, the attempt to control the other is part of our own self-assertion. Benjamin talks about the relationship between control and self-assertion in erotic life in the following way:

> We might call this the dialectic of control: If I completely control the other, then the other ceases to exist, and if the other completely controls me, then I cease to exist. A condition of our own independent existence is recognizing the other. True independence means sustaining the essential tension of these contradictory impulses; that is, both asserting the self and recognizing the other...In mutual recognition the subject accepts the premise that others are separate but nonetheless share feelings and intentions. The subject is compensated for his loss of sovereignty by the pleasure of sharing, the communion with another subject. (1988: 53)

The concept of 'recognition' is central to Benjamin's thinking. Recognition of the other involves an acceptance of separation and difference of self and other simultaneously with the recognition of the other for who they are and the self's dependency on that other. This is the case even for 'others' that are confronting and disruptive to self. Phoebe's relationship with Baphomet is just such a case of erotic intimacy. Whatever the ontological status of Baphomet, Phoebe's relationship with this deity has profound consequences for her self-understanding.

I argue that contemporary Pagan possession trances are similar to the experience of erotic intimacy described by Benjamin. They do not involve complete surrender of self to the possessing other. Nor do they involve a complete acceptance of all that the possessing other represents. Rather, they are a form of profoundly intimate, even erotic, union that provides a moment of mutual recognition. Benjamin puts it this way:

> In my view, the simultaneous desire for loss of self and for wholeness (of oneness) with the other, often described as the ultimate point of erotic union, is really a form of the desire for recognition. In getting pleasure with the other and taking pleasure in the other, we engage in mutual recognition. (1988: 126)

Such mutual recognition does not, however, result in a sense of sameness, but of valued difference within the moment of mutual recognition. Sexual desire and bisexuality are among the things that Baphomet represents. However, Phoebe remains monogamous and married. What is transformed is her understanding of these aspects of her self. She no longer fears her sexual desire, nor does she fear the possibility of being attracted to women. Phoebe understands herself as having been engaged in a form of 'shadow work.'

> Phoebe: [Baphomet] is an energy that's primal that's in all of us. To embrace it. Not to fear it. To embrace it. We've ignored it, we've been scared of it through society, through religion. There's the fine line between doing what's acceptable and what's not acceptable. Baphomet is in all of us. Baphomet is all God, or Goddess, he's everything. He has the qualities of all the Gods and Goddesses. But it's just the one name.

The ritualists at Faunalia seek to reinterpret those experiences and aspects of the self that have been traditionally associated with Satan in Christian and post-Christian cultures. Embodied pleasure, including sexual desire, have traditionally been portrayed as dangerous, as things to be feared. The 'fine line between what is acceptable and what's not acceptable' flags Phoebe's awareness that to move away from fear of these aspects of self requires a new and more complex moral engagement with sexuality and sexual desire. Baphomet is an extremely complex figure who represents much more than sexual desire, including things such as self-esteem, body image, aggression, and grief. However, all these facets are linked to the 'shadow self' – aspects that have been repressed, feared or demonised as dangerous and Satanic.

'Satanic othering' refers to the process by which an individual portrays another opposing person or group as completely evil and 'Satanic' (Harvey, 1997). One important social function of Satanic othering is to provide a cultural resource for dealing with one's own failings. Clarke draws on psycho-analytic literature to argue that projective identification is a psychological process in which 'destructiveness is disowned by projecting it onto others' (1999: 27). Unpalatable parts of the self are forced onto the 'other,' which then serves to protect the self from those parts of the self that he or she does not wish to experience or acknowledge. According to Kearney, a Catholic philosopher, this is a patterned social phenomenon.

> Most strangers, gods and monsters…are, deep down, tokens of fracture within the human psyche…They remind us that we have a choice: (a) to try to understand and accommodate our experience of strangeness,

or (b) to repudiate it by projecting it exclusively onto outsiders. All too
often, humans have chosen the latter option, allowing paranoid illu-
sions to serve the purpose of making sense of our confused emotions by
externalizing them into black-and-white scenarios. (2003: 4)

All this does not mean that Phoebe thinks there is nothing to fear in her work
with Baphomet. Nor does it mean that she thinks that she has all the answers.
To use Benjamin's (1988) terminology, Phoebe points to the need to both
assert herself as separate from Baphomet and to develop respectful relationships with other people to maintain a healthy sense of self.

Phoebe: I don't fear Baphomet anymore. What I do fear is losing myself
totally to that. I don't want to lose myself in ego. I have my moments of
ego, and I joke with Wildthorn. I don't want to be a handful of people
that I've come across over eight years that have lost themselves and now
are empty souls. I don't want to be the guru. Because, to me, we're all
gurus. We're all followers and we're all leaders.

Conclusion

Contemporary Pagan possession rituals focus on transforming the self through
embodied, emoted, performances. This reflects a broader social trend toward
a focus on self-development and transformation (Greenwood, 2000; Taylor,
2007). Drawing Down the Moon as practised by contemporary mainstream
Witches celebrates the pleasure of sensual life, Heathen seidr rituals are an
engagement in community and the possession rite of Baphomet engages with
the shadow self. One of the key differences between Pagan and Christian
and post-Christian cultures is their understanding of evil (Nussbaum, 1986;
Pagels, 1995). Christianity tends to see 'the good' as unified and pure, and
evil as something completely 'other.' Pagans, in contrast, understand life as
complex and sometimes contradictory. Good and bad are inevitably and
inextricably mixed. This idea was, according to Nussbaum, central to classical
Greek tragedies. Tragedy lies in the fact that when one person pursues 'the
good,' unpleasant things inevitably and unavoidably result for others (1986).
The possession rite of Baphomet provides a moment of reorientation from a
Christian to a Pagan understanding. This reorientation is not simply intellectual, rather it is primarily embodied, emoted and performed.

The Baphomet possession rite is understood by participants as an opportunity to engage with repressed parts of the 'shadow self,' such as sexual desire
and bisexuality. Other participants describe similar work on self-esteem,

poor body image, depression, aggression, and grief. These difficult and often disturbing aspects of the self have often been evaluated as evil and associated with Satan and Satanic 'others.' Arguing along similar lines, Pagels suggests that Satan should be understood 'as a reflection of how we perceive ourselves and those we call "others"' (1995: xviii). However, Satan is also understood as a symbol of 'radical evil' that is associated with deep violation of the moral law (Bernstein, 2002). The Pagan practice and theology of the Baphomet possession rite separates out these two aspects, exploring and honouring the shadow self while also being strongly committed to maintaining respectful, moral relationships.

The Baphomet rite provides an embodied, performed, emotionally intense moment of reorientation and re-evaluation of participants' understandings of good and evil that allows them to work with previously feared and repressed aspects of their self-understandings. This chapter has drawn on the psycho-analytic theory of Benjamin (1988) to analyse these processes. Homo-erotic desire may be named and acknowledged as part of the self, although the individual may choose to remain in a monogamous heterosexual relationship. The primary change is release from the *fear* of homo-erotic desire, and the grief and confusion that this may engender. Baphomet initiates continue to be very conscious of the ethics of respectful relationships, although they are probably equally as likely as any other group of people to be fallible in the performance of these ethics.

Overall, this chapter has demonstrated that contemporary Pagan spirit possession is an embodied practice 'with serious social, cultural, and political consequences' (Stoller, 1995: 7). When Baphomet enters the ritual, this is a moment that transforms the possessed priestess and the other ritualists 'both physically and symbolically.' The ritual engages with symbols that are delib-erately confronting and transgressive, representing aspects of self and society that have been repressed, feared and demonised. The ritualists themselves report that this is a rewarding and emotionally transformative experience with profound consequences.

NOTES

Introduction

1 For TV series, see, for example, Angel, Ghost Whisperer, Medium, Reaper, and Supernatural. For film, see Fry, 2008.
2 Although slightly dated, the literature reviews offered by Boddy (1994: 407–34), Smith (2001: 203–12) and Mayaram (2001: 213–22) provide a fairly exhaustive overview of the academic field up to the end of the twentieth century.
3 Ultimately, none of the approaches identified treats spirit possession in absolute isolation from the others. The academic frames identified here comprise analytical emphases which concentrate on one or a number of dimensions of spirit possession without necessarily denying the existence or validity of other interpretative approaches which focus upon different aspects of spirit possession.
4 The relevance of the hermeneutical or cultural turn for spirit possession studies is that it moves away from a concern with explaining spirit possession by reference to its psychophysical bases and instead concentrates on the interpretative dynamics and sign-based systems through which spirit possession both engenders meaning for and is rendered meaningful by those involved.
5 The emphasis upon Spirit-centred experience articulated by modern charismatic and Pentecostal forms of Christianity has, though, modified inherited possession paradigms (see, Csordas, 1994; Mariano, 2005).
6 The division of agential labour between self and spirit is not always uncontested and may be understood to oscillate relative to, for example, the maturity of the host, type of spirit involved and specific task performed.

Chapter 1

1 The authors wish to thank the Wenner-Gren Foundation for Anthropological Research for its generous support of this research.

Chapter 2

1 Mobutu renamed the country Zaire in 1971. In 1997, Joseph Kabila returned the name of the country to the Democratic Republic of the Congo (DRC).
2 The Kimbanguist trinity comprises Diangienda who represents Papa Simon Kimbangu who himself represented the Holy Spirit, Dialungana who represents

the Son and Kisolokele who represents the Father (see, Mokoko Gampiot, 2004: 228, 240).

3   Collected from the sacred pond of the 'New Jerusalem,' Nkamba water (*Maye ya Nkamba*) is used, along with Nkamba earth, for healing and cleansing purposes.

Chapter 3

1   Research and travel in Sudan in 2001 was facilitated by Dr Ali Abd al-Magid, former director of the Central Veterinary Research Laboratories, and generously funded by a grant from Butler University. Thanks also to Andrew Dawson, Wendy James and Lesley Sharp who read earlier drafts of this chapter and made substantive suggestions for improving the final version.

2   The term 'Red Wind' is preferred today by devout Muslims, who refuse to utter the word zar, believing it to be *haram,* forbidden in Islam.

3   In the past there were at least three forms, all based on belief in a particular type of spirit or 'Red Wind.'

4   In Khartoum in the 1960s, Constantinides found the Ethiopian spirit *Wazir Mama* (Minister of Mama) to be the 'emissary' of other spirits, the 'representative and overseer of all other zayran' (1972: 331). In Hofriyat, the small (pseudonymous) village in northern Sudan where she conducted field research in the 1970s and 1980s, Boddy described the Habbashi spirit *Wilad Mama* (literally 'the children of Mama' but invoked as a single spirit), as the 'vizier of the zayran' (1989: 280). Neither Boddy nor Constantinides elaborate further, though it is significant that the spirits they describe are *kabir,* which carries the double meaning that they are both high-ranking and old. To some extent, this role is now assumed by Bashir and, more recently, Dasholay – though as slaves and 'young/little' spirits they are quite different from earlier 'emissaries.'

5   Found in popular Sufi Islam as well as in zar, *khashf* is a type of clairvoyance which reveals otherwise hidden knowledge.

6   Azrag literally translates as 'Blue,' but is best idiomatically rendered as 'Black.'

7   Formal ceremonies – when drums are beaten and all of the zar spirits summoned – are today held only during the Islamic month of Rajab, known in zar as *Rajabiya.*

Chapter 4

1   Initially supported by the AHRC, recent fieldwork has been funded by the Ford Foundation through the Social Science Research Council, USA (SSRC) as part of an international comparative research project on transnational religion.

2   I use the spelling preferred by Tamils and as given at the Melmaruvathur Centre.

3   Interviews took place at the temple and in the homes of devotees during the period of August 2006 and July 2009.

4   Discussion of the relation between trance and possession in Tamil contexts is undertaken by Bastin, 2002; Diesel, 2002: 5–20; Nabokov, 2000; and Ward, 1984: 307–34.

5   Sacred ash, *vibhuti,* is used throughout ritual procedures, including on parts of the body that are going to be pierced. It is considered to have healing and

protective properties, as well as being imbued with the divine essence of the deity and is therefore another factor emphasising the permeability of the individual.

6   The *Kavadi* is a decorated wooden frame carried on the shoulders by male devotees from which hang small pots of milk to offer to the deity. Many *Kavadi* are like small shrines and heavy to carry. Women carry pots of milk or pots of fruit on their heads as they process to the shrine (see, David, 2008: 217–31; Geaves, 2007; Willford, 2002: 247–80).

Chapter 5

1   This chapter is based on data resulting from sixteen months of fieldwork in Havana, conducted between 2005 and 2008 on Cuban Spiritist practices and the role of the dead in Afro-Cuban religion. The research was funded by the UK's Economic and Social Research Council and the Royal Anthropological Institute. I thank my friends and informants in Cuba, especially Leonel Verdeja Orallo. In the interests of privacy, some of the names given in this text are pseudonyms. This chapter is dedicated to the memory of Teresita Fernández Fernández, astrologer and friend, and the first medium I ever interviewed.

2   Known more commonly as Palo Monte, *Reglas de Congo/Palo* is usually associated with Bantu-speaking slaves brought to Cuba from the east coast of Africa.

3   Unless otherwise stated, all references to Spiritism denote its Cuban form, *espiritismo cruzado*.

4   'Becoming' signifies a journey through which the medium gains awareness of the self and its boundaries.

Chapter 6

1   I wish to thank Andrew Dawson for his editorial suggestions and also Michel Foucault, whose chapter The Prose of the World, in *The Order of Things* (1994), breathed life into these pages.

2   Pandi Kooyil is part of a local economy of temples whose gods and goddesses are famous for specific boons and powers.

3   Pandi's title of *munisvarar* can be translated as 'he who is awakened having realised Isvarar' – another name of Shiva. The term *muni* (sage or saint) is also a title of the Buddha and carries connotations of the fury and anger Shiva directs at those who disturb the ascetic practices he often carries out on the cremation ground.

4   Vengidu clarifies this point because Pandi can also visit in the form of a *karuppu* – a dense, black shadow vaguely resembling a human. Typically, a *karuppu* visit is unpleasant, causing unbearable pressure on the chest.

5   Female orgasm is considered a necessary condition for conception in South India (see Daniel, 1984: 175). This orgasmic intensity also corroborates Pandi's affinity with Shiva whose eroticism is legendary.

6   In a thorough and excellent review of the literature on possession in modern India, Frederick Smith identifies five main paradigmatic approaches, each weighted by Eurocentric agendas: '(1) as a negatively inspired religious phenomenon, (2) as a psychological event, (3) as a social or sociopolitical event that trades in power relations, (4) as a type of shamanism, and (5) as a "real" incursion

of spirits or deities to be taken [uncritically] at face value and addressed with a full cosmological arsenal' (2006: 78).

7   See, Daniel, 1984, for an account of the 'indexical' prominence of South Indian semiotics.

8   For the way the birth of a child can have either deleterious or auspicious effects on prior generations, see, Kapadia, 1995: 82.

9   In South India, Munis are a class of fearsome spirits who serve as protective beings patrolling the perimeters of villages in the night. The diagnosis of *Muni aDi* is literally a discolouration in the shape of a hand on the middle of the back and blue lips, probably signs of heart attack due to shock. I was told that to cross a Muni on his nightly rounds is a frightening experience if one is not morally and ritually clean.

10 'Flowers on a vine' is an often used Tamil metaphor of continuity between the generations; especially generations of women (see, Trawick, 1990: 163).

11 That Pandiammal knew very well how to narrate a reproductive tale of the body was revealed when she described on another occasion and in vivid detail the home birth of her first granddaughter, which nearly killed Rajathiammal.

12 'To kill' (*kolai*) is the term women (and men) commonly used to describe Pandi-induced 'abortions,' as miscarriages are called in the region. The imagery of murder is crude and shocking to modern 'enlightened' sensibilities because it seems to impute a homicidal intent to the god. The metaphor is an honest description of the gore of a miscarriage outside a hospital setting.

13 Thevar women commonly raise a goat alongside a difficult pregnancy for sacrifice to a lineage deity after birth. Sudden blindness in animal or human is usually interpreted as a sign of grave moral wrongdoing.

14 According to Rajathiammal, her father, Veeramalai, was a Muppanar – a caste below Thevars. Writing in 1956, Louis Dumont identified the family in charge of Pandi Kooyil as the even lower caste of Valaiyan (1986: 259).

15 Here 'cow' (*maadu*) stands for 'woman' but carries no pejorative association as cows are auspicious beings in village life, a form of the goddess of wealth, Lakhsmi.

16 Women wash their hair on the last day of their menses. This ritual bath also marks the periodicity of their menses and is thus used as a mnemonic device to track menstrual cycles.

Chapter 7

1   The Word of Life was founded in 1983, and is now based on the outskirts of Uppsala, Sweden. It runs a school for children as well as a Bible school and a university, and sends missionaries to such places as Eastern Europe and South Asia. Its congregation claims that around 3,000 people visit its premises each week.

2   Prosperity Theology emphasises the connection between the possession of faith and 'material' prosperity such as good health and increased wealth. Though originally associated with American charismatics such as Kenneth Hagin, from the 1970s onwards it has become a globally diffused ideology (see, Coleman, 2000).

3   At the original and originating point of being born again, the ability to speak in tongues – receive baptism in the Spirit – becomes a significant authenticating 'sign' of the legitimacy of the experience.

4 'Conviction is confiction, the product or meta-product of a project of world-making engaged in with others' (Lambek, 2007: 74).
5 The meeting referred to here was held by Curt Lahti on 3 April 1987.
6 In the late 1970s, Parsley's original Bible study group formed what became known as Sunset Chapel, and later the Word of Life Church, Canal Winchester, Ohio.

Chapter 8

1 Fieldwork informing this chapter was made possible by grants from the British Academy and the Leverhulme Trust.
2 Kardecism arose in France in the mid-nineteenth century and is so-called after its founder Allan Kardec (1804–1869). Arriving in Brazil in the late-1800s, Kardecism is known both as *Kardecismo* and, more commonly, *espiritismo* (Spiritism).
3 For the martial connotations of this regimentation, see, Dawson, 2008: 183–95.
4 Although in continuity with much of what is elsewhere designated as 'New Age,' the Brazilian *nova era* nevertheless embodies a distinctive configuration of socio-cultural processes and spatio-temporal dynamics. Not to lose sight of this distinctiveness, I translate the term *nova era* as 'new era' rather than New Age (see, Dawson, 2007).
5 The manner in which the concepts of *modernity* in general and (the European-derived) *late-modernity* in particular play out in Brazil are contentious issues. With limited space, however, I can do no more here than acknowledge this point and signal familiarity with those who have contributed to ongoing debates in respect of this issue (see, for example, Martins, 2000: 248–74; Ortiz, 2000: 127–47; Tavolaro, 2008: 109–28).

Chapter 9

1 The Internet is an excellent source of secondary literature on *Shaman King*, with *Wikipedia*'s long entries conveniently listing characters, titles, dates of publication, and much more. Additionally, numerous fan sites provide information on various aspects of *Shaman King*.
2 I cite this edition (as chapter, volume: page) because it is the most famous and served as the basis of the anime.
3 An English summary of the manga is available in *Wikipedia* (*Wikipedia* c), while a Japanese summary of the anime can be found online at Television Tokyo (www.tv-tokyo.co.jp). Because the anime was aired well before the manga had been completed, their plots differ in their second halves.
4 I use the transliteration Takei himself suggested, although this is inconsistent and often deviates from any established system of transliteration. The modified Hepburn system usually employed to transcribe Japanese would, for example, mark lengthened vowels with either macrons or circumflexes. Takei, however, is very inconsistent when writing, for example, 'Yoh' (not 'Yô'), 'Ryu' (not 'Ryû') and 'Bokutou' (not 'Bokutô').
5 Anna is once said to work herself into a state of trance for one of her rituals, but she, too, is in fact fully conscious (16, II: 157–61).

6 Compulsory education until the age of 15 and increased employment opportunities for visually impaired women have rendered undesirable the strenuous work of an *itako*.

Chapter 10

1 Research was undertaken with the approval of the University of Tasmania Human Research Ethics Committee.
2 Photograph by B. Dalton.

BIBLIOGRAPHY

Adami, N. R. 1991. *Religion und Schamanismus der Ainu auf Sachalin: Ein Beitrag zur historischen Völkerkunde Ostasiens*. München: Iudicium Verlag.

Adler, M. 2006. *Drawing Down the Moon: Witches, Druids, Goddess-Worshippers, and Other Pagans in America*. Revised Edition. New York: Penguin.

Antoni, K. 2005. 'Izumo as the "Other Japan:" Construction vs. Reality', *Japanese Religions*, 30.1/2, 1–20.

Appadurai, A. 1996. *Modernity at Large: The Cultural Dimensions of Globalization*. Minneapolis: University of Minnesota Press.

Argyriadis, K. 2005. 'El Desarrollo del Turismo Religioso en la Habana y la Acusación de Mercantilismo', *Desacatos*, 18, 29–52.

Arruda, C., Lapietra, F. and Santana, R. J. 2006. *Centro Livre: Ecletismo Cultural no Santo Daime*. São Paulo: All Print Editora.

Asai, T. 1977. Koropokkuru, in K. Inada, T. Ôshima, T. Kawabata, A. Fukuda, and Y. Mihara Nihon eds. *Mukashibanashi Jiten*. Tokyo: Kôbundô, 362–3.

Asch, S. 1983. *L'église du Prophète Kimbangu*. Paris: Karthala.

Aston, W. G. 1972. *Nihongi: Chronicles of Japan from the Earliest Times to A.D. 697*. Tokyo: Charles E. Tuttle.

Balandier, G. 1955. *Sociologie Actuelle de l'Afrique Noire*. Paris: Presses Universitaires de France.

Banton, M. 1963. 'African Prophets', *Race and Class*, 5, 42–55.

Bargen, D. 1997. *A Woman's Weapon: Spirit Possession in The Tale of Genji*. Honolulu: University of Hawaii Press.

Barnet, M. 2001. *Afro-Cuban Religions*. Princeton: Markus Wiener Publishers.

Bastide, R. 1985. *As Religiões Africanas no Brasil*. São Paulo: Livraria Pioneira Editora.

Bastin, R. 2002. *The Domain of Constant Excess. Plural Worship at the Munnesvaram Temples in Sri Lanka*. New York: Berghahn Books.

Bauman, Z. 2005. *Liquid Life*. Cambridge: Polity.

Beck, U. and Beck-Gernsheim, E. 2002. *Individualization: Institutionalized Individualism and its Social and Political Consequences*. London: Sage.

Behrend, H. and Luig, U. 1999. Introduction, in H. Behrend and U. Luig eds. *Spirit Possession, Modernity and Power in Africa*. Madison: University of Wisconsin Press, xii–xxii.

Benjamin, J. 1988. *The Bonds of Love: Psychoanalysis, Feminism, and the Problem of Domination*. New York: Pantheon Books.

—. 1998. *Shadow of the Other: Intersubjectivity and Gender in Psychoanalysis*. New York: Routledge.

Berger, H. and Ezzy, D. 2007. *Teenage Witches*. New Brunswick: Rutgers University Press.

Berndt, J. 1995. *Phänomen Manga: Comic-Kultur in Japan*. Berlin: Edition Q.

Bernstein, R. 2002. *Radical Evil*. Cambridge: Polity Press.

Besnier, N. 1996. Heteroglossic Discourses on Nukulaelae Spirits, in A. Howard and J. M. Mageo eds. *Spirits in Culture, History and Mind*. New York: Routledge, 75–98.

Blacker, C. 1986. *The Catalpa Bow: A Study of Shamanistic Practices in Japan*. London: Unwin Paperbacks.

Blain, J. 2002. *Nine Worlds of Seid-Magic: Ecstasy and neo-Shamanism in North European Paganism*. London: Routledge.

Bloch, M. and Parry, J. 1982. Introduction: Death and the Regeneration of Life, in M. Bloch and J. Parry eds. *Death and the Regeneration of Life*. Cambridge: Cambridge University Press, 1–44.

Boddy, J. 1988. 'Spirits and Selves in Northern Sudan: The Cultural Therapeutics of Possession and Trance', *American Ethnologist*, 15.1, 4–27.

—. 1989. *Wombs and Alien Spirits: Women, Men, and the Zar Cult in Northern Sudan*. Wisconsin: University of Wisconsin Press.

—. 1994. 'Spirit Possession Revisited: Beyond Instrumentality', *Annual Review of Anthropology*, 23, 407–34.

—. 1998. Afterword: Embodying Ethnography, in M. Lambek and A. Strathern eds. *Bodies and Persons: Comparative Perspectives from Africa and Melanesia*. Cambridge: Cambridge University Press, 252–73.

Bolivar, N. 1990. *Los Orichas en Cuba*. La Habana: Ediciones Unión.

Bolivar, N. and Diaz de Villegas, C. G. 1998. *Ta makuende yaya y las relgas de Palo Monte: mayombe, brillumba, kimbisa, shamalongo*. La Habana: Ediciones Unión.

Bourguignon, E. Ed. 1973. *Religion, Altered States of Consciousness, and Social Change*. Columbus: Ohio State University Press.

—. 1976. *Possession*. San Francisco: Chandler and Sharp.

—. 1979. *Psychological Anthropology: An Introduction to Human Nature and Cultural Differences*. New York: Holt, Rinehart, and Winston.

—. 1995. 'Possession and Social Change in Eastern Africa: Introduction', *Anthropological Quarterly*, 68.2, 71–4.

Brandon, G. 1997. *Santería from Africa to the New World: The Dead Sell Memories*. Bloomington: Indiana University Press.

Braude, A. 1989. *Radical Spirits: Spiritualism and Women's Rights in Nineteenth-Century America*. Boston: Beacon Press.

Brown, D. D. 1994. *Umbanda: Religion and Politics in Urban Brazil.* New York: Columbia University Press.

Brown, D. H. 2003. *Santería Enthroned, Art, Ritual, and Innovation in an Afro-Cuban Religion.* Chicago: University of Chicago Press.

Brown, M. F. 1997. *The Channeling Zone: American Spirituality in an Anxious Age.* Cambridge: Harvard University Press.

Busby, C. 1997. 'Permeable and Partible Persons: A Comparative Analysis of Gender and Body in South India and Melanesia', *Journal of the Royal Anthropological Institute*, 3, 261–78.

Cabrera, L. 1998. *El Monte,* La Habana: Ediciones Universal.

Caldwell, S. 1999. *Oh Terrifying Mother: Sexuality, Violence, and Worship of the Goddess Kali.* New Delhi: Oxford University Press.

Camargo, C. P. 1961. *Kardecismo e Umbanda: Uma Interpretação Sociológica.* São Paulo: Livraria Pioneira Editora.

Canclini, N. 1995. *Hybrid Cultures: Strategies for Entering and Leaving Modernity.* Minneapolis: University of Minnesota Press.

Cavalcanti, M. L. V. de C. 1983. *O Mundo Invisível: Cosmologia, Sistema Ritual e Noção de Pessoa no Espiritismo.* Rio de Janeiro: Zahar Editores.

Chakrabarty, D. 1997. The Time of History and the Times of Gods, in L. Lowe and D. Lloyd eds. *The Politics of Culture in the Shadow of Capitalism.* Durham: Duke University Press, 35–60.

Chamberlain, B. H. 1981. *The Kojiki: Records of Ancient Matters.* Tokyo: Charles E. Tuttle.

Chandrasekharan, E. C. and Thirugnanasambandham, C. 2004. *Glory of Mother Divine–Amma.* Melmaruvathur: Adhiparasakthi Charitable, Medical, Educational, and Cultural Trust.

Chauvet, C. 2007. 'Pilgrimages of the Four Palaces: Reshaping Local and National Identities in Contemporary Northern Vietnam.' Paper presented at Modernities and Dynamics of Tradition in Vietnam: Anthropological Approaches, Binh Chau, Vietnam. December, 2007.

Chilson, C. and Knecht, P. Eds. 2003. *Shamans in Asia.* London: RoutledgeCurzon.

Clammer, J. R., Poirier, S. and Schwimmer, E. 2004. Introduction: The Relevance of Ontologies in Anthropology – Reflections on a New Anthropological Field, in J. R. Clammer, S. Poirier and E. Schwimmer eds. *Figured Worlds: Ontological Obstacles in Intercultural Relations.* Toronto: University of Toronto Press, 3–22.

Clarke, S. 1999. 'Splitting Difference: Psychoanalysis, Hatred and Exclusion', *Journal for the Theory of Social Behavior*, 29.1, 21–35.

Claus, P. 1979. 'Spirit Possession and Spirit Mediumship from the Perspective of Tulu Oral Traditions', *Culture, Medicine and Psychiatry*, 3.1, 29–53.

Cohen, E. 2007. *The Mind Possessed: The Cognition of Spirit Possession in an Afro-Brazilian Religious Tradition.* Oxford: Oxford University Press.

Cohen, E. and Barrett, J. 2008. 'Conceptualizing Spirit Possession: Ethnographic and Experimental Evidence', *Ethos*, 36.2, 246–67.

Cohn, N. 1970. The Myth of Satan and his Human Servants, in M. Douglas ed. *Witchcraft Confessions and Accusations*. London: Routledge, 3–16.

Coleman, S. 2000. *The Globalisation of Charismatic Christianity: Spreading the Gospel of Prosperity*. Cambridge: Cambridge University Press.

—. 2004. 'The Charismatic Gift', *Journal of the Royal Anthropological Institute*, 10.2, 421–42.

—. 2006. When Silence isn't Golden: Charismatic Speech and the Limits of Literalism, in M. Tomlinson and M. Engelke eds. *Ritual and the Limits of Meaning: Case Studies in the Anthropology of Christianity*. Oxford: Berghahn, 39–61.

—. 2010. Constructing the Globe: A Charismatic Sublime, in G. Hüwelmeier and K. Krause eds. *Traveling Spirits: Migrants, Markets and Mobilities*. London: Routledge, 186–202.

—. Forthcoming. Voices: Presence and Prophecy in Charismatic Ritual, in M. Lindhardt ed. *Practicing the Faith: The Ritual Life of Pentecostal-Charismatic Christians*. Oxford: Berghahn.

Comaroff, J. 1985. *Body and Power, Spirit of Resistance: The Culture and History of a South African People*. Chicago: Chicago University Press.

Comaroff, J. and Comaroff, J. 1999. 'Occult Economies and the Violence of Abstraction: Notes from the South African Postcolony', *American Ethnologist*, 26.2, 279–303.

Constantinides, P. 1972. Sickness and the Spirits: A Study of the Zaar Spirit-Possession Cult in Northern Sudan. Ph.D. Dissertation, University of London.

Couto, F. de La R. 2004. Santo Daime: Rito da Ordem, in B. C. Labate and W. S. Araújo eds. *O Uso Ritual da Ayahuasca*. Second Edition. Campinas: Mercado de Letras, 385–411.

Crapanzano, V. 1977. Introduction, in V. Crapanzano and V. Garrison eds. *Case Studies in Spirit Possession*, 1–39.

—. 2006. 'Postface', *Culture and Religion*, 7.2, 199–203.

Crapanzano, V. and Garrison, V. Eds. 1977. *Case Studies in Spirit Possession*. New York: Wiley and Sons.

Crites, S. 1971. 'The Narrative Quality of Experience', *Journal of the American Academy of Religion*, 39.3, 291–311.

Crocker, J. C. 1985. *Vital Souls: Bororo Cosmology, Natural Symbolism, and Shamanism*. Arizona: University of Arizona Press.

Csordas, T. 1994. *The Sacred Self: A Cultural Phenomenology of Charismatic Healing*. Berkeley: University of California Press.

—. 2009. Modalities of Transnational Transcendence, in T. Csordas ed. *Transnational Transcendence: Essays on Religion and Globalization*. Berkeley: University of California Press, 1–23.

Cutié Bressler, A. 2001. *Psiquiatria y Religiosidad Popular*. Santiago de Cuba: Editorial Oriente.

Dalby, A. 2003. *Bacchus*. London: The British Museum Press.

Daniel, V. 1984. *Fluid Signs: Being a Person the Tamil Way*. Berkeley: University of California Press.

David, A. R. 2008. 'Local Diasporas/Global Trajectories. New Aspects of Religious "Performance" in British Tamil Hindu Practice', *Performance Research*, 13.3, 89–99.

—. 2009a. 'Performing for the Gods? Dance and Embodied Ritual in British Hindu Temples', *South Asian Popular Culture*, 7.3, 217–31.

—. 2009b. 'Gendering the Divine: New Forms of Feminine Hindu Worship', *International Journal of Hindu Studies*, 13.3, 337–55.

Davis, W. 1980. *Dojo: Magic and Exorcism in Modern Japan*. Stanford: Stanford University Press.

Dawson, A. 2005. South American Indigenous Religions, in C. H. Partridge ed. *The New Lion Handbook of the World's Religions*. Third Edition. Oxford: Lion Hudson, 114–19.

—. 2007. *New Era – New Religions: Religious Transformation in Contemporary Brazil*. Aldershot: Ashgate

— 2008. Religious Identity and Millenarian Belief in Santo Daime, in A. Day ed. *Religion and the Individual: Belief, Practice, Identity*. Aldershot: Ashgate, 183–95.

De Boeck, F. 2005. 'The Apocalyptic Interlude: Revealing Death in Kinshasa', *African Studies Review*, 48.2, 11–32.

De Heusch, L. 1981. *Why Marry Her? Society and Symbolic Structures*. Cambridge: Cambridge University Press.

Devisch, R. 1994. '"Pillaging Jesus:" Healing Churches and the Villagisation of Kinshasa', *Africa*, 66, 555–86.

—. 2000. Les Églises de Guérison à Kinshasa: Leur Domestication de la Crise des Institutions, in A. Corten and A. Mary eds. *Imaginaires Politiques et Pentecôtismes*. Paris: Karthala, 119–43.

Diangienda Kuntima, J. 1984. *L'Histoire du Kimbanguisme*. Kinshasa: Editions Kimbanguistes.

Diesel, A. 2002. 'Tales of Women's Suffering: Draupadi and Other Amman Goddesses as Role Models for Women', *Journal of Contemporary Religion*, 17.1, 5–20.

Dror, O. 2007. *Cult, Culture, and Authority: Princess Lieu Hanh in Vietnamese History*. Honolulu: University of Hawaii Press.

Dumont, L. 1986. *A South Indian Subcaste: Social Organization and Religion of the Pramalai Kallar*. Delhi: Oxford University Press.

Durand, M. 1959. *Technique et Pantheon Des Mediums Vietnamiens (Dong)*. Paris: École Francaise d'Extreme-Orient.

Eade, D. and Garbin, D. 2007. 'Reinterpreting the Relationship Between Centre and Periphery: Pilgrimage and Sacred Spatialisation among Polish and Congolese Communities in Britain', *Mobilities*, 2.3, 413–24.

Eck, D. L. 1998. *Darsan: Seeing the Divine Image in India*. New York: Columbia University Press.

Eliade, M. 2004. *Shamanism: Archaic Techniques of Ecstasy.* Princeton: Princeton University Press.

Emoff, R. 2001. *Recollections from the Past: Musical Practice and Spirit Possession on the East Coast of Madagascar.* Hanover: Wesleyan University Press.

Engelke, M. 2007. *A Problem of Presence: Beyond Scripture in an African Church.* Berkeley: University of California Press.

English-Lueck, J. A. 2009. 'Deep Diversity and Global Flows: Silicon Valley and the Asian Pacific Region.' Paper presented at the International Conference of Anthropological and Ethnological Sciences, Kunming, China. July, 2009.

Erndl, K. M. 1993. *Victory to the Mother: The Hindu Goddess of Northwest India in Myth, Ritual and Symbol.* Oxford: Oxford University Press.

—. 2007. The Play of the Mother: Possession and Power in Hindu Women's Goddess Rituals, in T. Pintchman ed. *Women's Lives: Women's Rituals in the Hindu Tradition.* Oxford: Oxford University Press, 149–58.

Evans-Pritchard, E. E. 1950. *Witchcraft Oracles and Magic among The Azande.* Second Edition. Oxford: Oxford University Press.

—. 1956. *Nuer Religion.* New York: Clarendon Press.

Faivre, A. 1986. Esotericism, in M. Eliade ed. *Encyclopedia of Religions.* New York: Macmillan, 156–63.

Figarola, J. J. 2006. *La Brujeria Cubana: El Palo Monte, Aproximación al Pensamiento Abstracto de la Cubania.* Santiago de Cuba: Editorial Oriente.

Firth, R. W. 1967. *Tikopia Ritual and Belief.* Boston: Beacon Press.

Fjelstad, K. 1995. Tu Phu Cong Dong: Vietnamese Women And Spirit Possession in the San Francisco Bay Area. Ph.D. Dissertation, University of Hawaii.

—. 2006. We Have Len Dong too: Transnational Aspects of Spirit Possession, in K. Fjelstad and H. Nguyen eds. *Possessed By the Spirits: Mediumship in Contemporary Vietnamese Cultures.* New York: Southeast Asia Program Publications, 95–110.

—. 2010. Spirited Migrations: The Travels of Len Dong Spirits and their Mediums, in G. Hüwelmeier and K. Krause eds. *Traveling Spirits: Migrants, Markets and Mobilities.* New York: Routledge, 52–66.

Flood, G. 1999. *Beyond Phenomenology: Rethinking the Study of Religion.* London: Cassell.

Foucault, M. 1994. *The Order of Things: An Archaeology of the Human Sciences.* New York: Vintage Books.

Fry, C. L. 2008. *Cinema of the Occult: New Age, Satanism, Wicca, and Spiritualism in Film.* Bethlehem: Lehigh University Press.

Fujiwara, K. 2007–2008. *Seirei no Moribito.* 3 Vols. Tokyo: Gangan Comics.

Fuller, C. 1992. *The Camphor Flame.* Princeton: Princeton University Press.

Furuya, Y. 1994. Umbandização dos Cultos Populares na Amazônia: a Integração ao Brasil?, in H. Nakamaki and A. P. Filho eds. *Possessão e Procissão: Religiosidade Popular no Brasil.* Osaka: National Museum of Ethnology, 11–59.

Galvão, E. E. 1955. *Santos e Visagens: Um Estudo da Vida Religiosa de Itá, Amazonas.* São Paulo: Companhia Editôra Nacional.

Garbin, D. 2010. Symbolic Geographies of the Sacred: Diasporic Territorialisation and Charismatic Power in a Transnational Congolese Prophetic Church, in G. Hüwelmeier and K. Krause eds. *Traveling Spirits*, 145–65.

Garoutte, C. and Wambaugh, A. 2007. *Crossing the Water: A Photographic Path to the Afro-Cuban Spirit World*. Durham: Duke University Press.

Geaves, R. 2007. *Saivism in the Diaspora: Contemporary Forms of Skanda Worship*. London: Equinox.

Geertz, C. 1993. *Local Knowledge: Further Essays in Interpretive Anthropology*. London: Fontana Press.

Ginsburg, C. 1992. *Ecstasies: Deciphering the Witches' Sabbath*. London: Penguin Books.

Glick Schiller, N., Caglar, A. and Guldbrandsen, T. C. 2006. 'Beyond the Ethnic Lens: Locality, Globality, and Born-again Incorporation', *American Ethnologist*, 33.4, 612–33.

Goldish, M. Ed. 2003. *Spirit Possession in Judaism: Cases and Contexts from the Middle Ages to the Present*. Detroit: Wayne State University Press.

Goulart, S. 2004. Contrastes e Continuidades em uma Tradição Amazônica: As Religiões da Ayahuasca. PhD Dissertation, State University of Campinas.

Greenwood, S. 2000. *Magic, Witchcraft and the Otherworld*. Oxford: Berg.

Grimes, R. 2000. *Deeply into the Bone: Re-inventing Rites of Passage*. Berkeley: University of California Press.

Guimarães, M. B. L. 1992. A 'Lua Branca' de Seu Tupinamba e de Mestre Irineu: Estudo de Caso de um Terreiro de Umbanda. Masters Dissertation, Instituto de Filosofia e Ciências Sociais da Universidade Federal do Rio de Janeiro.

Hagedorn, K. J. 2001. *Divine Utterances: The Performance of Afro-Cuban Santería*. Washington: Smithsonian Institute Press.

Hallowell, A. I. 1960. *Ojibwa Ontology: Behavior, and Worldview*. New York: Columbia University Press.

Hanegraaff, W. J. 1996. *New Age Religion and Western Culture: Esotericism in the Mirror of Secular Thought*. Leiden: Brill.

Harris, H. 2006. *Yoruba in Diaspora: An African Church in London*. New York: Palgrave Macmillan.

Harvey, G. 1997. *Listening People, Speaking Earth: Contemporary Paganism*. London: C. Hurst and Co.

Hiltebeitel, A. and Erndl, K. M. Eds. 2000. *Is the Goddess a Feminist? The Politics of the South Asian Goddess*. Sheffield: Sheffield Academic Press.

Holbraad, M. 2007. The Power of Powder: Multiplicity and Motion in the Divinatory Cosmology of Cuban Ifá (or mana, again), in A. Henare, M. Holbraad and S. Wastell eds. *Thinking Through Things: Theorising Artefacts Ethnographically*. New York: Routledge, 189–225.

Howard, A. and Mageo, J. M. 1996. Introduction, in J. M. Mageo and A. Howard eds. *Spirits in Culture, History, and Mind*. London: Routledge, 1–10.

Hutton, R. 1999. *The Triumph of the Moon: A History of Modern Pagan Witchcraft*. Oxford: Oxford University Press.

Hüwelmeier, G. and Krause, K. Eds. 2010. *Traveling Spirits: Migrants, Markets and Mobilities*. London: Routledge.

Hüwelmeier, G. and Krause, K. 2010. Introduction, in G. Hüwelmeier and K. Krause eds. *Traveling Spirits*, 1–16.

Ishihara, M. 1985. *Shintei Gishi Wajinden, hoka Sanpen: Chûgoku Seishi Nihonden (1)*. Tokyo: Iwanami Shoten.

Ishii, K. 1997. *Dêtabukku: Gendai Nihonjin no Shûkyô: Sengo Gojûnen no Shûkyô Ishiki to Shûkyô Kôdô*. Tokyo: Shin'yôsha.

Ishizuka, T. 1959. *Nihon no Tsukimono*. Tokyo: Miraisha.

Jackson, N. and Howard, M. 2003. *The Pillars of Tubal Cain*. Milverton: Capall Bann Publishing.

James, W. 1979. *'Kwanim Pa. The Making of the Uduk People*. Oxford: Clarendon Press.

—. 2007. *War And Survival In Sudan's Frontierlands. Voices From The Blue Nile*. Oxford: Oxford University Press.

Johnson, D. H. 1988. Sudanese Military History from the Eighteenth to the Twentieth Century, in L. Archer ed. *Slavery and Other Forms of Unfree Labor*. London: Routledge, 142–86.

—. 1989. 'The Structure of a Legacy: Military History in Northeast Africa', *Ethnohistory*, 36.1, 72–88.

Johnson, P. C. 2007. *Diaspora Conversions. Black Carib Religion and the Recovery of Africa*. Berkeley: California University Press.

Johnson, P. C. and Keller, M. 2006. 'The Work of Possessions(s)', *Culture and Religion*, 7.2, 111–22.

Johnson, R. 1991. *Owning Your Own Shadow: Understanding the Dark Side of the Psyche*. San Francisco: Harper Collins.

Jules-Rosette, B. 1997. 'At the Threshold of the Millennium: Prophetic Movements and Independent Churches in Central and Southern Africa', *Archives des Sciences Sociales des Religions*, 99.1, 153–67.

Junior, A. M. A. 2007. Tambores para a Rainha da Floresta: A Inserção da Umbanda no Santo Daime. Masters Dissertation, Pontifícia Universidade Católica de São Paulo.

Kapadia, K. 1995. *Siva and Her Sisters: Gender, Caste, and Class in Rural South India*. Oxford: Westview Press.

—. 1996. 'Dancing the Goddess: Possession and Class in Tamil South India', *Modern Asian Studies*, 30.2, 423–45.

—. 2000. Pierced by Love: Tamil Possession, Gender and Caste, in J. Leslie and M. McGee eds. *Invented Identities: The Interplay of Gender, Religion and Politics*. New Delhi: Oxford University Press, 181–202.

Kardec, A. 2007. *The Mediums' Book*. Brasília: Conselho Espírita Internacional.

—. 2008. *The Spirits' Book*. Brasília: Conselho Espírita Internacional.

Keane, W. 2007. *Christian Moderns: Freedom and Fetish in the Mission Encounter*. Berkeley: University of California Press.

Kearney, R. 2003. *Strangers, Gods and Monsters: Interpreting Otherness*. London: Routledge.

Keller, M. 2002. *The Hammer and the Flute: Women, Power, and Spirit Possession*. Baltimore: John Hopkins University Press.

Kenyon, S. M. 1991. The Story of a Tin Box: Zar in the Sudanese town of Sennar, in I. M. Lewis, A. al-Safi and S. Hurreiz eds. *Women's Medicine. The Zar-Bori Cult in Africa and Beyond*. Edinburgh: Edinburgh University Press, 100–17.

—. 1996. The Past Imperfect: Remembering as Moral Practice, in P. Antze and M. Lambek eds. *Tense Past: Cultural Essays in Trauma and Memory*. London: Routledge, 235–54.

—. 2009. 'Zainab's Story: Slavery, Women and Community in Colonial Sudan', *Urban Anthropology and Studies of Cultural Systems and World Economic Development*, 38.1, 33–77.

Kim, C. 2003. *Korean Shamanism: The Cultural Paradox*. Aldershot: Ashgate.

Kishimoto, M. 1999–. 'Naruto,' *Shônen Jump* 1999. 43–. Tokyo: Shûeisha.

Klaniczay, G. and Pocs, E. Eds. 2005. *Communicating with the Spirits: Christian Demonology and Popular Mythology*. Budapest: Central European University Press.

Klass, M. 2003. *Mind Over Mind: The Anthropology and Psychology of Spirit Possession*. New York: Rowman and Littlefield Publishers.

Klimo, J. 1998. *Channeling: Investigations on Receiving Information from Paranormal Sources*. Second Edition. Berkeley: North Atlantic Books.

Knott, K. 2005. *The Location of the Sacred*. London: Equinox.

Kopytoff, I. 1971. 'Ancestors as Elders in Africa', *Africa*, 41, 129–42.

Kramer, F. 1993. *The Red Fez: Art and Spirit Possession in Africa*. London: Verso.

Krause, K. 2008. Spiritual Spaces in Post-Industrial Places: Transnational Migrant Churches in North East London, in M. P. Smith and J. Eade eds. *Transnational Ties: Cities, Identities, and Migrations*. New Jersey: Transaction Publishers, 109–30.

Labate, B. C. 2004. *A Reinvenção do Uso da Ayahuasca nos Centros Urbanos*. Campinas: Mercado de Letras.

Labate, B. C. and Pacheco, G. 2004. Matrizes Maranhenses do Santo Daime, in B. C. Labate and W. S. Araújo eds. *O Uso Ritual da Ayahuasca*, 303–44.

Lachatañaré, R. 2001. *El Sistema Religioso de los Afrocubanos*. La Habana: Editorial de Ciencias Sociales.

Laderman, C. and Roseman, M. Eds. 1995. *The Performance of Healing*. New York: Routledge.

Lambek, M. 1980. 'Spirits and Spouses: Possession as a System of Communication among the Malagasy Speakers of Mayotte', *American Ethnologist*, 7.2, 318–31.

—. 1981. *Human Spirits: A Cultural Account of Trance in Mayotte*. Cambridge: Cambridge University Press.

—. 2007. On Catching Up with Oneself: Learning to Know that One Means what One Does, in D. Berliner and R. Sarró eds. *Learning Religion: Anthropological Approaches*. Oxford: Berghahn, 65–81.

Lambek, M. 2010. Traveling Spirits: Unconcealment and Undisplacement, in G. Hüwelmeier and K. Krause eds. *Traveling Spirits*, 17–36.

Langdon, E. J. M. and Baer, G. Eds. 1992. *Portals of Power: Shamanism in South America*. Albuquerque: University of New Mexico Press.

Larsson, V. and Endres, K. 2006. Children of the Spirits, Followers of a Master: Spirit Mediums in Post-Renovation Vietnam, in K. Fjelstad and H. Nguyen eds. *Possessed By the Spirits*, 143–60.

Lawrence, P. 2003. Kali in a Context of Terror: The Tasks of the Goddess in Sri Lanka's Civil War, in R. McDermott and J. Kripal eds. *Encountering Kali: In the Margins, at the Center, in the West*. Berkeley: University of California Press, 100–23.

Leiris, M. 1934. 'Le Culte des Zars a Gondar (Ethiopie Septentrionale)', *Aethiopica*, 2.3/4, 96–103 and 125–36.

—. 1938. 'La Croyance aux Genies "Zar" en Ethiopie du nord', *Journal de la Psychologie Normale et Pathologique*, 35.1/2, 108–25.

Leslau, W. 1949. 'An Ethiopian Argot of People Possessed by a Spirit', *Africa*, 19.3, 204–12.

Levitt, P. 2007. *God Needs No Passport: Immigrants and the Changing American Religious Landscape*. New York: The New Press.

Levy, R. I., Mageo, J. M. and Howard, A. 1996. Gods, Spirits, and History, in J. M. Mageo and A. Howard eds. *Spirits in Culture, History, and Mind*, 11–28.

Lewis, I. M. 1986. *Religion in Context: Cults and Charisma*. Cambridge: Cambridge University Press.

—. 2003. *Ecstatic Religion: A Study of Spirit Possession and Shamanism*. Third Edition. London: Routledge.

Lewis, I. M., al-Safi, A. and Hurreiz, S. Eds. 1991. *Women's Medicine: The Zar-Bori Cult in Africa and Beyond*. Edinburgh: Edinburgh University Press.

Lindquist, G. 1997. *Shamanic Performances on the Urban Scene: Neo-shamanism in Contemporary Sweden*. Stockholm: Stockholm University Press.

LiPuma, E. 1998. Modernity and Forms of Personhood in Melanesia, in M. Lambek and A. Strathern eds. *Bodies and Persons: Comparative Perspectives from Africa and Melanesia*. Cambridge: Cambridge University Press, 53–79.

Luhrmann, T. 2007. How do you Learn to Know that it is God who Speaks?, in D. Berliner and R. Sarró eds. *Learning Religion*, 83–102.

Lum, K. A. 2000. *Praising his Name in the Dance: Spirit Possession in the Spiritual Baptist Faith and Orisha Work in Trinidad, West Indies*. Amsterdam: Overseas Publishers Association.

MacGaffey, W. 1983. *Modern Kongo Prophets: Religion in a Plural Society*. Bloomington: Indiana University Press.

Maderdonner, M. 1986. Kinder-Comics als Spiegel der gesellschaftlichen Entwicklung Japans, in M. Maderdonner and E. Bachmayer eds. *Aspekte Japanischer Comics*. Wien: Institut für Japanologie, 1–94.

Maity, P. K. 1989. *Human Fertility Cults and Rituals of Bengal: A Comparative Study*. New Delhi: Ahhinav Publications.

Makris, G. P. 2000. *Changing Masters: Spirit Possession and Identity Construction among Slave Descendents and Other Subordinates in the Sudan*. Evanston: Northwestern University Press.

Mariano, R. 2005. *Neopentecostais: Sociologia do Novo Pentecostalismo no Brasil*. Second Edition. São Paulo: Edições Loyola.

Marriott, M. 1976. Hindu Transactions: Diversity without Dualism, in B. Kapferer ed. *Transaction and Meaning: Directions in the Anthropology of Exchange and Symbolic Behavior*. Philadelphia: Institute for the Study of Human Issues, 109–42.

Martin, M. L. 1981. *Simon Kimbangu, un Prophète et son Eglise*. Lausanne: Editions du Soc.

Martins, J. de S. 2000. The Hesitations of the Modern and the Contradictions of Modernity in Brazil, V. Schelling ed. *Through the Kaleidoscope: The Experience of Modernity in Latin America*. London: Verso, 248–74.

Maskens, M. 2008. 'Migration et Pentecôtisme à Bruxelles', *Archives des Sciences Sociales des Religions*, 143, 49–69.

Maués, R. H. and Villacorta, G. M. 2004. Pajelança e Encantaria Amazônica, in R. Prandi ed. *Encantaria Brasileira: O Livro dos Mestres, Caboclos e Encantados*. Rio de Janeiro: Pallas, 11–58.

Mauss, M. 1934. 'Les Techniques du Corps', *Journal de Psychologie*, 32.3/4, 271–93.

Mayaram, S. 2001. 'Recent Anthropological Works on Spirit Possession', *Religious Studies Review*, 27.3, 213–22.

McGarry, M. 2008. *Ghosts of Futures Past: Spiritualism and the Cultural Politics of Nineteenth-Century America*. Berkeley: University of California Press.

Mélice, A. 2001. 'Le Kimbanguisme: Un Millénarisme Dynamique de la Terre aux Cieux', *Royal Academy of Overseas Science, Bulletin des Séances*, 47, 35–54.

—. 2006. 'Un terrain fragmenté: Le Kimbanguisme et ses Ramifications', *Civilisations*, 49.1/2, 67–76.

Metzner, R. 2008. *The Expansion of Consciousness*. Berkeley: Regent Press.

Mokoko Gampiot, A. 2004. *Kimbanguisme et Identité Noire*. Paris: L'Harmattan.

—. 2008. Kimbanguism as a Migrants' Religion in Europe, in A. Adogame, R. Gerloff and K. Hock eds. *Christianity in Africa and the Africa Diaspora: The Appropriation of a Scattered Heritage*. London: Continuum, 304–14.

Molyneux, G. 1990. 'The Place and Function of Hymns in the EJCSK', *Journal of Religion in Africa*, 20.2, 153–87.

Morin, K. M. and Guelke, J. K. 2007. *Women, Religion, and Space*. New York: Syracuse University Press.

Morris, I. 1970. *The Pillow Book of Sei Shônagon*. Harmondsworth: Penguin Books.

Moura da Silva, E. 2006. Similaridades e Diferenças entre Estilos de Espiritualidade Metafísica: O Caso do Círculo Esotérico da Comunhão do Pensamento (1908–1943), in A. C. Isaia ed. *Orixás e Espíritos: O Debate Interdisciplinar na Pesquisa Contemporânea*. Uberlândia: EDUFU, 225–40.

Murayama, S. 1980. Onmyôdô, in T. Sakamoto *et al.* eds. *Kokushi Daijiten*. Vol. 2. Tokyo: Yoshikawa Kôbunkan, 990–1.

Nabokov, I. 2000. *Religion Against the Self: An Ethnography of Tamil Rituals.* New York: Oxford University Press.

Napier, S. J. 1996. *The Fantastic in Modern Japanese Literature: The Subversion of Modernity.* London: Routledge.

Narayanan, V. 2000. 'Diglossic Hinduism: Liberation and Lentils', *Journal of the American Academy of Religion*, 68.4, 761–79.

—. 2007. Performing Arts, Re-forming Rituals: Women and Social Change in South India, in T. Pintchman ed. *Women's Lives*, 177–98.

Naumann, N. 1988. *Die einheimische Religion Japans. Teil 1: Bis zum Ende der Heian–Zeit. Handbuch der Orientalistik*, Vol.4.1.1. Leiden: E. J. Brill.

—. 1989. 'Die Wo-Königin Pi-mi-hu und ihr "Weg der Dämonen"', *Bochumer Jahrbuch zur Ostasienforschung*, 13, 309–26.

Ndaya, J. 2008. '*Prendre le Bic:' Le Combat Spirituel Congolais et les Transformations Sociales.* Leiden: ASC.

Ngo, D. T. 1996. *Dao Mau o Vietnam.* Hanoi: Nha Xuat Ban Van Hoa Thong Tin.

—. 2002. *Hat Van.* Hanoi: Nha Xuat Ban Van Hoa Dan Toc.

Nguyen, K. K. 1983. 'Vietnamese Spirit Mediumship: A Tentative Reinterpretation of its Basic Terminology', *Vietnam Forum*, 1, 24–30.

Nguyen, T. H. 2002. The Religion of the Four Palaces: Mediumship and Therapy in Viet Culture. PhD Dissertation, Indiana University.

Nicoletti, M. 2004. *Shamanic Solitudes: Ecstasy, Madness and Spirit Possession in the Nepal Himalayas.* Kathmandu: Vajra Publications.

Nieswand, B. 2005. Charismatic Christianity in the Context of Migration: Social Status, the Experience of Migration and the Construction of Selves among Ghanaian Migrants in Berlin, in A. Adogame and C. Weissköppel eds. *Religion in the Context of African Migration.* Bayreuth: Thielman and Breitinger, 243–65.

Nilsson, S. 1989. *Befria Mitt Folk.* Uppsala: Livets Ords Förlag.

Norton, B. 2000. 'Vietnamese Mediumship Rituals: the Musical Construction of the Spirits', *The World of Music*, 42.2, 75–97.

—. 2006. 'Hot-Tempered' Women And 'Effeminate Men:' The Performance Of Music And Gender In Vietnamese Mediumship, in K. Fjelstad and H. Nguyen eds. *Possessed by the Spirits*, 55–76.

Nussbaum, M. 1986. *The Fragility of Goodness.* Cambridge: Cambridge University Press.

Oesterreich, T. K. 1930. *Possession, Demoniacal and Other, among Primitive Races, in Antiquity, the Middle Ages, and Modern Times.* New York: R. R. Smith.

Ong, A. 1987. *Spirits of Resistance and Capitalist Discipline: Factory Women in Malaysia.* Albany: State University of New York Press.

Ortiz, R. 2000. Popular Culture, Modernity and Nation, in V. Schelling ed. *Through the Kaleidoscope*, 127–47.

Osella, F. and Osella, C. 1999. Seepage of Divinised Power through Social, Spiritual and Bodily Boundaries: Some Aspects of Possession in Kerala, in J. Assayag and G. Tarabout eds. *La Possession en Asie du Sud: Parole, Corps, Territoire.* Paris: EHESS, 183–210.

Otto, R. 1923. *The Idea of the Holy.* Oxford: Oxford University Press.

Otto, W. 1965. *Dionysus: Myth and Cult.* Bloomington: Indiana University Press.

Owen, A. 1989. *The Darkened Room: Women, Power, and Spiritualism in Late Victorian England.* London: Virago Press.

Pagels, E. 1995. *The Origin of Satan.* New York: Vintage Books.

Palmié, S. 2002. *Wizards and Scientists: Explorations in Afro-Cuban Modernity and Tradition.* Durham: Duke University Press.

Paper, J. 1995. *The Spirits are Drunk: Comparative Approaches to Chinese Religion.* Albany: State University of New York Press.

Peters, L. G. and Price-Williams, D. 1983. 'A Phenomenological Overview of Trance', *Transcultural Psychiatric Research Review*, 20.1, 5–39.

Pike, S. 2001. *Earthly Bodies, Magical Selves: Contemporary Pagans and the Search for Community.* Berkeley: University of California Press.

Phillipps, S. 1996. *Erzählform Manga: Eine Analyse der Zeitstrukturen in Tezuka Osamus 'Hi no Tori' ('Phönix').* Wiesbaden: Harrassowitz Verlag.

Placido, B. 2001. '"It's All to do with Words:" An Analysis of Spirit Possession in the Venezuelan Cult of María Lionza', *Journal of the Royal Anthropological Institute*, 7.2, 207–24.

Polari, A. de A. 1999. *Forest of Visions: Ayahuasca, Amazonian Spirituality and the Santo Daime Tradition.* Rochester: Park Street Press.

Prandi, R. 1991. *Os Candomblés de São Paulo: A Velha Magia na Metrópole Nova.* São Paulo: Editora Hucitec.

Pype, K. 2006. 'Dancing for God or the Devil: Pentecostal Discourse on Popular Dance in Kinshasa', *Journal of Religion in Africa*, 36.3/4, 296–318.

Rabelo, M. C. M., Mota, S. R. and Almeida, C. R. 2009. 'Cultivating the Senses and Giving in to the Sacred: Notes on Body and Experience among Pentecostal Women in Salvador, Brazil', *Journal of Contemporary Religion*, 24.1, 1–18.

Rasmussen, S. J. 2006. *Spirit Possession and Personhood among the Kel Ewey Tuareg.* Cambridge: Cambridge University Press.

Reynolds, H. B. 1980. The Auspicious Married Woman, in S. S. Wadley and S. B. Daniel eds. *The Powers of Tamil Women.* Syracuse: Syracuse University Press, 35–60.

Rietveld, H. C. 2009. Ephemeral Spirit: Sacrificial Cyborg and Communal Soul, in G. St John ed. *Rave Culture and Religion.* London: Routledge, 46–61.

Robinson, C. 1999. *Tradition and Liberation: the Hindu Tradition in the Indian Women's Movement.* Surrey: Curzon.

Román, R. 2007. *Governing Spirits: Religion, Miracles, and Spectacles in Cuba and Puerto Rico, 1898–1956.* Chapel Hill: University of North Carolina Press.

Rosenthal, J. 1998. *Possession, Ecstasy and Law in Ewe Voodoo.* Charlottesville: University Press of Virginia.

Rotermund, H. O. 1967. *Die Yamabushi. Aspekte ihres Glaubens, Lebens und ihrer sozialen Funktion im japanischen Mittelalter.* Hamburg: Monographien zur Völkerkunde V.

Rouget, G. 1985. *Music and Trance: A Theory of the Relations between Music and Possession*. Chicago: Chicago University Press.

Sánchez, R. 2008. 'Seized by the Spirit: The Mystical Foundation of Squatting among Pentecostals in Caracas (Venezuela) Today', *Public Culture*, 20.2, 267–305.

Santos, J. L. dos. 2004. *Espiritismo: Uma Religião Brasileira*. Campinas: Editora Átomo.

Saraiva, C. 2008. 'Transnational Migrants and Transnational Spirits: An African Religion in Lisbon', *Journal of Ethnic and Migration Studies*, 34.2, 253–69.

Sarró, R. and Blanes R. 2009. 'Prophetic Diasporas: Moving Religion across the Lusophone Atlantic', *African Diaspora*, 2.1, 52–72.

Sarró, R., Blanes, R. and Viegas, F. 2008. 'La Guerre dans la Paix. Ethnicité et Angolanité dans l'Église Kimbanguiste de Luanda', *Politique Africaine*, 110, 84–101.

Satô, N. 1981. 'The Initiation of the Religious Specialists Kamisan: A Few Observations', *Japanese Journal of Religious Studies*, 8.3/4, 149–86.

Schein, L. 1998. Forged Transnationality and Oppositional Cosmopolitanism, in M. P. Smith and L. E. Guarnizo eds. *Transnationalism From Below*. New Brunswick: Transaction Publishers, 291–313.

Schmidt, B. and Huskinson, L. Eds. 2010. *Spirit Possession and Trance: New Interdisciplinary Perspectives*. London: Continuum.

Sered, S. S. 1994. *Priestess, Mother, Sacred Sister: Religions Dominated by Women*. New York: Oxford University Press.

Sharp, L. A. 1993. *The Possessed and the Dispossessed: Spirits, Identity and Power in a Madagascar Migrant Town*. Berkeley: University of California Press.

—. 1995. 'Playboy Princely Spirits of Madagascar: Possession as Youthful Commentary and Social Critique', *Anthropological Quarterly*, 68.2, 75–88.

Shaw, R. 2002. *Memories of the Slave Trade. Ritual and the Historical Imagination in Sierra Leone*. Chicago: University of Chicago Press.

Shimazono, S. 1996. *Seishin Sekai no Yukue: Gendai Sekai to Shinreisei Undô*. Tokyo: Tôkyôdô Shuppan.

—. 1999. '"New Age Movements" or "New Spirituality Movements and Culture"', *Social Compass*, 46.2, 121–33.

Shimizu, S. 2004. Nihon Animêshon ni Komerareteiru Messêji, in K. Kusaka ed. *Entertainment Goes Pop!: UCLA Manga and Anime Course*. Tokyo: The Tokyo Foundation, 20–31.

Shoaps, R. 2002. '"Pray Earnestly:" The Textual Construction of Personal Involvement in Pentecostal Prayer and Song', *Journal of Linguistic Anthropology*, 12.1, 34–71.

Simons, R. C. 1973. *Floating in the Air, Followed by the Wind: Thaipusam – A Hindu Festival*. Filmmaker, G. Pfaff.

Sluhovsky, M. 2007. *Believe not Every Spirit: Possession, Mysticism and Discernment in Early Modern Catholicism*. Chicago: Chicago University Press.

Smith, F. M. 2001. 'The Current State of Possession Studies as a Cross-Disciplinary Project', *Religious Studies Review*, 27.3, 203–12.

—. 2006. *The Self Possessed: Deity and Spirit Possession in South Asian Literature and Civilization*. New York: Columbia University Press.

Smyers, K. 1999. *The Fox and the Jewel: Shared and Private Meanings in Contemporary Japanese Inari Worship*. Honolulu: University of Hawaii Press.

Spaulding, J. 1982. 'Slavery, Land Tenure and Social Class in the Northern Turkish Sudan', *The International Journal of African Historical Studies*, 15.1, 1–20.

—. 1985. *The Heroic Age in Sinnar*. Ethiopian Series Monograph no. 15. East Lansing: Michigan State University African Studies Center.

Spaulding, J. and Beswick, S. 1995. 'Sex, Bondage and the Market: the Emergence of Prostitution in Northern Sudan', *Journal of the History of Sexuality*, 5.4, 512–34.

Staemmler, B. 1999. The Shugendô, in J. Van Alphen ed. *Enkû 1632–1695: Timeless Images from 17th Century Japan*. Antwerp: Etnografisch Museum Antwerpen, 78–97.

—. 2009. *Chinkon Kishin: Mediated Spirit Possession in Japanese New Religions*. Hamburg: LIT Verlag.

Stoller, P. 1989. *Fusion of the Worlds: An Ethnography of Possession Among the Songhay of Niger*. Chicago: University of Chicago Press.

—. 1995. *Embodying Colonial Memories: Spirit Possession, Power, and the Hauka in West Africa*. New York: Routledge.

Styan, D. 2003. La Nouvelle Vague? Recent Francophone Settlement in London, in K. Koser ed. *New African Diasporas*. London: Routledge, 17–37.

Sugirtharajah, S. 1994. Hinduism, in J. Holm and J. Bowker eds. *Women in Religion*. London: Pinter, 59–83.

Sullivan, L. E. 1988. *Icanchu's Drum: An Orientation to Meaning in South American Religions*. New York: Macmillan Publishing.

Sylvan, R. 2005. *Trance Formation: The Spiritual and Religious Dimensions of Global Rave Culture*. New Edition. London: Routledge.

Takei, H. 1998–2005. *Shaman King*. 32 Vols. Tokyo: Shûeisha.

—. 2007. *Butsu Zone*. 3 Vols. Tokyo: Shûeisha.

Tarabout, G. 1999. Prologue, in J. Assayag and G. Tarabout eds. *La Possession en Asie du Sud*, 9–30.

Taussig, M. 1987. *Shamanism, Colonialism, and the Wild Man: A Study in Terror and Healing*. Chicago: Chicago University Press.

Tavolaro, S. B. F. 2008. '"Neither Traditional nor Fully Modern…" Two Classical Sociological Approaches on Contemporary Brazil', *International Journal of Political Cultural Sociology*, 19, 109–28.

Taylor, C. 2007. *A Secular Age*. Cambridge: Belknap Press of the Harvard University Press.

Television Tokyo. 'Sutôrî'. www.tv-tokyo.co.jp/anime/shaman/story.html. Accessed, 23 October 2009.

Ter Haar, G. 1998. *Halfway to Paradise: African Christians in Europe*. Cardiff: Cardiff Academic Press.

Tezuka, O. 1992. *Hi no Tori No. 1: Reimei–hen*. Tokyo: Kadokawa Bunko.

The Spiritual Beacon. 2001. 'To get Arul Vaakku (Oracle)'. 1.6/7, 1–8. www.adhipar-asakthi.org. Accessed, 10 August 2008.

Thomas, J. B. 2008. Manga to Shûkyô no Genzai: 'Nijûseiki Shônen' to Nijûissseiki no Shûkyô Ishiki, in K. S. Kenkyûjo ed. *Gendai Shûkyô 2008: Media ga Umidasu Kamigami*. Tokyo: Akiyama Shoten, 120–42.

Till, R. 2009. Possession Trance Ritual in Electronic Dance Music Culture: A Popular Ritual Technology for Reenchantment, Addressing the Crisis of the Homeless Self, and Reinserting the Individual into the Community, in C. Deacy and E. Arweck eds. *Exploring Religion and the Sacred in a Media Age*. Farnham: Ashgate, 169–88.

Tishken, J. E. 2002. *Prophecy and Power in Afro-Christian Churches: a Comparative Analysis of the Nazareth Baptist Church and the Église Kimbanguiste*. PhD Dissertation, The University of Texas at Austin.

Tomoe. 'Funbari ga Oka Tsûa Gaido', in *Rîra Rîra*. http://cabin.jp/reera/gaido1. html. Accessed, 23 October 2009.

Trawick, M. 1990. *Notes on Love in a Tamil Family*. Berkeley: University of California Press.

Tsujimura, S. 2008. Shôhi Shakai no 'Shûkyô:' Supirichuarubûmu no Kage de, in K. S. Kenkyûjo ed. *Gendai Shûkyô 2008*, 216–29.

Turner, E. 1992. Preface, in E. Turner with W. Blodgett, S. Kahona and F. Benwa, *Experiencing Ritual: A New Interpretation of African Healing*. Philadelphia: University of Pennsylvania Press, xi–xiii.

—. 1993. 'The Reality of Spirits: A Tabooed or Permitted Field of Study?' *Anthropology of Consciousness*, 4, 9–12.

Turner, V. 1969. *The Ritual Process*. New York: Cornell University Press.

Uehashi, N. 2006. *Seirei no Moribito*. Tokyo: Kaiseisha.

Valiente, D. 2000. *Charge of the Goddess*. Brighton: Hexagon Hoopix.

Vásquez, M. A. and Marquardt, M. F. 2003. *Globalizing the Sacred: Religion Across the Americas*. New Brunswick: Rutgers University Press.

Vertovec, S. 2000. *The Hindu Diaspora: Comparative Patterns*. London: Routledge.

Voeks, R. A. 1997. *Sacred Leaves of Candomblé: African Magic, Medicine, and Religion in Brazil*. Austin: University of Texas Press.

Wafer, J. 1991. *The Taste of Blood: Spirit Possession in Brazilian Candomblé*. Philadelphia: University of Pennsylvania Press.

Wallis, R. J. 2003. *Shamans/Neo-Shamans: Ecstasy, Alternative Archaeologies, and Contemporary Pagans*. London: Routledge.

Ward, C. 1984. 'Thaipusam in Malaysia: A Psycho-Anthropological Analysis of Ritual Trance, Ceremonial Possession and Self-Mortification Practices', *Ethos*, 12.4, 307–34.

Washington, P. 1995. *Madame Blavatsky's Baboon: A History of the Mystics, Mediums, and Misfits Who Brought Spiritualism to America*. New York: Schocken Books.

Wastiau, B. 2000. *Mahamba: The Transforming Arts of Spirit Possession among the Luvale-speaking People of the Upper Zambezi*. Fribourg: Fribourg University Press.

Weber, M. 1949. 'Objectivity' in Social Science and Social Policy, in E. A. Shils and H. A. Finch eds. *Max Weber: The Methodology of the Social Sciences*. New York: The Free Press, 50–112.

Werbner, P. 2002. *Imagined Diasporas Among Manchester Muslims: the Public Performance of Pakistani Transnational Identity Politics*. Oxford: James Currey.

Wikipedia a. 'Takei Hiroyuki'. http://ja.wikipedia.org/wiki/武井宏之. Accessed, 23 October 2009.

Wikipedia b. 'Shâman Kingu'. http://ja.wikipedia.org/wiki/シャーマンキング. Accessed, 23 October 2009.

Wikipedia c. 'List of *Shaman King* characters'. http://en.wikipedia.org/wiki/List_of_Shaman_King_chapters. Accessed, 23 October 2009.

Willford, A. 2002. '"Weapons of the Meek:" Ecstatic Ritualism and Strategic Ecumenism among Tamil Hindus in Malaysia', *Identities: Global Studies in Culture and Power*, 9.2, 247–80.

Winkelman, M. and Peek, P. 2004. Introduction, in M. Winkelman and P. Peek eds. *Divination and Healing: Potent Vision*. Tucson: University of Arizona Press, 3–25.

Wright, R. 2002. The Baniwa, in L. E. Sullivan ed. *Native Religions & Cultures of Central and South America*. New York: Continuum, 221–35.

Yamanaka, H. 1996. Manga Bunka no naka no Shûkyô, in S. Shimazono and K. Ishii eds. *Shôhi sareru Shûkyô*. Tokyo: Shunjûsha, 158–84.

Young, K. 1987. Hinduism, in A. Sharma ed. *Women in World Religions*. New York: State University of New York Press, 59–103.

—. 1999. Introduction, in A. Sharma and K. Young eds. *Feminism and World Religions*. New York: State University of New York Press, 1–24.

LIST OF CONTRIBUTORS

Simon Coleman holds a Jackman Chair at the Department and Centre for the Study of Religion, University of Toronto, Canada and is editor of the *Journal of the Royal Anthropological Institute*. He works on charismatic Christians in Sweden, London and Nigeria, and on pilgrimage to Walsingham, England. Simon's books include *The Globalisation of Charismatic Christianity* (Cambridge University Press, 2000).

Ann R. David is a Principal Lecturer at Roehampton University, London. Her primary interest is in dance anthropology and her research has focused on the performance of dance and ritual possession in British South Asian communities. Her interdisciplinary research has been widely published and she is currently completing work as a Research Fellow on an international anthropological project examining the religious lives of immigrant groups in London.

Andrew Dawson is Senior Lecturer in the Department of Politics, Philosophy and Religion at Lancaster University, England. He has degrees in religious studies, theology and social science from universities in England and the United States. Researching in the area of religion and society, his most recent book, *New Era – New Religions* (Ashgate, 2007), examines the rise and spread of new religiosity in Brazil. Andrew co-edits the journal *Fieldwork in Religion* and is currently writing an introduction to the *Sociology of Religion* to be published by SCM Press.

Douglas Ezzy is an Associate Professor in Sociology and Head of School at the University of Tasmania, Australia. His research focuses on contemporary Pagan practice and the sociology of morality. Douglas' most recent publications include *Teenage Witches*, with Helen Berger (Rutgers University Press, 2007) and 'Qualitative Interviewing as Embodied Emotional Performance' (*Qualitative Inquiry*, 2010).

Karen Fjelstad lectures in Anthropology at San Jose State University, California, USA. Her research interests include ritual transnationalism, spirit possession and migration, and therapeutic aspects of popular religions. She is currently conducting joint research with Nguyen Thi Hien, with whom she co-edited *Possessed by the Spirits: Mediumship in Contemporary Vietnamese Communities* (Southeast Asia Program Publications of Cornell University, 2006).

David Garbin is a Research Fellow at the Centre for Research on Nationalism, Ethnicity and Multiculturalism of the University of Surrey, England. His research interests include transnational religion, African and South Asian diasporas and youth and popular cultures in urban settings. David has recently written Symbolic Geographies of the Sacred: Diasporic Territorialisation and Charismatic Power in a Transnational Congolese Prophetic Church, in G. Hüwelmeier and K. Krause eds. *Traveling Spirits: Migrants, Markets and Mobilities* (Routledge, 2010).

Gillian Goslinga is an Assistant Professor of Anthropology at Wesleyan University, USA. She works in and on the ideological borderlands between reproductive technologies and so-called 'virgin birth' beliefs or god-assisted reproduction in the context of an aggressively modernising Tamilnadu. Feminist ethnographer and visual anthropologist as well, she is, broadly speaking, interested in mapping the processes that render subaltern knowledges subaltern. Gillian recently released her third ethnographic film, *The Poojari's Daughter*.

Susan M. Kenyon is Professor Emerita of Anthropology, Butler University, Indianapolis, USA. Educated in England (London University, BA Honours History) and the United States (Bryn Mawr College, MA, PhD Anthropology), she has carried out ethnographic research on the northwest coast of Canada, Indonesia, Costa Rica, and (most recently) St Kitts. Susan's most extensive studies, however, focus on Sudan, particularly the women of Sennar.

Diana Espirito Santo is a Postdoctoral Research Fellow at the Institute of Social Sciences, University of Lisbon, Portugal. Her current interests include the anthropology of religious knowledge and learning, and notions of personhood and materiality in Afro-Cuban and Brazilian religion. Among her recently published articles is 'Making Dreams: Spirits, Vision and the Ontological Effects of Dream Knowledge in Cuban Espiritismo', *Suomen Antropologi* (2009, 34.3, 6–24). Diana is currently writing a book on Cuban Spiritism.

Birgit Staemmler is a researcher at the Institute of Asian and Oriental Studies, Department of Japanese Studies, University of Tübingen, Germany. Her research is currently funded by the Horst und Käthe-Eliseit-Stiftung. Birgit's research interests include Japanese new religions, religion and new media and spirit possession and shamanism in Japan. She has recently published *Chinkon Kishin: Mediated Spirit Possession in Japanese New Religions* (LIT, 2009).

Nguyen Thi Hien is a member of the Institute for Culture and Arts in Hanoi, Vietnam. He is currently conducting joint research with Karen Fjelstad, with whom he co-edited *Possessed by the Spirits: Mediumship in Contemporary Vietnamese Communities* (Southeast Asia Program Publications of Cornell University, 2006).

INDEX